CE... ...TAL

Also available from Continuum:

Adorno: A Guide for the Perplexed, Alex Thomson

Deleuze: A Guide for the Perplexed, Claire Colebrook

Existentialism: A Guide for the Perplexed, Steven Earnshaw

Hegel: A Guide for the Perplexed, Andrew Chitty

Husserl: A Guide for the Perplexed, Matheson Russell

Levinas: A Guide for the Perplexed, B. C. Hutchens

Literary Theory: A Guide for the Perplexed, Mary Klages

Merleau-Ponty: A Guide for the Perplexed, Eric Matthews

Quine: A Guide for the Perplexed, Gary Kemp

Wittgenstein: A Guide for the Perplexed, Mark Addis

DERRIDA: A GUIDE FOR THE PERPLEXED

JULIAN WOLFREYS

continuum

Continuum
The Tower Building   80 Maiden Lane, Suite 704
11 York Road   New York
London SE1 7NX   NY 10038
www.continuum books.com

British Library Cataloguing-in-Publication Data
A catalogue record for this book is available from the British Library.

ISBN-10: HB: 0-8264-8600-2
PB: 0-8264-8601-0
ISBN-13: HB: 978-0-8264-8600-4
PB: 978-0-8264-8601-1

Library of Congress Cataloging-in-Publication Data
A catalog record for this book is available from the Library of Congress.

Typeset by Servis Filmsetting Ltd, Manchester
Printed and bound in Great Britain by Cromwell Press Ltd,
Trowbridge, Wiltshire

For Xu

J'ai tant aimé; J'ai besoin d'être aimée

CONTENTS

Preface and Acknowledgements   ix
Abbreviations   xii

Introduction   1
Jacques Derrida – 'un résau de traces'
I   confessions   1
II   autobiothanatography   4
III   this, therefore, will not have been
        'Jacques Derrida'   9

1. Deconstruction   13
Remains: to be thought or, deconstruction (is not) what you
think (it is)
I   construing deconstruction: de construrer/de
        constructionem   13
II   performativity   14
III   taking off from de-construction or, leaving home:
        de lobia   17
IV   beyond enclosure: de finire   19
V   post cards, envois   28

2. Différance and Writing   44
I   a letter, literally a   44
II   literal mnemonic   48
III   Derrida after Saussure   55
IV   spacing and temporality   58
V   writing, supplement and 'la brisure'   63
VI   trace and arche-writing   68
VII   khora   71

3. Art   79
   (Writing in [excess of]) Representation
   I   reflecting on a portrait or, drawing forth   79
   II   framing the subject   81
   III   subjectile   83
   IV   trait   87
   V   passe-partout   95
   VI   mimesis   98
   VII   loose threads   106
   VIII   representation   108

4. Literature and Being   115
   I   to literatize or, the equivocal seventh   115
   II   invention, singularity, historicity   119
   III   being-circular or, where one is, in literature 133
   IV   being in literature   139
   V   literature is citation   142
   VI   as if   144
   VII   the barn and the bonfire: the example of Hardy   147
   VIII   spectrality   153
   IX   being-haunted, in other words   163

Works Cited   166
Index   169

PREFACE AND ACKNOWLEDGEMENTS

This book will not set out the work of Jacques Derrida as if one could approach it thematically. One cannot read Derrida thematically. I cannot pretend to write such a book. It's impossible. One cannot approach any of the texts by Derrida as if, in doing so, certain patterns might be discerned, the purpose being to learn those forms of thought and then 'apply' them to whatever it is you think you want to read. One cannot fit Derrida into a methodological or formal analytical frame. The very idea ignores just about everything Derrida says or does in writing. However tempting such approaches – and such approaches to approaches, introductions, guides, surveys – might be, as soon as one assumes the possibility Derrida has not been read. Were there the space, had I been as faithful as possible to Derrida, I would pursue an analysis of what is different between the idea or concept of the introduction, from that of the guide or survey. As I cannot do this, I would ask you to begin to think those differences, between the introduction on the one hand and the guide or survey on the other, and what they imply.

To thematize or order Derrida on the pretence or misguided, however well intentioned, belief that one has to start somewhere with Derrida is to believe in the idea of the finite or containable, schematic representation of 'Jacques Derrida', 'the work or thought of Derrida', 'deconstruction', and so on. Such phrases imply that there is an organic whole, so many species belonging through genetic relationship to a genus, whether that genus is identified as 'deconstruction' or 'Derrida'. Such thinking is what Derrida describes as *logocentric*. It is a dominant form of thinking in the history of Western thought, or metaphysics from Plato at least, to the present day. And such thinking is precisely what in tireless and endlessly inventive fashion, Derrida exposes for its limitations. To produce a Derrida or a deconstruction would be therefore to ignore something fundamental to all of Derrida's acts of reading and thinking. All such gestures desire representation as the first and last word. They believe, mistakenly, that, behind all the variable expressions, one can unearth or find a single semantic kernel. It's like planting evidence where none existed. You can't put Derrida in the frame, you can't fit him up, so to speak.

It isn't enough to refuse the temptation of producing something in the space of an introduction though. You cannot simply refuse the call. Avoidance should be avoided, and one must accept an impossible responsibility, seeking to respond by working in what Derrida might describe as 'an idiom hesitating between chance and necessity' (SOR, 297). So, one strives to work in an idiom, if not in several. One does so within the idiom of the 'introduction', the 'guide', the 'survey', seeking to deform the idiom, to twist or translate it, to betray its injunctions, and offering a countersignature idiomatically to the idiom. You might therefore approach this volume as a series of chapters that move in a weaving manner, or as so many pieces of textile unfolding and refolding themselves onto and around one another. Ideas introduced will be dropped, and then taken up again in a different context. This gesture should be read as indicative of the fact that one cannot gather up Derrida's text and give some simplistic order or context to it. Derrida has shown, patiently and repeatedly, that no context is ever finite. No context excludes other contexts. One can never exhaust the resources of a context. Whatever idea or notion is found to have particular contexts will never remain in place in that context. It will instead transport itself into other contexts, transforming its meaning and identity.

The chapters seek to respect this way of thinking, and I attempt to be attentive to Derrida by disordering order within specific chapter structures, having recourse to strategic reiterations, and by seeking to maintain attention to some semblance of forms, order, whilst playing with that in what will be found, hopefully, an engaging, if provocative manner. The purpose is to make you think, but also to make you question *how* you think. In lieu of the purely thematic approach, writing proceeds here, between chance and necessity, as on the one hand I seek to economize on the seemingly endless weave of Derrida's thinking, pulling at a thread here and there, while on the other hand, folding the material back on itself, transforming the rewoven thread through moving between differing contexts. This is a patchwork of sorts. The stitches are picked apart, then rewoven.

I would like to thank the following for their thoughts and suggestions, for passing comments and for everything else that remains and which has found its way into this book, however secretly: Andrew Bennett, Caroline Blomfield, David Blomfield, Mary Ann Caws, Thomas Dutoit, Roger Ebbatson, Elaine Hobby, Brian Jarvis, John Leavey, Martin McQuillan, Martin Middeke, J. Hillis Miller, Bill Overton, Nils Plath, David Punter, Avital Ronell and Nicholas Royle. I would like to thank Sophie Cox for her diligent and painstaking editorial work. I would also like to thank Anna Sandeman for commissioning this book, and for being so supportive and encouraging an editor.

ABBREVIATIONS

AEL   *Adieu: to Emmanuel Levinas*. Trans. Pascale-Anne Brault and Michael Naas. Stanford: Stanford University Press, 1999.

AF   *Archive Fever: A Freudian Impression*. Trans. Eric Prenowitz. Chicago: University of Chicago Press, 1996.

AΠWD   '"*As if* I were dead"': An Interview with Jacques Derrida'. John Brannigan, Ruth Robbins, Julian Wolfreys, eds. *Applying: to Derrida*. Basingstoke: Macmillan, 1996. 212–27.

Atf   'A time for farewells: Heidegger (read by) Hegel (read by) Malabou'. Preface, trans. Joseph D. Cohen. Catherine Malabou. *The Future of Hegel: Plasticity, Temporality and Dialectic*. Trans. Lisabeth During. London: Routledge, 2005. vii–xlvii.

Avm   'At this very moment in this work here I am'. Trans. Ruben Berezdivin. Robert Bernasconi and Simon Critchley, eds. *Re-Reading Levinas*. Bloomington: Indiana University Press, 1991. 11–48.

C   'Circumfession: Fifty-nine periods and periphrases *written in a sort of internal margin, between Geoffrey Bennington's book and work in preparation (January 1989–April 1990)*'. Geoffrey Bennington and Jacques Derrida. *Jacques Derrida*. Trans. Geoffrey Bennington. Chicago: University of Chicago Press, 1993. 3–315

D   'Différance'. *Margins of Philosophy*. Trans. Alan Bass. Chicago: University of Chicago Press, 1982. 3–28.

D   *Dissemination*. Trans. and int. Barbara Johnson. Chicago: University of Chicago Press, 1981.

D^2 *Derrida: Screenplay and Essays on the Film.* Kirby Dick and Amy Ziering Kofman, dir. Foreword Geoffrey Hartman. New York: Routledge, 2005.

DFT   'Demeure: Fiction and Testimony'. Maurice Blanchot and Jacques Derrida. *The Instant of My Death/Demeure: Fiction and Testimony.* Trans. Elizabeth Rottenberg. Stanford: Stanford University Press, 1998. 13–103.

DO   'Deconstruction and the Other: an Interview with Richard Kearney'. Richard Kearney, ed. *Debates in Continental Philosophy: Conversations with Contemporary Thinkers.* New York: Fordham University Press, 2004. 139–56.

E   'Economimesis'. Trans. R. Klein. *The Derrida Reader: Writing Performances.* Ed. Julian Wolfreys. Edinburgh: Edinburgh University Press, 1998. 263–93.

EC   'Et Cetera . . . (and so on, und so weiter, and so forth, et ainsi de suite, und so überall, etc.)'. Trans. Geoffrey Bennington. Ed. Nicholas Royle. *Deconstructions: A User's Guide.* Basingstoke: Palgrave, 2000. 282–306.

FK   'Faith and Knowledge: Two Sources of "Religion" at the Limits of Reason Alone'. Jacques Derrida and Gianni Vattimo, eds. *Religion.* Stanford: Stanford University Press, 1998. 1–78.

FWT   *For What Tomorrow . . . A Dialogue.* With Elisabeth Roudinesco. Trans. Jeff Fort. Stanford: Stanford University Press, 2004.

GGGG   *Geneses, Genealogies, Genres and Genius: The Secrets of the Archive.* Trans. Beverley Bie Brahic. Edinburgh: Edinburgh University Press, 2006.

H.C.   *H.C. for Life, That is to Say . . .* Trans., with additional notes, Laurent Milesi and Stefan Herbechter. Stanford: Stanford University Press, 2006.

I   'Implications: interview with Henri Ronse'. *Positions.* Trans. Alan Bass. Chicago: University of Chicago Press, 1981. 3–14.

I:D   'Introduction: Desistance'. Trans. Christopher Fynsk. Phillipe Lacoue-Labarthe. *Typography: Mimesis, Philosophy, Politics.* Ed. Christopher Fynsk *et al.* Cambridge, MA: Harvard University Press, 1989. 1–42.

IHTS   ' "I Have a Taste for the Secret" '. Jacques Derrida and Maurizio Ferraris. *A Taste for the Secret.* Trans. Giacomo

Donis. Ed. Giacomo Donis and David Webb. Cambridge: Polity Press, 2001. 1–93.

J   'Justice'. Trans. Peggy Kamuf. Barbara Cohen and Dragan Kujundzic, eds. *Provocations to Reading: J. Hillis Miller and the Democracy to Come.* New York: Fordham University Press, 2005. 228–61.

JD   'Jacques Derrida, penseur de l'évènement: entretien par Jérôme-Alexandre Nielsberg', www.humanité.fr, 28 January 2004. n.p.

K   *Khora. On the Name.* Ed. Thomas Dutoit. Trans. David Wood, John P. Leavey, Jr. and Ian McLeod. Stanford: Stanford University Press, 1993. 89–130.

LG   'The Law of Genre'. Trans. Avital Ronell. *Glyph Textual Studies* 7. Baltimore: The Johns Hopkins University Press, 1980. 202–32.

LI   *Limited Inc.* Trans. Samuel Weber. Evanston: Northwestern University Press, 1988.

LJF   'Letter to a Japanese Friend'. Peggy Kamuf, ed. *A Derrida Reader: Between the Blinds.* New York: Columbia University Press, 1991. 270–6.

LNO   'Language is Never Owned: An Interview'. Trans. Thomas Dutoit and Philippe Romanski. Thomas Dutoit and Outi Pasanen, eds. *Sovereignties in Question: The Poetics of Paul Celan.* New York: Fordham University Press, 2005. 97–107.

MB   *Memoirs of the Blind: The Self-Portrait and Other Ruins.* Trans. Pascale-Anne Brault and Michael Naas. Chicago: University of Chicago Press, 1993.

MOPO   *Monolingualism of the Other or the Prosthesis of Origin.* Trans. Patrick Mensah. Stanford: Stanford University Press, 1998.

MP   *Margins of Philosophy.* Trans. Alan Bass. Chicago: University of Chicago Press, 1982.

M&S   'Marx & Sons'. Trans. G. M. Goshgarian. Michael Sprinker, ed. *Ghostly Demarcations: A Symposium on Jacques Derrida's Specters of Marx.* London: Verso, 1999. 213–69.

N   *Negotiations: Interventions and Interviews 1971–2001.* Trans. and ed. Elizabeth Rottenberg. Stanford: Stanford University Press, 2002.

OCF	*On Cosmopolitanism and Forgiveness*. Trans. Mark Dooley and Michael Hughes. Preface Simon Critchley and Richard Kearney. London: Routledge, 2001.
OG	*Of Grammatology*. Corrected edn. Trans. Gayatri Chakravorty Spivak. Baltimore: The Johns Hopkins University Press, 1998.
OS	*Of Spirit*. Trans. Geoffrey Bennington and Rachel Bowlby. Chicago: University of Chicago Press, 1989.
OT	*On Touching – Jean-Luc Nancy*. Trans. Christine Irizarry. Stanford: Stanford University Press, 2005.
P	*Psyché: Inventions de l'autre*. Paris: Galilée, 1987.
PC	*The Post Card: from Socrates to Freud and Beyond*. Trans. Alan Bass. Chicago: University of Chicago Press, 1987.
PIO	'Psyche: Inventions of the Other'. Trans. Catherine Porter. Lindsay Waters and Wlad Godzich, eds. *Reading de Man Reading*. Minneapolis: University of Minnesota Press, 1989. 25–66.
PM	*Paper Machine*. Trans. Rachel Bowlby. Stanford: Stanford University Press, 2005.
POO	'Passions: "An Oblique Offering" '. Trans. and ed. David Wood. *Derrida: A Critical Reader*. Oxford: Blackwell, 1992. 5–36.
RI	*Right of Inspection*. (1985) Photographs by Marie-Françoise Plissart. Trans. David Wills. New York: The Monacelli Press, 1998.
RM	'The *Retrait* of Metaphor'. Trans. F. Gasdner. Julian Wolfreys, ed. *The Derrida Reader: Writing Performances*. Edinburgh: Edinburgh University Press, 1998. 102–29.
RTER	*Rogues: Two Essays on Reason*. Trans. Pascale-Anne Brault and Michael Naas. Stanford: Stanford University Press, 2005.
SA	'The Spatial Arts: An Interview with Jacques Derrida'. Peter Brunette and David Wills, eds. *Deconstruction and the Visual Arts*. Berkeley: University of California Press, 1994. 9–33.
SAAA	*The Secret Art of Antonin Artaud*. With Paule Thévenin. Trans. and Preface Mary Ann Caws. Cambridge, MA: MIT Press, 1998.
SICL	' "This Strange Institution Called Literature": An Interview with Jacques Derrida'. Derek Attridge, ed.

Jacques Derrida, *Acts of Literature*. London: Routledge, 1992. 33–75.

SM   *Specters of Marx: The State of the Debt, the Work of Mourning, and the New International*. Trans. Peggy Kamuf. Int. Bernd Magnus and Stephen Cullenberg. London: Routledge, 1994.

SOO   'A Silkworm of One's Own: Points of View Stitched on the Other Veil'. Hélène Cixous and Jacques Derrida. *Veils*. Trans. Geoffrey Bennington. Stanford: Stanford University Press, 2001. 21–92.

SOR   'Sending: On Representation'. Trans. Peter and Mary Ann Caws. *Social Research* 49:2 (Summer 1982): 294–326.

SP   *Speech and Phenomena: and Other Essays on Husserl's Theory of Signs*. Trans. and int. David B. Allison. Preface Newton Garver. Evanston: Northwestern University Press, 1973.

SPC   'Shibboleth: For Paul Celan'. Trans. Joshua Wilner. Rev. trans. Thomas Dutoit. Thomas Dutoit and Outi Pasanen, eds. *Sovereignties in Question: The Poetics of Paul Celan*. New York: Fordham University Press, 2005. 1–64.

SPIP *Sur parole: instantanés philosophiques*. Saint-Étienne: editions de l'Aube, 1999.

TA   'The Three Ages of Jacques Derrida: An Interview', *LA Weekly*, 6 November, 2002. n.p.

TOJ   'The Time is Out of Joint'. Anselm Haverkamp, ed. *Deconstruction is/in America*. New York: New York University Press, 1995. 14–40.

TP   *The Truth in Painting*. Trans. Geoff Bennington and Ian McLeod. Chicago: University of Chicago Press, 1987.

TUS   'To Unsense the Subjectile'. Trans. Mary Ann Caws. Jacques Derrida and Paule Thévenin. *The Secret Art of Antonin Artaud*. Preface Mary Ann Caws. Cambridge, MA: MIT Press, 1998. 59–157.

TwJ   'Two Words for Joyce'. Trans. Geoff Bennington. Derek Attridge and Daniel Ferrer, eds. *Post-Structuralist Joyce: Essays from the French*. Cambridge: Cambridge University Press, 1984. 145–59.

WA   *Without Alibi*. Ed., trans. and int. Peggy Kamuf. Stanford: Stanford University Press, 2002.

WD   *Writing and Difference*. Trans. Alan Bass. London: Routledge and Kegan Paul, 1978.

WM   *The Work of Mourning*. Ed. Pascale-Anne Brault and Michael Naas. Chicago: University of Chicago Press, 2001.

INTRODUCTION

Jacques Derrida – 'un résau de traces'

Writing is not speaking.

Abdelkebir Khatibi

'He was born, he thought, and he died.' And all the rest is pure anecdote.

Jacques Derrida

'Now that deconstruction and interest in Derrida is largely moribund, what do you see the point of your work being?'

Impure anecdote

I CONFESSIONS

Two 'responses', then, with which we begin.

> I began, almost forty years ago, with a reflection on writing, on text. That which mattered to me from the beginning – although I would become a 'philosopher' by profession – was literary writing. What is it to write, I asked myself. What is it that takes place when one writes? In order to respond, I had to broaden the concept of text and try to justify this extension. 'There is no outside text' does not want to say that all is . . . writing, but that any experience is structured like a network of traces, which return to something other than themselves. In other words, there is no present which is not constituted without reference to another time, another present. The present-trace. It traces and is traced. (JD, n.p.)

What's the most widely held misconception about you and your work?

1

That I'm a skeptical nihilist who doesn't believe in anything, who thinks nothing has meaning, and text has no meaning. That's stupid and utterly wrong, and only people who haven't read me say this. It's a misreading of my work that began 35 years ago, and it's difficult to destroy. I never said everything is linguistic and we're enclosed in language . . . Anyone who reads my work with attention understands that I insist on affirmation and faith, and that I'm full of respect for the texts I read. (TA, n.p.)

You open a book, and it begins with two comments extracted from interviews. A voice appears to be here, even though the person speaking them is not, obviously. Writing arrives before the voice. By virtue of the text, there are the traces of that person's words in that person's absence. The present moment is divided. It can never be present fully, even the present in which I write or in which you read. When I wrote *here, there are traces*, and *the present moment*, each of those moments was a present, now irrecuperable. The present moment of writing, always changing, comes to pass, and in that inscription the present consigns, countersigns itself to its own displacement. It is *as if*[1] the present were marked by the appearance of the letters in the nanoseconds after I have pressed the keys and the cursor advances, fractionally ahead. But each and every present moment that I am describing, which I am describing through inscription even as I inscribe the description, is in process, having become traced in the words you are reading, traced by the traces of that present turning and returning to some other moment than that present. This description of what takes place here is not limited to the act of writing in any narrow sense. It is what structures the experience of, well everything.

To restrict that 'everything' with an example, a single instance on which we will risk the implication of everything, reflect on your reading of this passage.

First: who is the 'you' to whom I refer? It implies an unknowable number of yous, of readers, which number cannot be calculated. One cannot assume a totality or finite number of readers or, for that matter, readings.

Second: for every you who reads, there is a *now*, a present moment of reading. The movement and network of traces informing the times of writing also marks and is remarked by the experience of reading. By extension, the network of traces by which a present folds back onto, echoes with, or returns to some other place informs every experience of the present on the part of a subject.

Third: the present moment of a reading is incalculable. You will continue to read even when you close the book, when you put it down to do something else.

Fourth: though you are reading in a present the traces of the present in which these words are/were written can never be present as such, even though I am/was writing in the so-called present tense. That is a present without presence, and is only simulated by the 'present-trace', the trace of the present that is traced and which traces.

Fifth: neither you nor I are present at the moment when the 'voice', which is reported above by the collection of traces, and therefore writing, text, spoke those words. Jacques Derrida is not present. His words are remainders. They remain – to be read. They are reminders, every time one reads, that he is not present, that he can no longer be present.

And the same goes for the words I write. Written at a different time than the interviews cited above, and yet another time than those other times of transcription, printing and all the times of reading, what I will call 'my' words (with a deliberate naïveté) are here/there in my absence. My own present moment is thus inscribed in, as it inscribes itself into, that return of the traces to some other present than the present which this is (7:23 am, Tuesday, 8 August 2006). I will therefore have been absent, always already absent if you are reading this. There is no 'I' here. It is *as if* I were dead. It is always *as if* one is reading 'the traces of one who has just died . . . this was what Derrida meant by *writing* . . . this terrible *Unheimlichkeit* [uncanniness] . . . there and not there. Still here and, already, not here: now here and nowhere' (Gaston 2006, 1). To echo a remark from above, this does not mean to say that everything is linguistic. This should be clear, let's be clear about this. But not everything is clear. Otherwise, we wouldn't have to repeat the point. It hasn't been clear – ever. Had it been clear to those whose misreadings are stupid and utterly wrong, then not only would Derrida not have had to say what he says/said in the interviews above and in numerous other places, there would also be no need for books such as this 'introductory guide'. Although nothing could be clearer than the two reflective commentaries I cite above, we're not in the clear yet.

II AUTOBIOTHANATOGRAPHY

Jacques Derrida: this name has become virtually synonymous in some circles with the word 'deconstruction'. Derrida's publications have had an enormous, though not uncontested influence on literary study and other academic disciplines in the latter half of the twentieth century, particularly since the 1970s. Derrida first came to the attention of the English-speaking academic world in 1966, following a paper presented at a colloquium at Johns Hopkins University. The following year, 1967, Derrida published three books subsequently translated as *Of Grammatology* (1976), *Speech and Phenomena* (1973) and *Writing and Difference* (1978). These were followed in 1972 by three more in French, translated as *Dissemination*, *Margins of Philosophy* and *Positions*, securing Derrida's influence. This influence has subsequently spread beyond the study of literature and literary theory, to produce effects in film and cultural studies, in legal theory, in the study and theory of architecture and more generally throughout the humanities and social sciences. A professor of philosophy (he once remarked that he was not 'happy with the term *philosopher*'; DO, 140) Derrida's writing has, ironically, though perhaps not surprisingly, met with the greatest resistance – sometimes, more simply, a lack of comprehension – in philosophy departments throughout British and North American universities, and in French intellectual and political circles.

Derrida's own philosophical work began with a study in the mid-1950s of German philosopher Edmund Husserl, before turning to detailed, painstaking analyses of many of the canonical philosophers, from Plato onwards. His published works have also considered a broad range of literary writers, including Shakespeare, Joyce, Paul Celan, Jean Genet and Francis Ponge. *Glas*, a book presented in two columns, presents discussions side by side of Genet and Hegel. There is also discernible to some in Derrida's writing a turn, from the 1980s at least, to more overtly stated questions of ethics and politics, considerations of the identity of Europe, matters of globalization and its implications, the meaning of democracy, the future of the humanities and the role of the university in today's society. His work has also engaged in a sustained fashion with the discourse of psychoanalysis, particularly the work of Sigmund Freud, in numerous essays, *The Post Card: from Socrates to Freud and Beyond* (1987) and *Archive Fever* (1995). His writing is rigorously informed, simultaneously, by the great philosophical exegetical traditions and an experimental, playful exploration of tonalities and voices, and an interest in what he has called the 'non-verbal within the verbal'.

However, it is impossible to sum up Derrida's work. This is in small part because his published output in both French and in translation is so huge. In 1992, an annotated primary and secondary bibliography was published, which lists over 40 books in French alone, between 1967 and 1991. Not counting chapters in books or interviews, there were over 180 articles published during the same period. More significantly however, it is impossible to offer a summary because, despite views put forward in encyclopaedias, textbooks on literary theory, and in many classrooms, Derrida has neither articulated nor proposed a single theory or philosophical position. Rather, what can be said of his work is that each publication is a singular demonstration of a patient response to the contours, rhythms and turns of the subject being addressed. This being the case, it has to be recognized, if one attempts to read Derrida faithfully, that his writing necessarily transforms itself according to the given interest. As Derrida puts it ' "good" literary criticism, the only worthwhile kind, implies an act, a literary signature or countersignature, an inventive experience of language, *in* language, an inscription of the act of reading in the field of the text that is read' (SICL, 52). Because of this singular attentiveness on Derrida's part, it is therefore impossible to elevate the specificity of each analysis to the level of certain general rules.

This has led to a somewhat odd reception of Derrida's work. The initial phase of reception in both the UK and the USA was marked either by outright hostility, where Derrida had been characterized as an obscurantist charlatan, or by an attempt to extract from his writings certain repeatable practices, thereby producing a theory of analysis from his work, and it is this process that has come to be termed 'deconstruction', of which, as you will see in the first chapter, Derrida is repeatedly wary, marking a distance between himself and such methodological appropriations. It should not be thought however that Derrida has been simply misunderstood. Indeed, he has a number of faithful, careful readers.

Originally named Jackie by his mother, Georgette Derrida (née Safar), Jacques Derrida was born in El-Biar, Algeria, 15 July 1930. Born into a Jewish family who, under the Crémieux decree of 1875 were 'indigenous jews' of Algeria without rights to French citizenship, Derrida was doubly discriminated against. In 1940, Derrida experienced anti-Semitic discrimination at primary school as a result of the regulations of the Pétain regime, where, because he was Jewish, he was not permitted to raise the French flag, an honour usually given to the top pupil in the class. In 1942, one year after starting school at the Lycée de Ben Aknoun, Derrida was expelled. Being sent to another school, the Lycée Emile-Maupas, at which Jewish teachers barred from the public system worked, Derrida spent much of the year until spring 1943 secretly not attending school. Following the Allied landing and a period of dismantling Pétainist control by the De Gaulle–Giraud government, Derrida returned for four years to the Lycée de Ben Aknoun. A poor student, he preferred to play football, and was a voracious reader, reading at the time figures such as Rousseau and Nietzsche, who would later become significant in his writing and thought.

In 1948, Derrida passed his *baccalauréat*, at the Lycée Gauthier, Algiers, where he read for the first time Jean-Paul Sartre and Henri Bergson. Between 1949 and 1952, he was a boarder at the Lycée Louis-le-Grand, Paris. His first exposure to Paris and mainland France, Derrida's experience as a student was a difficult one, marked by poor physical and mental health, particularly in 1951–52. Having failed the entrance exam to the Ecole Normale Supérieure in 1950, he was subsequently admitted in 1952, when he came to know and work with Marxist philosopher Louis Althusser, who was to remain a close acquaintance for nearly two decades. In 1957, following success in the *agrégation*, the exam which qualifies teachers of higher education, Derrida travelled to the USA for the first time, to study unpublished work by Edmund Husserl at Harvard University. In June of that year, he married Marguerite Aucouturier, in Boston, Massachusetts.

Conscripted in 1957 for two years by the French army during the Algerian War, Derrida served not in the military but as a French and English teacher. This was followed by a teaching position for four years at the Sorbonne, during which time Derrida met French historian of ideas Michel Foucault and novelist Philippe Sollers, also publishing his first articles in the radical journal founded by Sollers, *Tel Quel*, an association maintained until 1972, when Derrida made an unequivocal break. In 1964, he was invited by Althusser and philosopher Jean Hyppolite to teach at the Ecole Normale

Supérieure, where Derrida remained for 20 years. Though responsible for organizing the first general assembly at the Ecole Normale during May 1968, and taking part in marches, Derrida did not give his support wholeheartedly to particular aspects of the protests.

Travelling frequently to conferences and colloquia from 1968 onwards, Derrida was offered a visiting professorship in 1975 at Yale University, a post he held until 1986, when, along with Yale colleague and literary critic J. Hillis Miller, he accepted another visiting post at the University of California, Irvine. At Yale, Derrida was identified in the media, along with Miller, Harold Bloom, Geoffrey Hartman and Paul de Man, as belonging to the so-called Yale School of Deconstruction. In truth, no such school existed, but was invented by media misperception and a misunderstanding of the nature of the critical work that Derrida, de Man and Miller were each, in their own fashion, pursuing. Such work was mistakenly given the name of 'deconstruction', as though this were a method, a programmatic form of analysis, or, indeed, a school of thought.

Back in France, Derrida and other philosophers organized at the Sorbonne the Estates General of Philosophy in 1979, while the following year he defended his *Thèse d'Etat*. Derrida had never formally completed doctoral work and the examination in 1980 addressed his published work. In 1981, Derrida helped organize the Jan Hus Association, aimed at aiding persecuted Czech intellectuals. While visiting Prague in the same year, to organize a secret seminar, he was arrested on the pretext of producing and trafficking drugs. As a result of François Mitterand's involvement, amongst other measures, Derrida was released and expelled from Czechoslovakia. Another significant organizational work took place in 1983, the founding of the Collège international de philosophie in Paris. Derrida was its first director, whilst also being involved in the Foundation against Apartheid, and the organization of an exhibition, 'Art against Apartheid'. In this year, Derrida was also elected as directeur d'études at the Ecole des hautes études en sciences sociales, Paris, a position he held until his official 'retirement' at the age of 67.

Jacques Derrida continued to travel extensively, lecturing, taking up visiting posts, participating in conferences, writing and publishing. Two moments of public notoriety attached themselves to Derrida, which speak more of both the public and the academic misunderstanding of his work, than they do of Derrida himself. The first, coming in 1987, became known as the 'Paul de Man Affair'. A friend and colleague of Derrida's at Yale, de Man died unexpectedly in 1983. Subsequently, a young Belgian researcher, Ortwin de Graef, discovered some articles written for the right-wing paper *Le Soir* by de Man, while a young man in Belgium during the Second World War. A couple of articles on national literatures expressed anti-Semitic sentiments. While none of de Man's subsequent publications show any traces of such thought, the discovery of the articles became the excuse for a media feeding frenzy, attacking so-called deconstruction and its 'practitioners' for being nihilist, irresponsible, aimed at destroying the humanities and even, in one or two extreme cases, fascistic. Few if any of these attacks adhered to even a basic reporting of the facts, and showed neither any sign of understanding nor any real willingness to read either de Man or Derrida's work whatsoever. Equally fuelled by misunderstanding and not reading was the 1992 'Cambridge Affair', in which, in an extremely rare occurrence, a small number of Cambridge dons started a campaign against the awarding of an honorary degree to Derrida. Several months of agitation led to letters of objection being printed in the national and international press. Eventually however, the vote went strongly in Derrida's favour, and the doctorate *honoris causa* was awarded on 11 June 1992.

These two incidents are symptomatic of the non-reception of Derrida, both inside the university and at large. They typically highlight the ways in which an author and his works can be received without ever having been read. This is ironic inasmuch as all of Derrida's life and work, regardless of subject, has been devoted to careful, diligent, patient acts of reading and not to hurried or journalistic analysis or what Derrida has referred to as 'reading on the fly'. However, as with so many commonplace terms, such as writing or text, Derrida has expanded radically our notion of the meaning of such words, and reading is no exception. In an interview, Derrida claimed never to have 'read' particular authors. This was not some coy gesture on Derrida's part but is, rather, typical of Derrida's insistence on how one addresses and analyses any textual form. For Derrida, the notion of 'reading' is one that implies a comprehensive commentary on a poem or novel in its entirety, an achievement which is impossible. One can never *finally* read or claim to have read a text in its entirety. One must continue carefully to read and re-read, because the act of reading is always marked by an ever-receding horizon. It is always to come.

III THIS, THEREFORE, WILL NOT HAVE BEEN 'JACQUES DERRIDA'

Where should one start, though, with the text signed *Jacques Derrida*? A biography tells us little or nothing of the work. Certainly, the text cannot be understood only by the biography or restricted to that life as if it were the first and final context. Wherever the biography marks itself on the text, the one is not the same as the other, and biography is not a replacement for close, patient reading of a paragraph or two. It is a narrative device sustained by the authority of raw facts and dates designed to stabilize the reception of an image, co-mingling public and private, as though in doing so one could provide a way into, or a substitute for, the writing of the person being discussed.

If one is to speak to the question of how Derrida reads and writes reading, we ought to begin by understanding that the question for the reader of Derrida is one of inventing ways to disrupt received narratives. Let us therefore conclude this introduction by turning towards the interest of the next chapter, *deconstruction*. The received narratives concerning this word amount to, or include, statements concerning its existence as a form of literary theory. It is a method of analysis, a school of thought, a programme for reading according to an interdisciplinary amalgam of linguistic, philosophical and psychoanalytic discourses. Regarding the origins of deconstruction, the received and institutional narratives strive to separate the philosophical from the linguistic or literary and stake claims in philosophy rather than language. As you can see though, if you reflect on the first of Derrida's two responses cited at the beginning of this introduction, there is no simple origin, no single source from which everything can be traced. Instead, what takes place between discourses and remains to be read as the motion, if you will, of the other, that gives to any discourse or institution its determining features whilst remaining other than, and heterogeneous to, those elements – this is what interests Derrida: that which is irrecuperable to any homogeneous order and yet which supports it, causing the identity, meaning, discourse, institution or ontology to take place.

As you will see in the following chapter, representations of deconstruction as method, school of thought, programme and so on, are *mis*representations for the reasons explained there. Consider instead though, the following commentary on deconstruction. Deconstruction, Derrida argues, not only teaches us to read literature more thoroughly by attending to it as *language* . . . through a complex play of signifying traces; it also enables us to interrogate the covert philosophical and political presuppositions of institutionalized critical methods which generally govern our reading of a text. There is in deconstruction something which challenges every teaching institution. (DO, 155)

There is much more to this quotation, and I shall consider it in the next chapter. For now however, notice how Derrida, in speaking of a provisional definition for 'deconstruction', emphasizes equally language, philosophy and politics, and by way of a further orientation a challenge to 'every teaching institution'. By institution, Derrida refers not only to the material manifestations such as universities, but also to the operative and normative discourses, from administrative protocols and procedures, to the discourses and disciplines, to which the various discourses pertain.

The question is therefore one of *inventing* new translations for reading and writing within the institutional, operating on and transforming them from within. Derrida has pursued repeatedly the effective *invention* or translations of such concepts. (*Invention* will be considered in the final chapter.) His purpose has been to

eviscerate and re-assemble them in difference, interrupt[ing] the received programs of perception, interpretation, and experience – and in the process of altering this past . . . hold open the space for the arrival of the unprecedented event, of a virtual or alternative 'future' to those [that are] programmatically foreseeable. (Cohen 2001, 2)

To the extent that a number of academics who claim to read Derrida have not recognized this means the broad contexts of Derrida's misreception have remained largely static. Insisting on transforming Derrida's patient acts of reading into methods, and circling around the same arguments concerned with the origins or provenance of Derrida's thought in the academic context, arguments have remained resolutely unattentive to the aporia, the gaps or impasses in their own structures. They have succumbed to the symptomatic procedures by which they seek to identify both Derrida and deconstruction.

If we can summarize Derrida in any way then, it is as the thinker of this aporia, as a thinker of the space, the gap, the deviation or swerve within any ontology, meaning or identity. His work repeatedly stresses that one can 'only respond by tracing the gap' and the 'histories of the gap' (Gaston 2006, vii). The gap is necessary to thought. It takes place as a place and as the possibility of a between; unbridgeable in itself it nonetheless opens itself, within a discourse, within an institution, within cultures and politics, in order to give place to the possibility of an other taking place, the unprecedented event by which transformation, translation, interruption have their chances. Reading after Derrida one must fall, be precipitated headlong into the gap, so as to avoid reappropriation (Gaston 2005, 97) so as to leave oneself naked and open to the unforeseeable in taking a chance on the precipitate decision.

It is in thinking the gap, each time in the patient reading or *invention* of a singular text, institution or situation, that Derrida avoids reappropriation, recuperation, not least in terms of 'theory' or programme. There is therefore never an objective position or 'metaposition' (Fynsk 2004, x). Instead, Derrida enters into an engaged, committed relation to the other by which his reading is guided resistant to any ready-made position. There is to his work an aspect of 'fundamental research' insisting, demonstrating repeatedly, tirelessly, the gap or unthought within any system, as this enables an interrogation of the 'structure of representation' (Fynsk 2004, x) by which the system, model, or institution maintains itself. In this fashion, in endlessly inventive and interruptive ways, Derrida opens the textual network of traces and the history of its silences, omissions, and absences, to an unexpected event of reading, and so to other readings to come, beyond the expectation of any programmable or predictable future or horizon.

Thinking without programme from within that structure, and yet with a smiling and affirmative resistance to the systems he inhabits, Derrida achieves a different 'level of reflection', which in any number of examples had previously been unavailable. In its exposure of the limits of any 'language', theory or philosophy, Derrida may seem to move to 'a new level of complexity or difficulty . . . [involving, for some] an irritating complication' (Fynsk 2004, xiii). However, for others, he offers profound possibilities for the transformation of the 'realities at stake' undergirding any practice through 'sustained attention to the grain of thought in its textual elaboration' (Fynsk 2004, xiii). Every text by Derrida is a profession of faith in the undecidable and what is to come. It entails a 'labyrinthine movement', a 'performative and at times vertiginous mobility', the 'explosive variants and viral elaborations' of which are the hallmarks of a movement and a spacing in pursuit of an 'irreducible element' (Cohen 2001, 6). It is through an attention to such movement, to irreducible elements such as the *performative, writing* and *singularity, literature, representation* and *being,* amongst other things, that we will speak.

NOTE

1. *As if* is highlighted throughout *Derrida: A Guide for the Perplexed.* This figure, *as if,* is an important figure or rhetorical/phenomenological trope in Derrida's writing. Taken in part from the Kantian category of *als ob* (as though, as if), the figure installs in writing the possibility of imagining a relation between experience or fact and a fictionalized experience. Thus the figure names a certain analogical, rather than mimetic correspondence. The *as if* names a 'fictional' condition, an imagined and therefore *phantasmatic* possibility that is not a lie, but which either has not happened, or which, more significantly, cannot be experienced as such. So, I cannot experience 'my death'. I can experience dying, but what I call my death is not available to me. In this, the death which I call mine is never mine, properly speaking, it is the impossible, unavailable (like language) to appropriation. *As if* institutes a form of 'hinge' if you will between the possible and the impossible. It names the spectral condition of imagination as the projection of fictions and narratives. So I can imagine a condition of being after death and yet still having consciousness of the *post-mortem.* Such an imagined condition is possible through the *as if.* To think this impossibility is to say or picture, or narrate a state *as if* I were dead. This is surely a fiction if ever there was one. We imagine an exorbitant fiction in the thought of a reflexive consciousness of the absence of consciousness, the absence or more precisely non-existence of the *me,* the *ego,* which thinks this.

   I discuss the thinking of the *as if* apropos death in the chapter on art, in relation to the subject of portraiture and representation of oneself. You might think through the implied analogy between language and death, in that they share the condition of never being owned (see the chapter on deconstruction for more on the impossibility of language being owned). In thinking through the analogy, what Derrida calls a relation without relation, there is much to be understood about Derrida's work, about the constant, reciprocal and always dizzying opening informing the intimacy between the one and the other, between language and philosophy, or between literature and being, between, let us say, linguistics and phenomenology.

CHAPTER 1

DECONSTRUCTION

*Remains: to be thought or, deconstruction (is not)
what you think (it is)*

We should not neglect the fact that some biographies . . . finally invest this authority in a book, which . . . represents the truth. The 'truth'.

Jacques Derrida

Deconstruction is not a school or an 'ism'. There is no such thing as 'deconstructionism': this is a word used by idiots.

Martin McQuillan

Deconstruction *n.* not what you think: the experience of the impossible: what remains to be thought: A logic of destabilization always already on the move in 'things themselves': what makes every identity at once itself and different from itself: a logic of spectrality.

Nicholas Royle

I CONSTRUING DECONSTRUCTION: DE CONSTRURER/DE CONSTRUCTIONEM

How to construe *deconstruction*? What *of construal* remains to be thought in *deconstruction*? How does *de* construe *construction*? Construction and construal share similar etymological sources. While the former signifies mostly material acts building or refers to a material style, it is structured or informed also by associations with grammar, with the arrangement of words according to syntactical rules. Furthermore, it is used metaphorically to imply reading or interpretation. The last two senses, pertaining to linguistic, analytical and formal functions, direct us to the second term, *construe* or *construal*. Again, the emphasis is on interpretation. It is also indicative, in a more archaic sense, of translation, and of comprehension or understanding. One may therefore not unreasonably construe an invisible link, metaphorically a structure that simultaneously spaces and yet connects *construction* and *construal*. One construes 'construction' but equally one may construct one's 'construal'. The passage between literal and metaphorical cannot be closed. It remains as it is, suggestive however, of a silent, yet nonetheless visible, *graphic* transference. A motion in writing takes place. This is *inscribed* between and across the two as that which *inscribes* both and yet which *proscribes* the absolute equivalence of one with the other without there being some remainder or difference, by which each is *described* from its other.

What is therefore *prescribed* is a remarking of that difference by which meaning arrives as the iterable remainder of the other. I am speaking *of* construction, and *of construal* therefore. Yet I am not outside these subjects. In writing *of* them, I am actively engaging in their own processes. I *construe*. I *construct*. And I do so, what is more, in a reciprocal fashion, weaving endlessly across the boundaries of each, and erasing the finite or permanent sense of a border. I am engaging not merely in description, or what would be called a constative speech act. I am also *doing* what I am describing with and in words. I am producing, constructing, what is known as a *performative speech act*. I am crossing a line once again, between forms.

II PERFORMATIVITY

Before we proceed further, we should reflect on what a performative speech act is. The performative is at the heart of deconstruction. Derrida formalizes a radical notion of the performative in addressing the instability of speech acts. His analysis of the performative in 'Signature Event Context' arrives as a response to J. L. Austin who distinguishes between constative and performative or illocutionary utterances. The former is an 'assertion' or 'description', while the latter is 'an utterance which allows us to do something by means of speech itself' (1999, 6–7).

Of performative utterances such as the 'I do' of the wedding ceremony, 'I name this ship', and so on, 'to utter the sentence . . . is not to *describe* my doing . . . it is to do it. None of these utterances is either true or false . . . When I say . . . "I do", I am not reporting on a marriage: I am indulging in it' (1999, 6–7). This is Austin's definition. However, Austin qualifies the definition, pointing out that some statements, whilst appearing to be performatives, do not necessarily fulfil that function. They are not felicitous. The example given by Austin is of an actor in a play. Were I in a play, film or television show saying 'I do' in a staged marriage, then this utterance would not be 'true' or serious (1999, 22). It would be what he terms 'parasitic' on the real performative speech act, but is not performative itself because it operates as a special exception, subject to different language rules (those of fiction).

Austin's inflexible and 'proper' sense of the limits and contexts of a speech act are questioned by Derrida. 'Is not', asks Derrida, 'what Austin excludes as anomalous, exceptional, "non-serious", that is *citation* . . . the determined modification of a general citationality – or rather a general iterability – without which there would not even be a "successful" performative?' (*MP*, 325). I will come back on other occasions – I promise – to both citation and iterability. For now though, it is important, albeit ridiculous, not to mention impossible, that I stick to the subject of the performative. Returning to Derrida's question, you might notice how it undoes Austin's assumptions, especially when Derrida continues by asserting that a 'paradoxical but inevitable consequence' of the forces of citationality and iterability is that what might be considered from Austin's perspective a so-called successful performative is in fact and 'necessarily an "impure" performative' (*MP*, 325). It is 'impure' precisely because in operating according to a given rule, law, institution or structure of officially and properly inscribed utterances, it is not genuine but parasitical, even in those instances where it is supposedly genuine and unique. When I say 'I do' or 'I promise' (as in the statement on English bank notes 'I promise to pay the bearer on demand the sum of . . .'), I am *citing*, reiterating, a formula the authenticity of which can only be attested to through the possibility of its being institutionally repeatable, the same every time. This is what makes the 'authenticity' of the performative 'impure'. As my parenthetical example of the statement on each and every bank note issued by the Bank of England (since 1833) shows, the promise is a performative of an act being carried out that the words anticipate and supposedly guarantee.

Or let's take Nicholas Royle's example: 'if I promise . . . to provide you, in due course, with an account of Derrida's work . . . it is always possible that this promise will not be kept' (2003, 27). Royle might have died before finishing the book. You might die before finishing reading the book. I might die before I finish writing the book in which you will read this commentary on the promise. Royle might not have meant what he said. He may not have been lying exactly, but he may not have been entirely serious. In the promise – and by extension any performative – there must be necessarily the chance that it can always fail. Hence the words on the bank note, which function structurally in a manner similar to Royle's, are merely the iterable citation of a fiction of deferred and generalized fulfilment. Neither true nor false, they still 'do' something, but their doing, their structural completion, is in fact haunted by the possibility that such an act might not be fulfilled and also by the fact that the statement can always be transferred outside some genuine or originary, unique context.

Derrida explains this by asking a further question. Could a performative succeed,

> if its formulation did not repeat a 'coded' or iterable statement, in other words if the expressions I use to open a meeting, launch a ship or a marriage were not identifiable as *conforming* to an iterable model, and therefore if they were not identifiable in a way as 'citation'? . . . given this structure of iteration, the intention which animates utterance will never be completely present in itself and its content . . . One will no longer be able to exclude . . . the 'non-serious' . . . from 'ordinary' language. (*MP*, 326–7)

Any utterance, sign or mark is always available to citation and iterability. This is the very premise of communication, whereby transmission sends beyond the supposedly 'proper context' of a unique event (such as writing my signature). Intrinsic to this possibility of communication, of sending or posting, is the opposite yet concomitant recognition that there remains *even before I have sent a post card, published an article, spoken to you on the phone*, 'the possibility that *any* performance may fail' (Howells 1999, 65). This is a condition of any articulation. The problem is that the performative relies, in Austin's theorization, on the presupposition of a 'self-conscious "I" . . . In order for a performative to be felicitous, I must mean what I say, and must know what I mean and that I mean what I say, with . . . no unconscious motives or reservations' (Miller 2001, 28–9). As far as Austin is concerned, the performative must 'be uttered by a fully self-conscious ego in complete possession of its wits and its intentions' (1999, 32).

The question of irony arises, inevitably. Irony would not be considered felicitous by Austin. There's a constant destabilizing force in irony, marking it with a radically undecidable condition that puts the onus of interpretation on the person hearing, receiving the communication, reading the letter, email or book. So, the performative cannot depend on consciousness. It can always have the power to produce unforeseen effects in its arrival, over which I have no control. In order to be truly, radically performative, the performative must operate as 'a "communication" which does not essentially limit itself to transporting an already constituted semantic content guarded by its own aiming at truth' (*MP*, 322). It is precisely, *ironically*, because irony relies on a certain parasitic citation or borrowing from seemingly antithetical statements, which logic would dictate cannot function simultaneously, that its performative force exceeds the limits of some proper form of communication and transport. And what goes for irony also goes, at least in principle, for all language. The performative is always already haunted therefore. 'Spooky and perverse' (Royle 2003, 29), the performative is always already structured by the *perverformative* (*PC*, 136). It acts perversely. It perverts intention. What haunts it is its failure, as I've said, but also its non-seriousness, its inability to guarantee fulfilling its intention, and also its failure, despite my best intentions, to remain felicitous, sincere, true to itself.

III TAKING OFF FROM DE-CONSTRUCTION OR, LEAVING HOME: DE LOBIA[1]

This still leaves us to confront the prefix, *de-*, from which I begin this chapter. In considering the *de-* of *deconstruction*, I am inviting you to investigate through an orientation around the contradictory and paradoxical semantic values of the prefix the ways in which language 'performs' its own deconstruction, problematizing the use of a term such as deconstruction in any purely constative fashion. Prefixes can have a habit of being ignored or underestimated in their force. This particular prefix, a Latin adverb and preposition, operates on words with which you might be familiar, but without necessarily being aware of the effects by the hinge or bracket that *de-* forms and causes to function. It has, most commonly, a private force, as for example in many of the most commonly misunderstood uses of *deconstruction*, that is, the opposite of construction, to take apart, to dismantle and so on. Beyond this immediate signification though, as a preposition and not simply a prefix (the latter being derived from the former), *de* may be translated variously, as: *down from, from, off, of* or *concerning*. The French preposition *de*, itself the offspring of its Latin parent, and announcing its variant filiation in the family resemblance (*la brisure*) but also announcing itself as a break or fracture (*la brisure*), a difference in short by which that resemblance has the chance of its appearance. Both resemblance and departure therefore, connectedness and break, similarity and otherness: all find themselves at work and haunting the structure of *de*, even as in its many appearances as a mere prefix that *de* appears to offer itself as a, perhaps undecidable, countersignature. That which is deconstruction concerns, comes from, takes off from, or is, in a certain way, *of* construction.

As each of these formulations acknowledge, there is in *deconstruction* equally, if not more so than in its conventional misuse having to do with a somewhat mechanistic and utilitarian or applied 'taking-apart', the silent announcement of an interest in constructions, construals and so on. Specifically, what is written in the term is an apprehension of that which is *in* and *of* construction, which makes it all hang together *as if* it were a unified, full, non-differentiated identity. What is announced in the affirmative countersignature of *deconstruction*, of that concerning construal and construction, is the work of an analysis that *de*-pends (hangs on, suspends itself from) on the close and patient tracing of construction and construal. Everything *depends* on the close and patient reiteration of grammatical, semantic, syntactical, material, ideological, cultural, historical, political, hieratical, ontological, phenomenological (*etc.*) structures and forms. It is to look for that which desists and so is already *decongruous* (to coin a word) within the *de congruo* assumption of harmony within any form, structure or identity. As a consquence, it is through analysis that there occurs an opening of that form or meaning beyond itself, taking off from the non-rational or incongruous difference within the selfsame on which all such identities *depend*. I do not *decongruate* however, any more than I *deconstruct*. For

> the *dé* does not determine . . . perhaps . . . the *dé* dislodges . . . radically, in an uprooting that would gradually dislocate the whole series, which seemed merely to be modifying a common

stem and assigning complementary attributes to it. A powerful meditation on the root, on . . . a-radicality . . . here is what we might follow, among other paths. (I:D, 1)

Perceiving what is at stake therefore in the question of deconstruction, we need to start by 'dislodging' so-called 'deconstruction' from the habitual. Taking off from what the *de* authorizes in its countersignature, we must expel ourselves from its house, from the economies that would control the institution and make of it a habit or technique, to which we become habituated.

IV BEYOND ENCLOSURE: DE FINIRE

What I have sketched so far should suggest to you that 'deconstruction' is inimical to a closure, to the *fin* of de*fin*ition, both in the operations of whatever we think we mean when we speak of deconstruction, and in the very act of definition itself, as a means to bring about an end to the undecidability concerning this most overused and equally most obscure, most enigmatic of words. As its prefix should now illuminate for you, there is that *in* de-finition, specifically as articulated in the *de-* in relation to the *finite* that moves one away from the closure of such finality. And this of course is taking place nearly simultaneously, albeit silently and perhaps invisibly, every time one speaks of a *definition*. In the act of de*fin*ition there is another gesture, *de*finition's countersignature, which torques and opens beyond itself any attempted act of defining, giving meaning or identity to something, someone, some concept. And this applies perhaps nowhere more so than to *de-construction*, to deconstruction in deconstruction, were such a thing imaginable.

Therefore, I know of no other way to begin than by repeating myself apropos 'deconstruction'. A word associated with Jacques Derrida, it is moreover a word given in a number of contexts as a master term for 'what Derrida does'. It thus becomes a determination and identification signalling a critical practice, an approach to the act of reading, interpretation and, therefore, a methodology. This is to a large degree a fallacious assumption and yet it persists.

Deconstruction is conventionally recognized as a school or method of criticism. Equally conventionally – which in some cases means without thinking or avoiding thought – when thought of as a school, method or critical programme, deconstruction is (mis)-

understood to have been developed by Derrida. At the same time, where this misperception still persists, there is the occasional expression of a desire that 'it' (this assumed, so-called deconstruction) would vanish. The desire is not articulated directly but takes place as something of a performative commentary (it is performative to the extent that what it expresses is the desired state longed for beneath the seeming affirmation of fact). As it was put to me in March 2006, 'now that deconstruction is moribund, what is the purpose of continuing to read Derrida?' Had the second part of the statement, the question, been asked on its own this would have elicited a very different kind of response to the one I gave, the one which, in some detail and with some elaboration I feel compelled to repeat. However, that I am repeating myself takes place because of that inaugural clause: *now that deconstruction is moribund.* Not a question but an assertion, its rhetorical mode is one of disingenuous bullying – or it would be if one felt bullied. Equally, one might say it sounds like a wish. The statement amounts to a performative. For it does not so much describe a situation merely (this would be a constative speech act, operating on its subject from outside, as in the statement, 'the sky is blue'), as it takes on the form of an acting out or 'doing' – hence *performative.* It says, I wish or I want deconstruction to be moribund. It says that however, from a quite stunning lack of comprehension. What it hides in its bluster of certainty is the anxiety of the person asking the question, someone who despite the desire to appear a good reader nonetheless wants to close the book on deconstruction.

The commentary is pointless, exposing its own overly nervous symptomatology in being asked at all. Let me schematize the logical problematic here in four gestures that describe a frame or inscribe a tombstone of sorts in which to present the symptomatics of desire from which the interrogation is generated. First:

- if there were a methodology, a school or programme called deconstruction and, furthermore,
- supposing such a thing were to exist (a convenient fiction so as to provide a target for the stupidity that undergirds the excuse not to read), then
- if it – or they – were moribund, nearly dead, having lost all sense of purpose or vitality, were becoming obsolete, if it were declining, dying, on the way out, waning, past its best or sell-by date,

on its last legs, past it, having seen better days, dilapidated or in the words of Michael Palin, shagged out after a long squawk – why, then
* there would be no need, there would never have been a need for the protocol of such a rhetoric in the first, second or indeed, any other place.

Deconstruction r. i. p.

I use this anecdote because the misunderstanding is all the more appallingly and hilariously inaccurate because it is so pervasive (not to suggest pernicious), widespread and eagerly accepted. With misunderstanding arrives misrepresentation and one is caught in a critical hall of mirrors. Take, for example, this following 'definition', which the dictionary of the software package 'Worldbook' offers: 'a method of literary criticism', it proclaims, 'applied especially to poetry, in which the text is reduced to its basic linguistic and semantic elements'. Equally inaccurate, the sixth edition of the *Columbia Encyclopedia* claims that the 'term "deconstruction" was coined by French philosopher Jacques Derrida in the 1960s'. One can perhaps forgive encyclopaedias or dictionaries for a degree of journalistic, which is to say non-specialist, error. Surely though, such a thing is more amiss when an academic makes such a gaffe.

Where should we begin then? Perhaps with the word itself, although this guarantees nothing, of course. Before anything else, deconstruction is not a neologism. Derrida affirms the word as something found, one might say an *objet trouvé*. It is, he remarks, 'a very old word in the French language' (*A∏WD*, 224). It is a verb and noun: *déconstruire, déconstruction, se déconstruire*. The first and third versions are visibly suggestive of the English *construe* as much as they are construction. Immediately therefore you may glimpse the otherwise invisible trace that moves between construction and construal. That last form, the self-reflexive verb, that's particularly nice: (it) deconstructs (itself) but not 'one deconstructs oneself' or even implicitly 'I myself deconstruct myself'. As Derrida comments, the reflexive condition of the verb signalled in that *se* does not attest to 'the reflexivity of some ego or consciousness'. In being precisely *not* this seductive and traitorous trace of the subject tempting you to misconstrue meaning and so situate an identity, therein lies 'the whole enigma'. For reflexivity is announced, or is glimpsed announcing itself as that which comes to pass or takes place without the operative presence of a subjectivity (LJF, 274).

Deconstruction is not solely French. The word can be found in the *Oxford English Dictionary*, derived from the French to be sure but an English term nonetheless. According to the *OED*, the first known written appearance of the word in English is in 1882. As with its French predecessor, it has legal connotations. Here is the citation used by the Dictionary from that year: 'A reform the beginnings of which must be a work of deconstruction'. Deconstruction presages reform therefore, it comes before reform as its beginning. Inaugurating or initiating a legal or political activity of transformation, deconstruction clears the ground, opens up to the possibility of change structure, institution, discourse or organized machinery of thought and habit. The English then appears almost the same as the French. It is the same and yet not the same: deconstruction/déconstruction. What a difference an accent makes, I am tempted to suggest and, while not making too much out of this, it is perhaps important that we observe the accent, its graphic, mute appearance. It offers a sign in writing, a mark or trace irreducible to any voice. The accent says nothing, and yet it may be read as 'speaking volumes' as the idiom has it. That accent and its non-translation might be said to mark economically and in a violent fashion the fortunes of deconstruction.

Whatever it may or may not be, deconstruction is always immanent in the conceptual languages of Western metaphysics. If there is an 'it' to 'deconstruction', then it is at work in language, it is not distinct from the very forms of expression, articulation, identity or meaning that it inhabits, *as if* it were some alien parasite dependent on its host and yet without which the host has no meaning. That every structure, institution, form, identity is different from every other, this must necessarily infer that anything which we might identify by the name of deconstruction must, in being intrinsic to those forms or meanings, neither be thought outside those structures, whether semantic or epistemological, ontological or cultural, nor brought to bear as some device on the analysis or 'taking apart' of the same identities or determinations. As Derrida remarks, 'operating necessarily from the inside, borrowing all the strategic and economic resources of subversion from the old structure, borrowing them structurally, that is to say without being able to isolate their elements and atoms, the enterprise of deconstruction always in a certain way falls prey to its own work' (*OG*, 24). Here, Derrida identifies the 'intrinsic' nature of what is taken to be the deconstructive element that exists already before any reader or analyst. At the same time, he also addresses acts of reading deconstruction as the enterprise to be undertaken. Simultaneously however, because of the immanence of deconstruction within the languages and structures of our cultures and identities, then reciprocally it follows that any effort to pursue the 'enterprise of deconstruction' must also be inflected by its own parasitical, deconstructive element, if only in the language which one brings to bear as the analytical medium operating on the subject or object of analysis and interpretation.

This is what has been missed frequently in the reading of Derrida. In being missed, language falls prey in precisely the manner described in the foregoing quotation to its own auto-recuperative ineluctability. Despite this, and despite the many cautions and *caveats* issued by Derrida over a period of 40 years or so, it remains true to say that deconstruction is associated with the texts of Jacques Derrida, especially his earlier publications from the 1960s, where he first employs the term. The term is used, as Derrida has had occasion to comment, in particular situations as a possible translation for two German words, *Destruktion* (destruction) and *abbau* (dismantling, quarrying, decomposition, breakdown, disintegration), used by Martin Heidegger. As Peggy Kamuf points out, 'Derrida had initially proposed [the word deconstruction] in a chain with other words – for example, difference, spacing, trace – none of which can command the series or function as a master word' (Kamuf 1991, xvii). So, while deconstruction is neither a concept nor a thing and does not name a methodology, it is moreover not a key signifier. Deconstruction is one term among many used by Derrida in his writing. Among the other terms used are *hymen, écriture, différance, text, trace, arché-écriture*. Some of the preceding terms will be considered elsewhere in the present volume. It should be borne in mind though, that none of these words, deconstruction included, is privileged over any other. They are all used on different occasions, in different and differing contexts, without any term assuming an absolute value of use over any of the others. The use of the words is dictated by the object of analysis or text being analysed, and according to the range of contexts – historical, philosophical, conceptual, discursive – which determine the shape and structure of the object, subject or text in question.

Geoffrey Bennington remarks on Derrida's choice of analytical 'levers' in the form of particular words, and their subsequent fortune. We have taken, he says, 'a series of terms from Derrida, who took them from texts read not according to a program or a' method . . . but, at least in (irreducible) part, according to the flair and the chance of encounters with what is bequeathed or repressed by the tradition'. Bennington then continues: 'these terms are singular in the sense that they remain more or less attached to the text from which they were taken, and never achieve the status of meta-linguistic or metaconceptual operators' (Bennington 1993, 267). As Derrida identifies that which falls prey to its own work, so Bennington highlights the impossibility of assigning to words such as deconstruction, writing, difference and so on the status of meta-linguistic or metaconceptual motifs. Such terms do not operate beyond, above or outside the textual or conceptual frames and networks in which they are found or employed. They, and still others, do not mean the same thing, nor do they serve the same purpose, yet they operate in Derrida's strategic textual analyses, interruptions and inventions, in similar dislocating ways to describe the unfolding of the functioning of the structure of a concept, institution, identity or meaning.

In part, Derrida's purpose in exploring the structure of a structure is to show how all structures rely on a centring or grounding principle, idea, concept which, though never examined as such, guarantees the identity, meaning, value of the structure. To show the structurality of structure however is not to deconstruct a text. You cannot deconstruct a text, as you can analyse it from, say a Marxist or feminist, or a structuralist position. Derrida does not offer us a method of reading called 'deconstruction', which, once learned, can be applied to anything we choose to read. As Derrida reminds us, 'the concept of structure and even the word "structure" itself are as old as . . . Western science and Western philosophy' (*WD*, 278). The concept and word are thus part of the very fabric of our thinking, yet about which we barely give a thought when we employ concepts. They inform silently almost all, if not every, epistemological and semantic procedure by which we function and navigate the world in which we live. Yet, to cite Derrida once more, '[s]tructure – or rather the structurality of structure – although it has always been at work, has always been neutralized or reduced, and this by a process of giving it a center or of referring it to a point of presence, a fixed origin' (*WD*, 278). Derrida's concern has been with exposing the ways in which such reference to presence or origin have been maintained in the history of Western thought, whether that history is expressed through the texts of philosophy, what we call the literary, or, as is the case in a number of his later essays, in forms and institutions such as government, the university, national identity, the concept of the gift or the idea of mourning. On the subject of presence or origin as organizational lodestones, '[t]he function of this center was not only to orient, balance, and organize the structure . . . but above all to make sure that the organizing principle of the structure would limit what we might call the play of the structure' (*WD*, 278).

A text, a structure, an idea, an institution, a philosophical or epistemological model: all contain in themselves that which disturbs and is in excess of the serenity, the self-assuredness of the full, simple identity as such. That which may be generalized as a system or model is defined by the laws of self-identification or by generic determination. What departs from generality, what breaks the law of genre is precisely what announces the singularity of a text. On a number of occasions, Derrida's writing has performed the tracing of the contours of whatever it takes to be its object of analysis. In such a process, which effectively doubles the writing being delineated in a transformative fashion, Derrida alights upon a single term, word or concept. For example, in one essay, given initially as a largely extemporized lecture at the Centre Georges Pompidou, Paris, November 1982, Derrida took two words from Joyce's *Finnegans Wake* – 'he war' – exploring their structural, semantic and epistemological significance to the text. Specifically, he asks the question: 'how many languages can be lodged in two words by Joyce?' (TwJ, 145). In so doing, Derrida is not only asking the question of languages – French, English and so on – but also of discourses that are to be read as embedded in these two words.

In the previous paragraph, I have stressed the idea of singularity. If you return briefly to the remark of Bennington's previously cited, you will notice that he talks of specific motifs or figures in their singularity. The notion of singularity will arise repeatedly throughout this book, as will the related matter of iterability, that process of transmission and repeatability formalized by Derrida, where the sign, text, concept is capable of being transmitted, communicated and so repeated beyond any supposedly finite context. Nicholas Royle offers us a lucid account of the importance of thinking singularity, beginning with the literary text but opening this out to consider the question of being: 'Everyone writes – and reads – differently, in their own, singular fashion', writes Royle. By extension, '[e]veryone has their own way of doing, thinking, feeling or experiencing things . . . it might be a singular situation' (Royle 2003, 119–20). Singularity however 'entails a double-bind', as Royle argues (2003, 120). For, as Derrida argues, while an event 'only happens to me' (C, 305), an 'absolutely pure singularity . . . would not be available to reading' (SICL, 68). Reading in this case implies transmission, communication, sending or posting, writing, textuality, memory, the concept of the archive, the formation of laws and institutions, repeatability in general, in fact, beyond the original context of their inscription. Thus the singularity of a text or even an identity may be read only as these are both available beyond the 'unique' moment of their taking place and also, in terms of literature and institutional forms, their relationship as singular entities to institutional and conventional laws that govern identification grounded in similarity or resemblance.

Language is of course a general system. It belongs to no one. Language, as Derrida says, is never owned (LNO). 'I have only one language; it is not mine' (*MOPO*, 1). How it is used may signal a certain singularity however: 'one cannot, for a thousand all too obvious reasons, compare my experience, my history, or my relation' to the English language to Derrida's 'experience and history and to his experience of the' French language (LNO, 101). Yet communication can on occasions take place, however faultily, even though language 'is never owned' and cannot be appropriated (LNO, 101). There must be 'a respect for the idiom', for the singular (LNO, 102). It is precisely the play and the tension between the singular and the general, the singular and the iterable, by which one proceeds without the rush to universalize or generalize. For what Derrida and I share, in common with you, and you, and Celan, Shakespeare or Abdelkebir Khatibi, is that we or, indeed, anyone ought to be able to declare that 'I have only one language and it is not mine; my "own" language is, for me, a language that cannot be assimilated . . . My language, the only one I hear myself speak and agree to speak, is the language of the other' (*MOPO*, 25).

With regard to this question of singularity and the other, if we return briefly to the essay 'Two Words for Joyce', we can illustrate this point, showing how it is precisely what is idiomatic in Joyce's use of language that attests both to the singularity of a work such as *Finnegans Wake* and, seemingly paradoxically, to how that very uniqueness or singularity is comprehensible and possible only in relation to reading and particular formalized systems such as language, grammar, syntax, translation. Such possibility also announces the declaration that language is not owned, it is always the other's. Reading 'he war' Derrida essays a 'first translation': 'HE WARS – he wages war, he declares or makes war, he is war, which can also be pronounced by babelizing it a bit . . . by Germanizing, then, in Anglo-Saxon, He war: he was – he who was . . . ' and so on to hearing in these words the utterance of YAHWE, before catching at the Germanic resonance *wahr*, meaning true, real or genuine (TwJ, 145). Thus through a certain performative 'babelization' of the words, a loosening of their polysemantic resonances across national tongues and identities, Derrida finds and responds to the Babel of all language, the war of tongues and nations initiated after a fashion by the fall of the tower of Babel in the Old Testament. In this though, Derrida is doing no more than unveiling the logic of Babel and the war economy that informs language in its production of meaning. He finds what is already underway in the language. For *Finnegans Wake* is already a contest of tongues, of genealogies and the histories of warring families. The general system of language is shown to operate through a war economy. Derrida does not *invent* meaning in the sense of producing something original and unique, for the first time. Instead, he gives to *invention* its other meaning, one which though less obvious is nonetheless in that word, the sense of finding what is already there but archived, buried, encrypted. In this manner, borrowing from the resources found in a given place, and putting them to work often counterintuitively within and against their locations, Derrida transforms the reception and perception of the text, the concept, the institution, theme or whatever, through examining how that single figure or phrase operates in the structure as a whole, in excess of the structure.

The figure in question then, far from calming down the production of a single meaning in the overall economy of the text, troubles that logic, making the univocal meaning undecidable. As I have sought to suggest through the prefix *de-* this is what is already at work in language. It is not some operation one imposes on language. Deconstruction is not a method. In unfolding the structurality of the structure, Derrida thus makes plain the aporia within the structural logic, on which the structure depends for its transmission, yet which it suppresses everywhere. In opening the structure's play to its own movement – already installed in the structure and not imposed from some supposed 'outside' – beyond the centre which the text is conventionally assumed to approve, or on which it is otherwise grounded, Derrida's discussion performs the already performative textual oscillation within the structure. It is such oscillation which conventional and institutional acts of reading seek to damp down, often through institutionally approved methods and techniques of reading that aim to emphasize the harmony of identity, at the cost of difference and undecidability. So, to reiterate: the exemplary reading cannot be rendered as a methodology, a technique, because, in being faithful to the contours of what is being analysed, the exemplary critique or analysis never applies a theory. On the other hand, the analysis is always already applied, in that it applies itself responsibly to its text. It offers the rigorous delineation of that which is in question, which, when performed, transforms the text, concept, institution, through the focus on that which moves the structure but which is not necessarily logical within the economy of the structure.

V POST CARDS, ENVOIS

Resisting any positivist or constructivist tendencies implicit in the conventional critical determination of deconstruction, Derrida has this to say:

> You know the programme; [deconstruction] cannot be applied because deconstruction is not a doctrine; it's not a method, nor is it a set of rules or tools; it cannot be separated from performatives . . . On the one hand, there is no 'applied deconstruction'. But on the other hand, there is nothing else, since deconstruction doesn't consist in a set of theorems, axioms, tools, rules, techniques, methods. If deconstruction, then, is nothing by itself, the only thing it can do is apply, to be applied, to something else, not only in more than one language, but also with something else. There is no deconstruction, deconstruction has no specific object . . . Deconstruction cannot be applied and cannot not be applied.

So we have to deal with this aporia, and this is what deconstruction is about. (*AП*WD, 217–18)

One the one hand . . . on the other hand . . . This formula is, it might
be argued, that which formulates the law of undecidability. The undecidable is that which is irreducible to any determination, and
Derrida's oft-used formula is one that maintains the undecidable in
the face of any demand for determination or identification. He situates the paradoxical within a particular model, thereby destabilizing
the truth or unequivocal value of that model, so: there is no applied
deconstruction because deconstruction is not a method. At the same
time, there is nothing other than deconstruction at work within any
structure, form, meaning or identity. The only programme here is the
refusal of a pro-gramme, a writing that arrives before (*pro-*), in
advance or ahead of the act of writing (*gramme*), as a propaedeutic
establishing in response to some other writing or text the need not to
read those prior texts. Thus, when Derrida comments, 'you know the
programme', he is commenting ironically on the by-now programmatic nature of the response to the very idea, and the concomitant
rejection, of deconstruction-as-programme, thereby operating ironically and performatively within the very kinds of utterance that
programme deconstruction.

Derrida's careful exposition of deconstruction turns on what
appears to be a formal paradox in his statement, then. Logically, an
ontological statement such as 'deconstruction is . . . X' should not
be able to accommodate two diametrically opposed positions. This
is particularly the case where one formulation begins 'deconstruction is', while the other insists that 'deconstruction is not'.
Conventionally speaking, such logic and the economy of its function
as the proposition or assertion of a truth, requires on the part of the
thinker a decision of an 'either/or' nature. An identification is
needed, which, in being put in place, resolves matters through the
establishment of a proposition or identity which is homogeneous,
self-contained, having a hermeneutically closed totality, within the
structure of which no element exists which is at odds with other elements of the formulation. Thus if something cannot exist, such a
statement presupposes that one cannot then say that it only exists in
the selfsame form.

Yet 'deconstruction', inasmuch as it names anything, names a
spacing that takes place simultaneously between or within meanings

or identities as the condition of their articulation . At the same time it comments also on the seemingly impossible condition of two identities, two meanings existing within the same location which differ from cach other, and both of which disable the possibility of their resolution into a totality or undifferentiated unity. Logical coherence opens within itself not as its collapse but as a revelation of the very condition of its expression or articulation. The condition of deferral, spacing, differentiation within a given concept does not require that I or anyone else observe it in order for it to take place or be a constituent element in the structure of a concept or practice. That which from particular logics of thought appears paradoxical or incoherent exists already. Not a thing as such, it takes place as the condition for thinking a notion, an ontology, model or form. This *taking place*, this spacing and deferral is called by Derrida variously *writing*, *text*, *différance* and, of course, *deconstruction*. It is an opening within identity (structural, conceptual, ontological, epistemological, ideological), whereby the very thought of that identity is seen to be made possible only through the incorporation necessarily of the signs of its non-identity or other, which informs every aspect of the form as a form. Moreover, those elements, for want of a better word, are not separable. They are not identifiable as absolutely separable terms. Instead they enfold one other mutually, touching on, and being interwoven into, each other. They do so at every instant of whatever the network of signs you seek to trace, and are everywhere irreducible to a single concept, idea or key term, the identity of which might somehow be shown were I to seek to 'regress' in an act of analysis 'back' towards some supposedly single, original, central or grounding element or nucleus. 'Deconstruction' is not therefore a structural term in any simple relational sense.

In deconstruction, one might say language, discourse, system, institution, conceptualization, ontology – all confront their own internal limits. They fall back on the economy of determination in the face of their own ruinous remainders, which nonetheless remain as so many traces of the undecidable. Here it might be suggested is the work of deconstruction. Here is deconstruction at work, and it is this which one must seek to read without attempting to stay its force. It is 'what remains unread or unreadable within the elaboration of concepts and workings of institutions' (Royle 1995, 160). *What remains unread*. This important phrase announces the endless commitment to reading at the heart of Derrida's work. There is always work to be done. There is always some remainder to come, to be given over to the lucid patient attempt to cover the ground once more. Derrida's perception of that which reading entails, as a very definition of reading, amounts to an acknowledgement of the inexhaustible reserves within 'the elaboration of concepts and workings of institutions', as well as in literary or philosophical texts. Such inexhaustibility may well seem abyssal. It may also entail our exhaustion while demanding that we return to the act of reading. But in such an idea of endless work is what amounts for Derrida to the ethics of reading, the purpose being not simply – if at all – to dismantle meaning but more significantly to show how a structure or system maintains invisibly its form and identity and so to begin or presage a work of reformation. Reformation does not take place if one stands outside a system, pretending to observe it from some other place objectively or dispassionately. Reading involves interesting oneself, involving oneself in the form, in-forming oneself one might say, or becoming *inter-ested: situating oneself as a being* (es-) *as a being whose being is defined by being between* (inter-), *between one identity and another, between one temporal location and another.*

Reading therefore opens to one a chance to reflect on the way in which any given or presumed ontology or identity is only ever a coming into being, a momentary collocation or occasion of traces that trace and are traced, opening meaning or the present to a haunting installation. More than this, perceiving the ineluctable translation of the self through its becoming, one might reflect that *where one is* (to use a phrase to which I give consideration in the chapter on literature), is marked, determined momentarily by the secret arrival of an other that occurs in reading. But of course, one cannot say for sure, and 'therein lies literature's secret, the infinite power to keep unde-cidable and thus forever sealed the secret of what it/she [*elle*] says' (*GGGG*, 18). What remains unread is inescapably a question of this secret, and reading remains that which opens one to a certain gift, 'as experience of the law that comes from the other . . . of the law whose giver is none other than the coming of the other, in this test of uncon-ditional hospitality which opens us to it before any condition, any rule, any norm, any concept, any genre, any generic and genealogical belonging' (*GGGG*, 48). What remains unread therefore is not that which the future holds as the final promise of the closure of reading. It is that which is always to come, always coming at any given moment of reading. Within any present or presence, there is the other, the haunting revenant. This is the secret of literature.

Because of this condition, it is impossible to programme reading. What passes for reading 'by the book', according to repeatable regulations is not properly a reading. Reading is irreducible to a consistent process, the stratagems and motions of which remain the same throughout its space and the time of its occurrence. Moreover, and as a provisional definition, this heterogeneous multiplicity of the unread, not-read, the unreadable and the as-yet-to-be-read is discernible within both discourse and, to stress the point again, 'the elaboration of concepts and workings of institutions'. If I stress this matter of reading institutions and concepts repeatedly it is because perhaps before anything else one must disabuse oneself of the idea that all Derrida does is talk of textuality or that his work has no bearing on cultural, material, historical or political forms as these manifest themselves in the world we inhabit, and by which we in turn are shaped.

The question therefore is not only one of tracing patiently that which inhabits language or writing according to some narrow or conventional definition. It is also a matter of that which makes possible the practical, political and historical or ideological operation of, for example, the idea of the university, the matter of a truly universal human rights, or the articulation of national identity, subjects on which Derrida has written urgently and cogently. Although it is impossible for me to speak to every issue in Derrida's work (and in many cases do nothing more than gesture towards some of its most politically insistent areas), it must be indicated in the guise of a guide possible other pathways, routes which had not been assumed to exist. There is that which 'has not been read, what remains unread or unreadable' in the articulation of social and political organization, whether one speaks of the university, government, the idea of democracy, notions of nation and so on, to which attention must be given.

If such matters have been generally glossed over in the institutionalization of deconstruction this is doubtless because what is at the heart of Derrida's thinking is deeply disturbing. It is an uncanny, perhaps appalling recognition that we are not, as Derrida has it in the essay 'The *Retrait* of Metaphor', 'like a pilot in his ship' (*R*M, 103). While Derrida is speaking here of the illusion that we believe we steer metaphor rather than figurally language dictating our course, the principle of illusionary mastery is at the heart of the need to master, to control the veering transport, the drift and slippage of Derrida's writing, to make it conform to our sense that we are in charge, we are behind the wheel. Hence, we see the need for the production of a method, so-called deconstruction. However, as Derrida has observed apropos a too hasty act of reading, there is 'no excuse for contenting oneself with flying through a text . . . the effect of thus skimming . . . on the fly are not limited to the hastily formed impression' (M&S, 228). The need to resist 'reading on the fly'. It doubtless also informs a response of Derrida's in the documentary *Derrida*. When asked of the books in his home library whether he has read most of them, Derrida replies, 'No, No. Only three or four. But I read those four really, really well' (D^2, 97). Here we read signalled in this seemingly off-hand remark the responsibility entailed in reading, a responsibility one has to the word 'deconstruction' if one aspires to be the good reader.

If reading remains to come deconstruction is untimely. This is why it haunts, interests itself in spectrality. It is the sign of a certain ghostly passage, an arrival or return from the past or future that disables and disjoints the present moment from within itself. Deconstruction takes place, then as that which can always arrive. It is that which is always already remarked within any identity or structure. It construes itself as other and its difference from any 'itself' at different times. Deconstruction, if it is anything at all, is the necessary spacing of a writing that reiterates its own displacements. Comprehending this remains the good reader's responsibility, and to which comprehension must come the response in the guise of a transformative critique. This is why, more than ever, it remains to be remarked, repeating oneself once more, if only in order to resist the 'hastily formed impression' that 'deconstruction is not a theory or a project. It does not prescribe a practice more or less faithful to it, nor project an image of a desirable state to be brought about' (Bennington 1988, 7).

We might sum up the hastily formed impression as bad reading (*PC*, 4), not reading, allergic reactions to reading and the avoidance of reading. One might even include amnesia, in the form of forgetting precisely what Derrida says. This question of forgetting has played a huge part in the fortunes of deconstruction in the histories of its reception or non-reception, its transmission and translation within and across institutional forms. Despite this, what takes place in deconstruction's singular acts is 'an affirmative form of resistance that points towards a new understanding' – of reading, of engagement, of ethical commitment and 'political practice' (Fynsk 2004, 56). Good reading is therefore all one has to oppose to all the symptoms observed as the reactions to deconstruction. Derrida touches on this matter in the following statement:

> I am not sure that deconstruction can function as a literary method as such. I am wary of the idea of methods of reading. The laws of reading are determined by that particular text that is being read. This does not mean that we should simply abandon ourselves to the text, or represent and repeat it in a purely passive manner. It means that we must remain faithful, even if it implies a certain violence, to the injunctions of the text. These injunctions will differ from one text to the next so that one cannot prescribe one general method of reading. In this sense deconstruction is not a method. (DO, 155)

Derrida's observation issues a *caveat* and an injunction concerning how one proceeds in reading. Notice also that Derrida cautions us to remain faithful to the text. A text cannot mean anything you care it to mean, as some parodists of deconstruction, idiots who speak of deconstructionism and other journalists have stated. You would think this is clear enough. To reiterate: there can be no method of reading that proceeds in the same fashion on every occasion because texts differ and dictate their readings if one is being faithful to, and responsible for their alterity. There is no methodology because every text exemplifies itself. It attests to its singularity, and not to some abstractable model of text, the rules of which hold true in every instance. This to make the point again is the aporia with which the reader has to contend in the name of a responsible critical intervention.

For all such foregoing reasons one cannot and one must not summarize meaning or pretend to encapsulate it. The responsible reader must not determine the literary simply as a range of effects, any more than she or he can hope to do this with or in the name of deconstruction. Were the reader to seek to do so, he or she would be seeking to produce the overhasty impression, to provide potted versions of thought. To formulate the hasty impression is to put an end to thinking by placing it in a nutshell (Caputo 1997, 31). This leads me to another comment of Derrida's that he begins through allusion to that demand on the part of some for the nutshell approach to thinking (not so much seeing the world in a grain of sand as transmitting the history of Western thought in a tee-shirt slogan), with the inaugural phrase 'in short':

> In short, deconstruction not only teaches us to read literature more thoroughly by attending to it as language, as the production of meaning through différance and dissemination, through a complex play of signifying traces; it also enables us to interrogate the covert philosophical and political presuppositions of institutionalized critical methods which generally govern our reading of a text . . . It is not a question of calling for the destruction of such institutions, but rather of making us aware of what we are in fact doing when we are subscribing to *this or that institutional way of reading.* (DO, 125; emphasis added)

At this moment, I have a strong urge to erase everything from this chapter except this quotation. Leaving it at the top of the chapter's first page, I would then invite you to write your own chapter in the space which is currently taken up with the sentences and paragraphs making up the content of this chapter. Imagine, something like an exam question would appear:

> What is deconstruction? What – *is* deconstruction? What is? Deconstruction? Discuss the difference between these three questions in the light of the foregoing extract. With extremely close reference to the text, discuss the understanding of deconstruction developed from this passage. Candidates may refer to the works of Derrida, particularly with   developing their understanding of the words *différance*   *ion, traces.* You must consider the relationship sign.   'da between language, specifically the language of h   ˜uage (and not as a convenient medium for the repre.   ` real world, more or less), and the question of the 'covˑ   ˑl and political presuppositions of institutionalized criˑ   ∧ ˜hich generally govern our reading of a text'. Give parˑ   ˑtion to what the philosophical and political presuppositiˑ ˑˑ institutionalized critical methods are or might be. Provide examples through a detailed examination of the presuppositions that generate your

own institutionalized critical methods, considering first what might be meant by the terms philosophical and political.

Some exam question you're no doubt thinking. As 'question', it exceeds what one is expected to demand conventionally or institutionally in the form of the examination. Implicitly therefore it invites you to attend to its own language as a complex play of signifying traces, and in turn expects you to turn your attention to the relation between the formal and the philosophical or political. In doing so though, it overflows the limit institutionally subscribed to in this or that way of reading, and so seeks to disorientate and reorientate your relation to the question of the question as this is subscribed to, and inscribed by institutional ways of reading. It therefore touches on the covert presuppositions of the critical method or methods. Nowhere more so perhaps than in the exam question are the demands institutionally for the nutshell to be imposed and closed exposed blatantly. One is adjudged relatively an inhabitant or outcast of the institution according to such demands, the very protocols of which issue injunctions to narcissistic repetitions of the self-same, whereby one is conjured as a subject of institutional philosophies, politics and laws, to articulate the extent to which one is that subject, and always subjected to such laws. In short, one must answer the question in order to be bounded in a nutshell, as Hamlet says, but a nutshell that is waiting patiently for one's own deformation. If we attend to language as language and not merely a medium of representation and seek to follow the complex play of signifying traces that thread through language to the philosophical and political presuppositions of the institution, then we may come to understand how an identity is produced for us, and how we participate actively in the shaping of our institutional identities.

In a sense, although I have only just articulated this – I promise you – it is the implicit motivation haunting this book. It is what drives me to repeat myself, to state again that deconstruction is not a methodology, and to cover terrain I have covered in different ways, more or less overtly, in encrypted and disguised manifestations for quite a few years. And I don't even feel that I've begun to answer the question, though I do believe I have caught sight of some of the ways one might put the question to work, in order to irritate and disrupt what we are in fact doing when we are subscribing to this or that institutional way of thinking. This in part is why, although Derrida's publications cannot be confined to literary study or the interdisciplinary interplay and tensions between, say philosophy, linguistics, literature and history, in the present volume I will be limiting myself to the immediate consideration of some of the ramifications of Derrida's thought for what we call writing, literature and art. This is engaged with not to carry on business as usual and so to produce a Derrida who can operate as a neutralized poetics of analysis within the *tekhne* of the institution. Rather the desire here is to engage with Derrida so as to open the work of what Christopher Fynsk defines with regard to Derrida's readings as an 'interrupting exposition' (2004, 36), which amount singularly, repeatedly, and together, to 'an opening to language that is an opening *of* language' (Fynsk 2004, 36) with regard to all the inexhaustible reserves of what we call history, ideology, ontology, politics, philosophy, aesthetics as their traces might chance to surface in the de-forms and disguises of the *literary*.

The work of *nutshelling*, of putting something to work in a neutralized and accommodated way, is not necessarily pernicious or repressive, even if it is what Derrida would call the sign of auto-immunization. Systems take into themselves just enough that is potentially harmful in order to assimilate the 'poison' and make it work within the system in question. Difference and otherness are thus given a home, on the condition of their being transformed and made to conform to the law of the house, to the institutional economy by which identities maintain themselves, systems continue to function. In no small measure, this begins to explain the historical transformation, and subsequent transmission, of deconstruction thought as a method with goals, aims and outcomes that can be repeated and so conform to acts of measurement. (Is the machine running well, does this incorporation or 'upgrading' serve the purposes of maintaining function and production?) By providing for deconstruction a stable meaning, placing it in the nutshell, in short making it into an institutionally tolerated mode of reading, the university can, and has in specific cases, fashion a deconstruction after its own image, for epistemological and ideological purposes. One can also observe such activities at work in governments, nations, families and elsewhere. Again, this is not a deliberate plan, necessarily. However, to insist on this matter, it is an inescapable condition of the economic procedures of various institutional forms in the repetitive maintenance of the ontological imperatives that inform and underpin the grammar and syntax of those establishments, organizations or societies. In the case of deconstruction, the university can best operate if deconstruction can be made into a reading method more or less akin to other methodologies. Taught as a set of theorems, procedures and practices, 'it' can be then applied to whatever acts of reading you like, producing in the process one more set of competent analyses, all of which generate another set of finalized and stable meanings.

It is perhaps a sign of how inappropriate so-called deconstruction is to such procedures that it has resulted in so many vehement responses, so many death wishes both inside and outside higher education. Despite the efforts to transform deconstruction though, it remains as so many instances of affirmative resistance. The openness, the experience of undecidability and the idea of an endless multiplicity performed in inventive acts of reading can be seen as quite disturbing. As readers however, we are confronted with this ineluctable demand for response and responsibility in the absence of any calculable determinants. One cannot decide on the undecidable. One cannot calculate what is incalculable, or which might arrive without any warning. It is perhaps for this very reason that Derrida has offered a provisional representation of deconstruction in the following terms: 'deconstruction [is] that which is – far from a theory, a school, a method, even a discourse, still less a technique that can be appropriated – at bottom what happens or comes to pass [*ce qui arrive*]' (TOJ, 17). That which arrives, which is always arriving, is impossible to pin down, locate or predict.

Never single or homogeneous then, deconstruction should involve a patient attempt to trace what remains unread, to risk a reading in the face of the undecidable. Stressing the work of language but not its being privileged over that conventionally understood as extra-linguistic, Derrida makes the political and historical dimensions clear in what will be the final, postal arrival here. As Derrida contends, the premises of a discourse 'are not absolute and ahistorical'. He continues:

> They depend upon socio-historical conditions, hence upon non-natural relations of power that by essence are mobile and founded upon complex conventional structures that in principle may be analyzed . . . and in fact, these structures are in the process of transforming themselves profoundly and, above all, very rapidly (this is the true source of anxiety in certain circles, which is merely

revealed by 'deconstruction': for before becoming a discourse, an organized practice that *resembles* a philosophy, a theory, a method, which *it is not*, in regard to those unstable stabilities or this destabilization that it makes its principal theme, 'deconstruction' is firstly this destabilization on the move in, if one could speak thus, 'the things themselves'; but it is not negative. Destabilization is required for 'progress' as well. And the 'de-' of *de*construction signifies not the demolition of what is constructing itself, but rather what remains to be thought beyond the constructivist or destructionist scheme). What is at stake here is the entire debate, for instance, on the curriculum, literacy, etc. (*LI*, 147; emphasis in original)

Everything remarked in this chapter is traced in Derrida's italicized emphases. Reconstituting a reading of those emphases would amount to an act of construction as long as this volume, if not longer. What goes for any discourse in general goes most especially for the idea of deconstruction when imagined *as if* it were or could be rendered as a discourse *comme les autres*. As you are now aware, this is 'the true source of anxiety in certain circles, which is merely revealed by deconstruction' (*LI*, 147). Effectively, Derrida construes the movement of deconstruction within the conventional assumptions concerning discourses considered as 'organized practice[s]', in reading the historical and other non-natural conditions and relations by which such institutionalized languages come to be structured as philosophies, methods, theories and so on. He thus traces that 'destabilization on the move' in the discursive structures of a discourse. In this, the statement passes from being a constative speech act to being a performative one. Put another way, it does not so much 'tell' as 'show' in its own motions, motifs and the contours that they describe. And in the end, though firstly, Derrida identifies this 'destabilization on the move' in the ' "de-" of deconstruction', seeing in it *what remains to be thought, what remains to be read*.

You don't need me to tell you this though. If you take the responsibility entailed in reading to spend some time with the texts of Jacques Derrida, you will find that there is no stable, perpetually recurrent method, no reproducible structure of critique. There is though a seemingly endless affirmation of the need to take responsibility for acts of an endless and endlessly responsible attentiveness. *It concerns, it is a matter or case of*, taking responsibility for one's response, of not rushing to the decision which will already have struck you.

Am I getting under your skin yet?

It's all a question or a matter of what arrives to solicit you, *of what acts on you,* what resonates disturbingly. Never quite visible nor invisible, hovering at the limits of visibility, legibility, readability, it comes down, as you might say, to a question of the idiom.

In using the phrases I have highlighted and repeated I am drawing on the French idiom *Il s'agit.* One can translate it as 'it's a matter of', 'it's a question of', 'it concerns', 'it has to do with', 'it acts on'. The phrase is a conjugation of *s'agiter,* the reading of which can be forced as 'to be agitated', 'to agitate oneself', 'it agitates itself'. The frequency of the idiom in Derrida should however give one pause. Conventionally translatable by phrases such as I have indicated, there is that which oscillates in the French wholly unavailable in its English counterparts, not least because of its being formed from a reflexive verb: *s'agiter.* The verb is performative. It agitates itself, it is a case of agitation, which is, itself, agitating. Agitation acts on itself, on its verb. If you stop to consider the resemblance, albeit partial, between the French and the English verb *to agitate,* then you might begin to glimpse what concerns us here, what troubles the French usage. For Derrida it is a matter of what takes place as an agitation but one not caused by someone, not operated by some consciousness. The agitation, the motion or communication concerning us here, is a matter of an internal agitation always already taking place, coming to pass and at work within language, within conceptualization, which we might write in translation as follows: (*it*) *agitates* (*itself, the-itself*). This is the agitation, if you will, at work in the matrix prefix *de-.*

Agitation or *solicitation* (literally a shaking) takes place within the structure or frame of a given concept, term, word, notion, identity, meaning and so on, by which certainty, truth, univocality, all are made to tremble. It operates on identity and meaning semantically and philosophically in the undecidability it installs even in the smallest meaning bearing traces, such as the prefix or what Derrida calls a *philosopheme* (a conceptual unit or unity). It is a question therefore to write and wager on the taking place of a solicitation at the heart of what Derrida would identify as any conceptual or epistemological *homohegemony* (the power, dominance or sovereignty of the selfsame, of auto-identification) on which much of what Derrida calls the *mondialatinization* (a world-latinization of discourse) of thought relies. The *bad reader* (*PC*, 4) seeks to avoid what acts on him or her. He or she rushes to evade responsibility for what is a matter of concern, yet finding him- or herself all too easily *agitated* at the turn of nearly every page. If we are not to resign ourselves to the role of the bad reader, it is to such attentiveness that we, in turn, owe our attention, 'everywhere and always' (*OCF*, 53), and to which we must respond decisively, *as if* everywhere and always there were the signs of a *coup de donc*.[2]

NOTES

1. I am playing here in a somewhat bastard Latin on *dislodge*. *Dis-*, meaning *in twain, asunder, abroad, away, in different directions*, gave way etymologically to *de-* in those places where the private sense of reversal, separation, undoing, or taking apart, or a departure from something, is operative. As with certain examples of *de-*, *dis-* functions to produce compound verbs from their simple forms when the sense produced has to do with a reversal of an action or effect. *Lodge*, originally in Latin either *laubia* or *lobia* (hence my usage), is used to indicate a temporary rather than a permanent dwelling. My concentration in this chapter is on the ways in which 'deconstruction' as, incorrectly, method or programme of analysis is produced through two 'lodging' effects. On the one hand, it is taken into the house, into the institution of higher education for example, and so habituated or domesticated according to the laws and economies of that habitation. It will be noted that I play on *habit* and *habitual* as terms associated with habitation, inhabit and so on, such words deriving from *habitus*, meaning either to have or to be, to be constituted by. One's clothing is, archaically, one's habit; it constitutes the external form of one's being (as in the sense of uniforms, where what one does is conflated with who one is). But habit – as in inhabit, abode (the *abide*, again a term for one's habitation or dwelling, is where one *bides*, where one stays, one's abode, but to *bide* is also to maintain, to dwell or insist on) – is where one lives. What is habitual is what is homely, familiar, repeatable. It is what one inhabits, where one dwells, because the habitual is what is ordered, made customary through repetitive and regulated usage – hence deconstruction as '*school* of thought' (note the institutional and architectural metaphor), as methodology, theory, programme. Where one inhabits institutionally is the place by which one is occupied (another double sense, occupation being one's work and also the place one inhabits, *inhabit* having the now obscure transitive sense, *to occupy*). What takes place therefore in the section following the heading currently discussed is a construction of how the 'house of deconstruction', so to speak, comes to be constructed, as a necessary stage in making it possible to depart from this construct through the remainder of the chapter.

2. *Coup de donc*: it's one of those resolutely untranslatable phrases in Derrida's text. *Coup de donc* (*MP*, xxix) arrives at the end of the essay 'Tympan', which serves as a preface of sorts to *Margins of Philosophy*. A cut is made, an incision, which is also an inscription. One starts and so decides on the undecidable. One begins to economize in writing, by writing, or speaking, delivering a blow, the circumcision as decision. But a decision can only arrive in the face of something, some event. Decision is always a response, it is that which wounds and announces a boundary or border that leaves the trait which it enacts, even as it remarks it, on the blank page. Literally, the fall or blow of the 'therefore' implies a very Derridean logic, which you should attempt to read in the instantiating sentence of the first essay 'proper' of *Margins of Philosophy*, 'Différance': 'I shall speak, therefore, of a letter' (D, 3).

If you're reading the sentence attentively, the operation of *therefore* should strike you as grammatically odd, especially if you meditate on the placement of the sentence in which this word acts as a kind of hiccup to the common sense of order, sequence, logical and temporal organization, notions of starting point, beginnings and so on. This being the *first* sentence in effect, the *therefore* has no place in this sentence. It disorders order and priority, from the very start, signalling a prior location, a (dis)place(ment) in effect that haunts from the first this first statement. *Therefore* signals an absence, a past which has never been present, and appears to indicate also the 'start' as not a beginning place but in fact a response to an unheard comment or statement.

Turning back to the phrase *coup de donc*, what might be said *therefore* is that the logic of the first, the origin, source, genesis and so on is always already internally disrupted in that there is never truly a *first* time. It does so in all its senses, the arrival of the word marks a conclusion, it announces sequence, cause and effect, its arrival being in consequence of something. It implies inference. It admits that I am saying something by reason of . . . Even were I to write a sentence on a blank page at the very beginning of what will become the first page of a book I have not yet written, in some manner what befalls me is response to some prior other. To say 'I' is to respond. Therefore.

The first word, the first touch of pen to paper, finger to key. My first word in a seminar, on the phone, saying 'yes' or 'hello'. This may be a thought of mine, my searching for the right words. It may be more systematically my deliberate attempt to begin a book on Derrida by searching for the apposite beginning as a response to whatever I take at that time to be the 'principal' idea, text or thought that allegedly governs all others in Derrida's texts. However, none of this is *originary*. Nothing gets going for a first time. Therefore, let me repeat myself. Let me insist therefore that the therefore of the supposedly first time befalls me every time I begin *as if* for the first time, which therefore must be understood as a convenient fiction, in the wake of which I am constantly following, always after belatedly. Such belatedness is the condition of all reading and writing, marked as these acts are by never being on time, always being subject to the *après-coup*. (Lit. an after-blow, meaning *afterthought*. Strictly speaking the phrase, utilized as a translation in some contexts for the Freudian concept of *nachträglichkeit* or belatedness, is a tautology, as all thought is an afterthought.) This is the counter-logic of the *coup de donc*, in which the *donc* signals a temporal and spatial displacement, a deferral and differentiation, and with that the invisibility of the *après* of the Francophone idiom.

CHAPTER 2

DIFFÉRANCE AND WRITING

. . . what remains here [is] . . . the displacement of a *question*, a certain system somewhere open to an undecidable resource that sets the system in motion.

Jacques Derrida

For what is put into question is precisely the quest for a rightful beginning, an absolute point of departure, a principal responsibility.

Jacques Derrida

I A LETTER, LITERALLY A

There is no justifiable starting point for reasons to be explained. One can never begin strictly speaking because one must always account for 'the deferral within the now of writing' (*WD*, 300). I will speak, therefore, of a letter (D, 3; *SP*, 160).[1] And what a difference a letter makes. That letter is *a*. Without any beginning that can be justified, and in a first chapter that addresses itself to the subject of writing amongst other things, the first letter of the alphabet seems as good a place from which to depart as any other. Thus, I start conventionally. 'I begin', with a conventional opening, starting with what begins, a letter, in a series and structure that is an institutional form. Learning the alphabet, one is 'instituted', placed in relation to a system of writing by which one begins as a subject-in-language, who communicates through the coherence and convention, the habit and customs of the system, the institution of writing that gives voice to the 'I', so that 'I' can begin. And so, to reiterate: I begin both *with and from* a conventional and conventionally recognized starting point of sorts. Not a single starting point however so much as two, you will notice. Not wholly separate and yet somewhat separable: *with* and *from*. Everything *depends* 'from' this you might say, had you recalled parts of the previous chapter. Everything hangs by that thread, that *fil*iation, a filiation which also names affiliation – something other than, breaking off from, the closed system or weave. You will have noted that I emphasize these two distinct terms, *with* and *from*, two prepositions to do with the same moment. However, they mark that moment differently. One signals conjunction, the other departure. The beginning is disrupted from within itself, by its own gesture and in its own inaugural gesture, which is also a response to that conventionally understood first letter. Why? This will come down to the question of what writing is, what it can do, and what its effects and movements might give us to read.

If I write here somewhat elliptically, this is done for a purpose: to draw attention to what I am doing and, in so doing, to invite you to pay close attention to the act of writing, and the motions by which it proceeds. If there is no justifiable beginning, and one must begin only by convention or habit as that which pre-exists or pre-dates any 'true' beginning, then we are already underway in a system and a law that dictates how we proceed. Every 'beginning' is marked, traced and haunted by that which stands before it, and which, though invisible and apparently mute, is that to which we therefore respond, and from which we depart through the myth or fiction of a start, a beginning, an opening, an *incipit* – *as if* one could start from zero. Yet something makes that system, that law and the structures of both possible. Possible, we might say, in the first place. We shall call this *différance*. Différance is not difference. Or to put this differently, there is a difference between différance and difference. What this difference is does not come down simply to the retention of that acute accent over the *e* in the first word. It is not as though in retaining it I had wished to admit silently and graphically of some material maintenance or trace of 'foreign' difference that refuses stubbornly to be either accommodated or domesticated within English (you will have seen though how the residue of another's tongue resides in your mouth, whenever you utter the prefix *de-*). At least it is not merely with this in mind that the accent remains as the sign of another's tongue. Were we to stay within the other's language there would still be difference at work. There would still remain a dislocation if you will. An articulating non-resemblance between apparently similar appearances would be in place as that which displaces.

Were I to write for example that *différance* is not *différence*, there would still be a difference between the italicized French words irreducible to any question of accent. The accent stays the same but the difference remains. In writing of différance some critics dispense with the accent *as if* this affirmed a translation, so: differance. Such a gesture presupposes an unproblematic transport across borders. *As if*, imagine such a fiction, that which had the appearance (and only the appearance) of a concept could be transposed across languages and cultures, keeping intact all that was at work in the French while giving it an English home and expecting somehow that the processes, suppositions, contexts, histories and etymologies would continue to operate in much the same way. However, even were one to do this (and I for one will not), this would still not produce any untroubled resemblance between differance and difference. The difference remains. Différance remains, although it cannot be located as such as we will come to see, however indirectly. (NB If the way in which I am saying something seems obtuse, obscurantist, this is not the case, not deliberately at any rate. I am struggling to express something requiring a degree of precision and rigour.) The difference, moreover, between différance and difference is not just graphic either, although it is this markedly. It is not only a matter of a material or formal difference afforded by the introduction of the letter *a* where there should be an *e*. In coining what has the appearance of a 'neologism' that bears a striking similarity to an already existing word and to which he has referred as a 'non-concept' (DO, 142)[2] Derrida is not merely playing either *with* or *in* writing, even though one of the things he is attempting is to invite his readers to rethink the very idea of writing, of what it is and what it does, as we shall see later in this chapter.

Nor I hasten to add should *play* be mistaken for frivolity. In a precise manner the 'play' observed and traced is the torque producing meaning or what we call idiomatically the 'give and take' (thereby indicating reciprocity, an I-you structure, a 'being-two-to-speak', a self and other) in and between the many and disparate forms, structures, ideas or institutions on which he has written. Referring specifically to 'Différance', the new spelling puts into play *what* is already at work, not merely in language and what language achieves, but how it does this. Though a 'neologism' or perhaps more accurately a neo*graphism* on Derrida's part, he insists in a note to *Writing and Difference* that the idea of différance, the thinking of the notion, comes to him as part of his reading. It is not conjured by Derrida but crystallizes in the guise of this neographic and quasi-conceptual trace as an imposition placed 'upon us by a reading of Husserl' (*WD*, 329 n.5). In a certain manner, this graphic disfigura-tion of a common word bears in it a play that signs the entire history of Western thought, of the philosophical thinking of Being from the pre-Socratics at least to the twentieth century.

However, regarding for the moment only the matter of language, Derrida raises the question of play on a number of occasions. The term is of great importance. It should not be mistaken or misread as a refusal or avoidance of the serious. It must not be read as mere punning or the avoidance of intellectual engagement for the sake of some semantic jocularity. As already telegraphed above, when you read *play* in the text bear in mind the *play* or torque between two or more elements or components in a machine. Though not play itself, différance might be called very cautiously that which, always already on the move in any system, brings about or makes possible the motion between the moving parts of that system, method of trans-port or communication, institution, or structure, thereby giving them meaning together which they otherwise lack.

Returning to difference, specifically what takes place between *a* and *e* and in the substitution of the former for the latter. The difference that goes untranslated is always that which remains to be read. This is a phrase you'll encounter a lot in this book. The difference that stays silently and resolutely French in différance has to do with both semantic and conceptual difference. It operates at and on both the linguistic and philosophical levels, to make a broad and doubtless crude distinction, but one which touches on the impossibility of separating the one from the other if one is attentive to Derrida. It might be said that it is precisely on this issue that certain commentators on Derrida and many more detractors have remained indifferent, so to speak. For with regard to différance the question is double from the very start. It has to do on the one hand with writing and on the other with the language of philosophy, specifically ontology, that branch of philosophy dealing with the meaning of Being as just observed. (To take a brief detour here: as we will see, Derrida will refer to the difference produced by *différance* between the ontic and the ontological, the ontic being, which philo-sophical term relates to the real existence of entities, rather than their phenomenal existence as considered in ontology.) Or to put this in another fashion, caught up in that *a* is an attentiveness to the intimate and simultaneous intertwining of fundamental formal and philosophical concerns that Western philosophical systems cannot address. In the neologism there is to be read the question of the formal or material – that which goes by the name of writing – within the philosophical which constitutes or makes possible the articulation of ontology (and with that Being or identity) and yet which exceeds any ontological or, more broadly, philosophical enquiry. As Derrida has it, 'the term *différance* cannot be defined within a system of logic – that is, within the . . . system of philosophy' (DO, 143).

II LITERAL MNEMONIC

Initially delivered as a lecture in 1968, 'Différance' appears as the inaugural essay of *Marges de la philosophie* (1972; *Margins of Philosophy* 1982). This is not the first appearance of Derrida's non-conceptual motif, however. The first use came in 1965, in an essay on Antonin Artaud, 'La parole soufflée', which was later published in *L'écriture et la différence* (1967; *Writing and Difference* 1978). Approaching this essay, the matter of language and translatability are of great concern. Much gets lost in any translation of course, but apropos the work of this neologism and the silent graphic interruption of the voice that the *a* installs, it is important to observe that '[u]nlike English, French has not developed two verbs from the Latin *differre*, but has maintained the senses of to differ and to defer in the same verb, *différer*' (Kamuf 1991, 59). There is thus to be borne in mind a simultaneous concern with spacing and temporality. The problem is further compounded within one language, when one realizes that, when spoken at least, in French there can be heard no difference between *différance* and *différence*, hence my insistence on the fundamentally silent and graphic nature of Derrida's *literal* interruption. That *a* leaves a trace as it is inscribed of what might be called the *literal mnemonic* of the other. There is an inscribed memory if you will, the trace of another that interrupts and ruins as it undoes the 'system' named by difference conventionally. This *literal mnemonic* serves as both remainder and reminder, of the spatial within the temporal and the temporal within the spatial, as both make semantic and conceptual meaning possible. (A digressive interruption: I am tempted to suggest that this *literal*, this self-reflexive and performative letter that is self-reflexive and performative in that it expresses its own being-literal, its being a letter and being one in a series of letters, to which system we give the name alphabet, is also a *littoral*. It is a figure of the margin, of the double boundary or border, which connects and separates – land and sea for example, or spatial and temporal distinction.) Thus whatever difference there is between the two terms is and 'remains purely graphic' (D, 3). A distinction that is addressed in 'Différance' (to be given further attention below) is at work between speech and language and, more specifically, speech and any non-verbal system of signs apprehended in the term writing. (In this sense, writing assumes an expanded meaning beyond marks on a page, screen, or other medium for the transmission of signs, whether made by pen, pencil, stone, brush, ink, key or whatever.) For this reason at least, one cannot *sensu stricto* speak of the term, 'which is literally neither a word nor a concept' (D, 3; for reasons to be explained), as a neologism – hence my placing the word above in quotation marks. It is instead, as I have already insisted above, a 'neographism' (D, 3). Whatever difference is being signalled in this 'gross spelling mistake' (D, 3) though, 'it cannot be heard. It cannot be apprehended in speech'. And yet, despite this audacious mutism, the graphic transgression is intended to *re*mark – to mark again rather than to comment upon – that which produces 'a kind of insistent intensification' (D, 3) of the play between graphic signs.

Such play exists between any signs. The very idea of the sign and its communicative or semantic efficacy is predicated on the fact that it exists, that it works and has force *only* in a system of signs such as language and, furthermore, that the meaning of any sign is only comprehensible in its difference from other signs. The difference between signs is what makes meaning possible. 'In a language', for example, 'in the *system* of language, there are only differences' (D, 11). Meaning is not intrinsic to the sign. Even were I to see a sign, for example what I assume to be a single word in Japanese or Russian, or perhaps a petroglyph, my incomprehension of that sign would still admit to its being a sign within a system, the significance of which emerges only out of a network or differential structure to which I am not privy at the time of this hypothesized encounter. Additionally, the sign (pictorial, verbal, graphic) is only ever understood as standing in for something. *Cow* is on the page but that which it signifies is not. So the sign functions only because, on the one hand, it is in a structural and therefore spatial relationship, while, on the other, its operation in that spaced differential alludes or refers to, or represents (re-presents)

some 'thing'. The 'thing' may be 'real' or material, an empirically veri-
fiable object such as a table, a banana or that cow. Or the 'thing' may
in fact be a concept rather than a material object, the existence of
which, though indicated in language through a particular sign, is not
physical but metaphysical, beyond the physical or material world in
which beings exist, such as truth, goodness, evil or God.

The sign thus stands in for a deferred presence, one not immediately present. Between sign and thing a structure exists, which can
only take place because of the difference, the differentiation between
sign and thing, and the always-implied deferral of the presence that
the sign attempts to supplement. When I write *I* here, you (whoever
you are), imagine someone who, though not present, perhaps no
longer alive even, is indicated through that *I*. The sign leads you to
infer an anterior presence. Thus *that cow and I* operate similarly
within the system of language. Yet we are not the same. (At least I
don't think so.) And *you*, dear reader (however many or few of *you*
there are, and however many times *you* are there), understand that
difference between *I* and *cow* not empirically but structurally in the
difference between the two signs, which are themselves differentiated
further within the broader system of signs called language.

Such an understanding of the structure of language and of signification is not Derrida's originally. It comes from the work of Swiss
linguist Ferdinand de Saussure,[3] to whose structural linguistic model
Derrida is responding in part in 'Différance'. Thus, it can be observed
in this small and local instance that Derrida does not 'originate' a
position, theory or hypothesis. In responding to another's text, his
text enters into a differential system of relations and semantic determinations in a similar, though obviously far more complex, manner
to the *I-cow* differential, with all that structure's implications. The
implied network of textual relation already in place becomes more
complicated still if we acknowledge those texts to which Derrida
refers, either with direct citation or allusion, or otherwise in the reference to a proper name, such as *Freud, Heidegger, Husserl, Levinas,
Koyré, Hegel, Heraclitus* or *Nietzsche*. Derrida (whose own name is
functioning in the same way in the text you are reading) is not referring to the dead philosophers but to the texts that are signed by and
in their names. Drawing attention to the fact that the proper name is
not proper, not some unique property, but a sign available to iterability and other effects common to all signs belonging to a system
of language, Derrida remarks apropos Nietzsche, Freud and Levinas,

'these "names of authors" here [are] only indices – [in] the network which reassembles and traverses our "era"' (D, 21). And of course, more indirectly still, the texts that appear under those names are not origins either. As networks of signs and complex irreducible signs themselves, these and every other text are also implicated in networks of reference and relationship, of spacing and deferral. All of which is made possible by différance. Moreover, every text is and remains singular even though, paradoxically, its singularity is only perceivable through the possibility of its iterable condition, the possibility that it can be transmitted, and communicates itself beyond any supposedly original or finite context. In its singularity, the text is an other. It is wholly other from every other text. As Nicholas Royle puts it: 'Every literary work is singular, and every reading of such a work is singular' (2003, 119). Even the inscription of something as apparently straightforward as a proper name on the cover of a text or on a title page only comes to have meaning within a differential structure. Meaning is only produced by difference.

Where, it might be asked, does such a structure of differences produced and maintained in their play by differences end? Where does it begin? The answer to both these questions is that it doesn't. To take just one more example, were we to turn to the text of Heidegger to which Derrida refers we would then have to take account not only of that which Heidegger reads or alludes to, but also to the concepts to which the philosopher refers, and from there to the structures or networks of ideas, concepts and so on which inform, order and make possible each and every one of the concepts in that text. And so on, and so on, and so on . . . One does not reach either an origin or a conclusion therefore. We cannot read toward either a final truth or ultimate central meaning. Nor can we trace back from text to prior text until we arrive at some supposedly originary text. Supposing that the hunt for the anterior source were to lead back to the earliest extant written text, say by Aristotle, Plato or even a fragment of one of the pre-Socratics – Anaximander or Heraclitus for example. Neither this fragment nor the name by which it is identified would be the origin for the very reason already implied and anticipated – that this apparently originary text is itself a response and belongs to an already existent structure or network.

This is implicitly at work when Derrida addresses Heidegger's reading of the Anaximander fragment (D, 23). Derrida's commentary arriving in response and in relationship to those texts – a relationship of difference rather than one of similarity it has to be said, or what Derrida might call a relation without relation – does not offer a reading that produces a meaning or offers mastery of its subject. Instead it makes manifest as a published text its place in the network or structure, in which it is always already implicit (before it was ever presented or published its possibility existed because of différance). Its unfolding of the traces, the differences, of the text of the other – by which I am signifying not only the text of 'Heidegger' or 'Anaximander' but any and every other text, network or structure implicit in those texts – thus enters into that structure in which it was immanent and opens beyond itself the *protention*[4] of all the traces, the differences that are woven into that mesh.

There is therefore no end or beginning in such a network, or what Derrida calls in the opening page of 'Différance', the 'sheaf'. He chooses this word because it

> seems to mark more appropriately . . . the assemblage [which] has the complex structure of a weaving, an interlacing which permits the different threads and different lines of meaning – or of force – to go off again in different directions, just as it is always ready to tie itself up with others. (D, 3)

Though not the sheaf, network of structure, différance signifies that which makes possible the knotting and unknotting, the folding and unfolding, of the lines of meaning or force in any given structure. And this is so, whether the structure is a written text such as a book, or an institutional structure and the laws and rules that determine the shape, meaning and identity of such a form. In the notion of any institutional form or structure such as the law, medicine, hospitals, the nation, the university, consciousness, identity – or most funda-mentally, language itself – a structure is always at work or, if you will, in play. Such play both makes possible the institution, its meaning and identity, but also, when perceived, gives the lie to the idea that the institution is seamless, organic, an undifferentiated whole. Furthermore, apprehension of the structurality of structure (as Derrida puts it) means that one cannot assign an origin or single meaning for that structure.

This is why Derrida begins the essay with the letter *a*, the so-called 'first letter, if the alphabet . . . [is] to be believed' (D, 3). His introduc-tory note of scepticism undercuts the assumption that the alphabet simply *begins* inevitably or naturally with *a*. Of course, conventionally we assume and agree that *a* is the *first* letter, but there is no logical reason for this. Consensus on what comes first is just that – arbitrary cultural agreement. The rest of the alphabet does not follow inevitably from *a*. Nor is it generated from or by the letter, *as if* that letter were a point of genesis. Without wishing to sound repetitive or to insist too much on this, *a* is not *first*. It is merely, arbitrarily, a nodal point in a particular network or sheaf, much like the fiction of the 'name of the author'. As a nexus, lines of meaning and force flow through it. They are undone and produced by it. But this is equally so of every other letter in the alphabet, without there being any hierarchical priority or significance that is assignable to any one letter. Pausing to reflect on Derrida's strategic inaugural gambit, we must also admit that the opening gesture of the essay, one in which response and structure are already enfolded, is unjustifiable. There is no logical reason for starting with a letter, even if that is the first letter of the alphabet. As Derrida's gesture illustrates in a performative fashion, one must start. But *where* one starts is indefensible strictly speaking. The opening is not a beginning. Rather it is an act of making visible a structural node, responding to a point which is immanent, and which could be supplanted by any other. The origin, the beginning, the start – none are absolute positions. One merely identifies a starting point or, equally, an origin or source, retrospectively, so as to impose a logic or economy, an order, or form on the narrative one wishes to present. To put this differently one merely 'economize[s] on the abyss', as Derrida puts it in a different context (*TP*, 37).

Derrida is not the first to observe this. So as to demonstrate the respect one must give to singularity and not simply assume a family resemblance between disparate texts we can take a literary example, even if this appears to be a detour. In a different manner and out of very different contexts, George Eliot proposes a similar hypothesis. In her last novel, *Daniel Deronda* published in 1876, Eliot 'begins' the first chapter with that device that sits on the page between the chapter title and the so-called beginning of the chapter, the epigraph. In Eliot's case this is not a 'found' text. It is not a citation drawn from another text even though it is given in such a manner on the page *as if* to suggest that this were the case. It is not cited as an authoritative voice returning from a prior moment, as is the convention with epigraphs. It is an invention of Eliot's and thus a fiction. Eliot plays on the fiction of the epigraph and the power of its imposition as a voice from before the beginning in order to permit the beginning at the same time as it defers any illusion of an absolute start or origi-nary moment. Eliot's fiction of an epigraph has this to say:

> Men can do nothing without the make-believe of a beginning. Even science, the strict measurer, is obliged to start with a make-believe unit, and must fix a point in the stars' unceasing journey when his sidereal clock shall pretend that time is set at Nought. His less accurate grandmother Poetry has always understood to start in the middle; but on reflection it appears that her proceed-ing is not very different from his; since Science, too, reckons back-wards as well as forwards, divides his unit into billions, and with his clock-finger at Nought really sets off *in medias res*. No retro-spect will take us to the true beginning. (1970, 35)

Eliot's wry commentary unveils the necessity of the concept of *one true beginning*. At the same time its fictional status quietly yet graph-ically undercuts the very idea that one can situate just such a start-ing point. As she establishes through that phrase *make-believe* indicating the silent role of fable within supposedly objective, empir-ical and factual truth, the fiction of the origin is nothing more than this. For the novelist, even science with its claims to absolute and universal truth succumbs to, and is delimited by, the work of narra-tive with its excessive, strategic signs, and the location of science in its being understood as a narrative in a network of differential rela-tions, historically and culturally produced. And the signs of narra-tive *are* excessive in relation to the truths of science, because they can accommodate and apprehend other manifestations of truth for which science is otherwise unable to account. Once more, this example, in which the roles of retention and protention as condi-tional aspects of human consciousness play a part, demonstrates how the beginning is not only strategic and provisional but also no 'true' origin. It is instead divided (*from the start* we might say) in that gesture of 'reckoning'. In the face of undecidability a decision has to be made. By this gesture, absolute authority is undermined from within itself. It differs and defers. In perceiving this, one understands how any sign, of which *a* is exemplary, in its potentially infinite sub-stitutability, 'exceeds the order of truth' (D, 6).

Thus Derrida provocatively risks everything in his argument through the exemplarity of something seemingly so innocuous and undeniably commonsensical as the so-called first letter of the alphabet. He does so precisely to illustrate both the supplementary and reiterable condition of which I have been speaking. (On *supplementarity*, see below.) Furthermore, he plays on this chance in order to illustrate that because 'in the *system* of language, there are only differences' everything in the articulation of the non-concept of différance is 'strategic and adventurous' (D, 7). 'Strategic',

> because no transcendent truth present outside the field of writing can govern . . . the totality of the field. Adventurous because this strategy is not a simple strategy . . . according to [the attempt to reach] a final goal . . . [or] a theme . . . (D, 7)

As the example from Eliot demonstrates, neither is science outside the 'field of writing' nor can it make claims to a 'transcendent truth' that would govern 'the totality of the field'. The 'adventure' is thus in the complexity of the strategy that narrative undertakes and into which it weaves itself through the 'make-believe' of beginnings, whilst starting out, again and again, through the gesture of response to something other, and therefore 'beginning' through repetition, through the idiom of the beginning.

III DERRIDA AFTER SAUSSURE

Why, you might ask, this insistence on the problem of the sign and writing? Why do I insist on this focus? Let us come back to a specific issue in 'Différance' highlighted in Derrida's response to Saussure. Or, to be more precise, let us return to the response inscribed in the text of Derrida to the text of Saussure. This has to do with the very word that the essay bears as its title. Derrida's *neographism* does not simply support or supplement Saussure's understanding of language as a system of differences. It also figures – or perhaps *performs* – graphically an evaluative invention into one important dimension of Saussure's work, which dimension and its critique Derrida anticipates in his spelling mistake and which he continues to unfold throughout the essay in a number of differing contexts.

Citing Saussure, Derrida reminds us that the human subject is inscribed by and in language. He or she is effectively a function or effect of language. Not only is this a formal condition but also a historical and material matter of the subject's determination. It might be put that there is no subjectivity without some language, whether by that term one refers to speech or some other system of signs. Equally the idea of a consciousness that does not perceive itself according to some differential play marking – and marked by – the difference between self and other is unimaginable. For consciousness or the subject to 'be' he or she must enter into 'the system of the rules of language as a system of differences' (D, 15). Citing Saussure further, Derrida acknowledges in agreement with the linguist that language pre-exists the spoken word. Speech can only occur if a system or network is already in place. However, while Saussure separates speech from language, prioritizing language in the binary opposition he defines, nonetheless he still understands language not as graphic but as essentially phonic, that is to say spoken. For Saussure, language is still 'spoken language minus speech' (1974, 37). In this assumption, Derrida departs from Saussurean linguistics. Arguing that language is a form of writing in the broadened sense he has given this notion to incorporate any system of signs or network of communication, Derrida rejects the privilege accorded to language in Saussure's *phonocentric* model of the system of language.

Derrida deploys the term *phonocentrism* to signify the priority in Western thinking afforded speech in the binary opposition speech/writing. While writing will be addressed more fully further on in this chapter, a brief explanation of the hierarchical economy is required here. The tradition of Western thought is phonocentric in its assumptions as Derrida shows at length in *Of Grammatology*. In this Derrida examines rigorously the suppression of writing and notions of networks of signification and the concomitant elevation of voice as the bearer and sign of Being, spirit and presence. While writing is revealed primarily in the philosophical tradition as a debased, secondary and necessary, if 'evil', supplement[5] to convey thought when the human voice cannot be heard or when the human 'origin' of the voice cannot be present to articulate a particular body of thought, this prejudice carries beyond the philosophical text into Western thinking in general, as Derrida demonstrates in his critiques of Saussure and structural anthropologist Claude Lévi-Strauss. The metaphysical, or as Derrida also terms it *logocentric*, discourse of the West, by which we support and propose notions and practices through reference to supposedly universal concepts (such as 'Truth', 'Beauty', 'Good', 'Evil' and so on) is inescapably phonocentric for

Derrida. Related closely to this is the notion of *logocentrism*, another neologism of Derrida's. *Logos* means either truth or word, and Derrida coins the term in order to identify that process by which rational or theological discourse refers back to some originary or governing concept or to the word of God. As with phonocentrism it relies on the idea of speech as the present manifestation of Being. In logocentric reasoning the signification of truth comes through speech and is inextricably tied to speech. Thus, logocentrism 'is also a phonocentrism' and vice versa, of course (*OG*, 11).

Phonocentrism 'merges with the historical determination of the meaning of being in general as *presence*, . . . [which is always implicitly] the self-presence of . . . consciousness, [and] subjectivity' (*OG*, 12). Such 'proximity of voice and being, of voice and the meaning of being, of voice and the ideality of meaning' (*OG*, 12), means that unthinkingly we have entered into and perpetuate the logocentric tradition. To make the point once more, as the proof of consciousness and being to itself (hearing oneself speak), and therefore of presence also, speech becomes the expression of the meaning of being. Writing is only a detour or deferral of this misperceived sense of unmediated presence. While more recently such phonocentric thought has concentrated on or been reflected in issues of consciousness and subjectivity (as in the example of Saussure as we have seen, or in the phenomenology of Husserl), in more explicitly theological eras and contexts, 'all the metaphysical determinations of truth . . . are more or less immediately inseparable from the instance of the logos, or of a reason thought within the lineage of the logos' (*OG*, 10).

For Derrida Saussure effects a break with tradition up to a point. However, that point is precisely where Saussure sees language in verbal and phonetic terms, rather than in the more radically graphic sense. Saussure can only offer a binary analogy when he remarks that 'language is a system of signs that express ideas, and is therefore comparable to writing' (1974, 16). In his insistence on the phonic element in language and the priority given that, Saussure is not alone however. As *Of Grammatology* maps out, and not without irony perhaps, Saussure is merely one more subject to enter into the system of signs and differences called language. That Saussure's text makes this observation is of radical importance in the decentring of humanist thought. Such decentring marks the text and is the sign of its historicity. Furthermore, it should not go unremarked that the decentring force of the Saussurean text is symptomatic of other challenges to essentialist or universalist humanist discourse of that era in the texts of Freud and Nietzsche. However, this very historicity is also a sign, a complex and indelible trace if you will, of the legacy of Western logo- and phonocentrism. Saussure does not choose *how* he enters the tradition of thought. Another in a long line of its subjects, he is both produced by and subjected to its rational, mastering economy.

In this way, Saussure is led to make remarks such as 'poetic texts are invaluable documents in the study of pronunciation' (1974, 36). Writing is secondary, servile even, in that it only serves to be put to work. Writing supports research into and promotes our understanding of spoken language and what Saussure calls phonology. The written sign is only ever an index to sound, to so-called 'living language' (1974, 37). It follows from this, as well as Saussure's interest in the use of signs in the 'imperfect' representation[6] of sound – and his tacit acceptance of writing as phonetic therefore – that writing is perceived as exterior to any subject, presence or consciousness – that it is, in fact, the sign of a materiality opposed to the spirit and also dead. In Saussurean linguistics, the dead-matter of writing is simply the *'external evidence'* (1974, 35) of once-live speech. It is a corpse to be exhumed and dismembered in the search for the signs or remnants of human spirit. That Saussure chooses such a word as 'external' for written and printed texts is itself telling. Elsewhere writing is defined as 'artificial' while language is 'natural', and so on (1974, 32). The project of such a structural linguistics in its phonocentrism thus becomes a work of retrospective teleological archaeology. Through its inherited privileging of presence, being and consciousness as these are implied by the voice, it is designed and destined to obliterate the spatial differences and temporal deferrals that it has introduced into the thinking of language, and so to obscure the play of différance by its logo- and phonocentric imperatives.

IV SPACING AND TEMPORALITY

Always already as silent as the grave, writing nevertheless bears eloquent witness to that invisible 'force' which haunts language, and therefore literature, as well as all other sign systems. As the inheritance of the historico-semantic play in the French announces, the oscillation between notions of differing and deferring are spectral through and through, haunting the French tongue with its Latinate traces like an ineffaceable quasi-genetic rem/a/inder. (Derrida has remarked that différance is neither simply structuralist nor geneticist, but gives rise to both forms of thought and the differences between them; I, 9.) Irreducible to any sign, structure, concept or 'thing', what I am calling with crude imprecision a 'force', is that which silently is at play and makes possible the spacing and temporalization that is named provisionally 'différance'. As Derrida has described it in an interview, différance is 'not a distinction, an essence, or an opposition, but a movement of spacing, a "becoming-space" of time, a "becoming-time" of space. . . . Hence a certain inscription of the same, which is not the identical' (*FWT*, 21). This 'certain inscription of the same' informs Derrida's thinking in so many ways, not least in his formalization of the notion of iterability. But for now it can be said that différance produces this possibility. Repetition takes place but never without some transformation, without transport or translation, and thus the affirmation of an otherness or alterity within the same. Such otherness maintains the spectral survival beyond any merely living moment, presence or meaning. Even if I say the same thing, if I repeat *verbatim* (as it were), that repetition is altered in itself and by its being repeated through the spacing and temporization of its being reiterated. What is articulated is thus the same, yet not the same.

So, reiterating an earlier sentence: I will speak, therefore, of a letter. Silently the 'first' words of Derrida's essay 'Différance' have returned. Spirited away from their supposedly 'original' context (but which? the lecture presented on 27 January 1968, the different instances of publication in French, the publication in translation, whether David Allison's or Alan Bass's?), they appear here. You might have been forgiven for thinking that the words were 'mine', concerning the material of this chapter. They do, though, even though the words are the same and yet not the same as Derrida's. Spaced ([di]sp[l]aced, I might write and so produce a graphic effect that cannot be carried in the voice) – differing and deferred – from anything resembling an originary moment of articulation and, in referring back while retaining the trace not only of themselves but everything that is considered in 'Différance', they remain the same without remaining the same. And this being so, one has to admit that in its protensive immanence 'différance' produces from that opening sentence everything written here.

In a certain way 'in' the work of language, yet not simply linguistic, or otherwise as that which allows meaning, identity or ontology to take place while remaining always other, 'différance' certainly cannot be thought on the basis of *logos*, genesis, origin or metaphysical concept. Not an it, 'it' does not 'reside' outside or prior to any structure. It is not thinkable as an *a priori* ideality. What Derrida strives to illustrate graphically from the first spoken presentation and the first printed page of 'Différance' is precisely the conditions of différance and the impossibility of any conventional recuperation of the term according to the logic of mainstream Western thinking. The silence and thus the expressly *graphic* difference between the *a* and *e* only functions graphically 'within the language and grammar which is as historically linked to [the very idea of so-called] phonetic writing as it is to the entire culture inseparable from phonetic writing' (D, 4).

However, let me stress once more: the insistence on the graphic element should not be mistaken as a sign that Derrida is only concerned with language in itself, whether in its oral or written aspects. As the discussions of subjectivity and consciousness should have made clear, the play of différance is assumed to take place not only in linguistics or in literary texts and their structures, but also in the ontology of being, and of course in the very thinking of ontology itself. In addition, 'historico-institutional structure[s]' (SICL, 71) and the thinking of such networks cannot take place without différance. (A few of these 'historico-institutional' networks or 'sheafs' – the literary, art, politics, ethics, identity, being – will be considered elsewhere in the present volume.) One such 'historico-institutional structure' is what we call, doubtless with too much unreflective haste, 'literary theory'. Another, equally unconsidered, is the 'French intellectual scene' of the 1950s and 1960s. From within such a 'scene', which in reality is not *one*, not a single undifferentiated and homogeneous moment or event, but multiple occasions, interventions and encounters, the Derridean text emerged as a ceaseless motion and provocation. It appeared also as a number of countersignatures to the dominant, the same and the identical exemplified by what Derrida has subsequently described as the many 'schematic and simplified' discourses of the era modelled on Saussurean linguistics.

Thus différance makes identity and meaning possible, and yet it 'is not' (D, 21), as Derrida has it in a deceptively simple affirmation. 'It' is 'not', though it is not nothing, because différance is not reducible to, or containable by, some ontology given systematic form in the guise of a language supposedly at work outside and not produced by the work, the motion that is différance. At the same time, therefore, although différance is nothing as such and impossible to apprehend in any direct manner, 'the thought of *différance* implies the entire critique of classical ontology'. With that, there is also the critique of 'the ontology of presence . . . which is to say the ontology of beings and beingness' (D, 21). '[I]nterrogated by the thought of *différance*', being is shown to be comprehensible not as some discrete condition or abstract notion, but as always a material, grounded and singular experience of difference and deferral. Who I am or what I am can only be articulated as a spatial difference from whoever is not-I. However, this is not all. For being is irreducible to any equation with organic, biological form or existence. Indeed, it is différance that makes possible the difference between notions of being and those of existence. Being pertains solely to the human animal.

As an identity, I am not you, as already suggested. What I am though is not simply a relationship of differing consciousness from every other consciousness presently in existence. Determined by language, other networks of signs and all the traces that comprise the networks we call culture, history, ideology and so on, *I* is a consciousness the meaning of which bears in it and in the ways in which it thinks, reflects and articulates any notion borne by particular historico-institutional structures. *I* is thus both a *sheaf* of folds and a ceaselessly changing node within a complex of networks, the meaning and identity of which never come to rest, and which are produced by différance – the différance that makes 'me' different not only from you or her, but also from myself. Additionally, because the thinking of différance does not accommodate the possibility of origin, the identity gathered in the sign *I* cannot be traced back to some founding moment or other identity by which mine is defined or rationalized.

Although différance *is not* then, neither is it simply a negative. Though pertaining to beings, to beingness and the concept and ontology of Being, différance is not a provisional name for the unnameable in Derridean discourse. This 'unnameable', Derrida cautions, 'is not an ineffable Being which no one could approach: God, for example'. Yet this unnameable, provisionally given the name différance, is that 'play which makes possible nominal effects' in addition to everything we have already considered – and everything else on which we have not begun to touch (D, 26). Before moving on, I will risk a provisional, strategic schematic reiteration of what différance puts into play, without of course its being identifiable or reducible to some stable concept or entity, always the same. Indeed, given that différance is unnameable, then even this name remains unstable. It is only one chosen on a particular occasion as a term that could be substituted by other non-synonymous figures, motifs or tropes. It is not a master term but ultimately undecidable, merely one sign that does service within the mesh that is language. The schematic and provisional definition is not my own. Instead, I take the equally unjustifiable risk of schematizing an already schematic series of determinations provided by Derrida, in an interview conducted by Henri Ronse:

> *First*, *différance* refers to the (active *and* passive) movement that consists in deferring by means of delay, delegation, reprieve, referral, detour, postponement, reserving. In this sense, *différance* is not preceded by the originary and indivisible unity of a present possibility. . . . What defers presence is announced or desired in what represents it, its sign, its trace.
>
> [. . .]
>
> *Second*, the movement of *différance*, as that which produces different things, that which differentiates, is the common root of all the oppositional concepts that mark our language, such as . . . nature/culture. . . . As a common root, *différance* is also the element of the *same* . . . in which these oppositions are announced.
>
> *Third*, *différance* is also the production . . . of these differences. . . . [Conversely] these differences . . . are the effects of *différance*; they are neither inscribed in the heavens, nor in the brain . . . they are [not] produced by the activity of some speaking subject.
>
> [. . .]
>
> *Différance* – *fourth* – therefore would name provisionally [the] unfolding of difference . . . of the ontico-ontological difference. (I, 8–10)[7]

Four provisional definitions, four sides of a framework, within the context of which one might believe that one could situate différance.

Yet, each 'definition' is different, and différance produces the difference, by which each 'definition' or 'determination' can be produced and yet spaced and displaced by every other 'definition' and 'determination'. The spacing of the structure involves also the displacement of its other elements, which can only take place temporally. In giving way to its successor, each 'definition', depending on every other 'definition', is deferred in its 'definite' its 'finite' condition. Derrida announces this of course in that simultaneity of the active/passive binarism in the first 'definition'. As soon as definition appears to get underway it is problematized immediately by the pairing which in their definition depend on the motion, the deferral, the reprise, the reserve, of différance that haunts what Derrida calls the 'present possibility', the desired 'presence' implicit in supposedly absolute and stable signs such as active/passive. These are signs, traces 'in themselves' (if we can say this of their deferred and displaced conceptual referents), which are of course already constituted in relation to one another, and by the effects of *différance*.

Thus, the first definition arrives as an anticipation of the second definition. In this anticipation it arrives improperly, a supplement before the principal determination of différance as naming that 'common root of all the concepts that mark our language, such as ... nature/culture' or, let us remind ourselves, active/passive. The third definition then folds back onto the first two, unfolding the implications of spacing and temporality that is ascribable neither to the metaphysical nor the human, neither to some universal truth or law, nor the work of some consciousness. And lastly, fourth, Derrida acknowledges again what is always already implicitly at work, and what he has just seemed to enact, to perform and so anticipate in his previous responses, all of which build on one another, weaving in and out, constructing and unpicking, construing and *de*construing, in what might be described as the deconstructive construal of the construction of meaning, in order that the process may itself be unfolded according to the provisional name that serves to announce the motion that makes possible the ontico-ontological difference.

V WRITING, SUPPLEMENT AND 'LA BRISURE'

At this juncture, let us turn our attention in a more sustained manner to the question of writing, of what it is and what it does. Earlier in this chapter, I sketched in passing the sustained suspicion concerning the perception of writing in the Western philosophical tradition identified by Derrida. An exteriorized representation of speech, writing was to be distrusted because of its transmissibility and repetitiveness beyond the immediacy of voice, the presence of the subject and the origin of spoken articulation, amongst other things. In short, writing exceeded and thereby exposed the limits of the phono- and logocentrism on which logic, rationality and theology in the West were grounded. This 'history' of writing and logocentrism and its theoretical premises are addressed exhaustively by Derrida in Part I of *Of Grammatology*, 'Writing before the Letter', before he turns to an extensive reading of Jean-Jacques Rousseau's exploration of language and the nature of writing, principally in his *The Essay on the Origin of Languages*, in Part II, 'Nature, Culture, Writing' (*OG* I, 194; II, 95–116). This is still to remain with a somewhat narrow conception of writing as the graphic mark on page, rock, computer screen and so on, a conception which Derrida expands as is also intimated above. While it is necessary to remain with the restricted definition of writing a little more in the present chapter (and indeed to have recourse to thinking the material effects of particular writing systems and their manifestation throughout this book), we will open up that definition towards its conclusion. In doing so, we will have cause to return to particular issues already announced that anticipate the directions of the rest of the present chapter, while also opening to our enquiry various terms such as *trace, arche-writing, la brisure* and *supplement*.

Toward the end of *Grammatology*, in the fourth chapter of Part II, Derrida observes that the 'verb [*suppléer*, translatable either as] "to supplant" or "to compensate for" defines the act of writing' (*OG*, 280). Once again therefore, as with the notion of differing/deferring, there are two meanings, two translations within the same language and within the same term and idea marking that apparently homogeneous and undifferentiated identity. On the one hand, *to supplement* means to add to something. One writes because one wishes to add to something previously written or said, in order to clarify, to provide additional definition, should the 'first' or 'original' determination either be or appear lacking in some manner, or else unclear, ambiguous, indeterminate. On the other hand, the verb *to supplement* signifies a replacement for that which came before it. The supplement does not merely compensate for a lack, it supplants that which preceded it.

(In effect, it might be noted in parenthesis that both definitions can be shown to be proven in the present paragraph. However 'accurate' or 'incorrect' my paraphrase and summary, I am both adding to that which Derrida has written, and also at the same time replacing it, as though it were in some manner lacking, ambiguous, unclear. In doing so, and despite whatever intention I may have, if one remains in the orientation of logocentric thought, I help to support the idea that writing as supplement is untrustworthy, a secondary addition and replacement. In writing this chapter, I am intimating that Derrida's own writing is inadequate, lacking, obscure, too difficult to be read instead of reading this 'guide'. Nothing in fact could be further from the truth. And furthermore, I am writing this parenthesis because what I have already written as a supplement in both senses of the word 'requires' or 'demands' a subsequent supplementary gesture to clarify and illustrate. Thus, one writing supplements another, it adds to and paradoxically replaces, and this, in principle, leads not to some closure but to some endless, reiterable process of supplementary signs, differing and deferring from one another, and so on, and so forth, etc. etc., . . . But to come back to the verb *suppléer* and to the passage in question,)

Derrida chooses to highlight the verb because it appears, with the meaning of 'to overcome', in the text of Rousseau. Rousseau employs to term 'overcome' to account for writing's 'failed' attempt to represent that which is supposedly proper to the spoken word, its sounds and accents, inflections and so on. This is writing's deficiency for Rousseau and also a threat to (phonetic, phonocentric) language. According to Rousseau writing is 'elaborately prolix' (well, we've just witnessed that in the parenthesis above) and therefore has the potential to drain language of its power (Rousseau cit. Derrida *OG*, 281). Writing is therefore comprehensible as a supplement. It replaces present speech – that which *is* present, occurring in a proximal space rather than at a distance, and that which occurs temporally *in* the present – and therefore the presence indicated by speech, that 'necessary' presence of the speaker, as is argued in the previous chapter (to which this chapter, or this part of this chapter at least, might be considered a supplement). Writing supplements, it adds to, thereby apparently exposing, an inadequacy (that full presence is never in fact full, complete) while simultaneously replacing that allegedly irreplaceable here and now, the '*hic et nunc*' of 'living' speech (*OG*, 281).

If only this were so, in fact. Arguably, because of the play of *différance* so-called living speech is already indelibly marked, or perhaps better yet re-marked, by the traces and the effects of writing's *supplementarity*. The condition of this broadened notion of writing-as-supplementary informs any spoken articulation, even in the moment of hearing-oneself-speak. However small the gap, temporally or spatially, there exists a disunity – between thought and sound, between articulation and comprehension. A breach is at work that makes articulation and therefore transmission and communication possible. There can be no absolutely present moment, nor an undifferentiated presence in the taking place of speech. Speech will therefore always already have been contaminated and determined by writing in its broadened sense.

Moreover, without wishing to suggest a somewhat mystical apprehension to the arrival of articulation in the subject, where language comes from, how the idea forms and comes to be given linguistic structure is never simply from oneself, but from some other place, *from some other*. As we have seen with the structures and encryptions of words such as *différer* in French or *supplement* in English meaning is never simple or full. There is always the trace of some other meaning, some other identity, at the structural and pre-subjective level of language. Definition, usage and context only serve to 'damp down' or occlude the oscillation, the disunity within apparent linguistic unification. Returning to the 'living' speech however, and to cite Gayatri Spivak in her 'Translator's Preface' from *Of Grammatology*, speech, supposedly that living thing that ensures and bears in it presence, complete and self-sufficient identity present to itself, identity of the subject who speaks, 'carries within itself the trace of a perennial alterity'. Thus, what holds true for 'the structure of the sign' also holds true of the 'structure of the psyche' as we have just intimated. Such a formation is caught succinctly in the words of a character from John Banville's *Eclipse*, Alexander Cleave. Pausing to reflect on being as he has cause to do so often, and capturing the temporal spacing of being's becoming in the process, Cleave asks 'what makes for presence if not absence? – I mean the presence of oneself as a remembered other' (Banville 2000, 46). It is to this structure or network that Derrida 'gives the name "writing"' (Spivak 1998, xxxix). Speech is thus a manifestation of writing in this sense: for, as Spivak has it, the sign, whether inscribed or spoken, is 'always already inhabited by the trace of another sign that never appears as such' (Spivak 1998, xxxix). It bears and so relays the traces of language, but never as a presence, only as the signs of some differentiation and deferral or delay in the system and by which the system is maintained. In order for speech to take place, there has to be that disunity already announced – displacement as replacement, as addition and therefore supplement – of the signifier and the signified.

This disunity or dislocation is called by Derrida the hinge (*la brisure*), which 'marks the impossibility that a sign, the unity of a signifier and a signified, be produced within the plenitude of a present and an absolute presence' (*OG*, 69). *La brisure* can signify in addition a crack, a fragment, a break (or a joint, the break which makes of an otherwise single piece of material the joint allowing that form to be an articulated structure), and also a heraldic mark of cadency. This last, interestingly, is that variation in a coat of arms signifying the descent of a branch of the family from one generation to another, and thus a difference or alterity (one might even risk saying a disunity or non-identity of sorts) within the familial sameness or identity. The *brisure* is thus both break, difference, spacing *and* that which allows for the structure, the meaning or identity to be figured and to represent – to re-present – itself, though never as present or presence. Differentiation and deferral are announced even as they serve to articulate, to write and inscribe. To risk a reading, I would argue that one treat the *a* of différance as precisely this hinge, break or joint, which arrives in writing to articulate the disunity and yet familial relation between deferral and differentiation, between spatiality and temporality. Spacing and temporality come into play through that very fragment which takes place, signifying the alterity or otherness acknowledged by Spivak. The hinge or break that makes writing possible is also the sign of that writing that is the not-self within the self allowing for the subject's identity to be articulated.

Being's apprehension thus hinges on the difference in any ontological determination, that to which Derrida refers as 'a "becoming-space" of time, a "becoming-time" of space . . . Hence a certain inscription of the same, which is not the identical'. Being 'written' by the process of différance being is a writing, a constant becoming. Or as Stephen Dedalus thinks to himself when walking, eyes closed, across the beach in the third episode of *Ulysses*: 'You are walking through it howsomever. I am, a stride at a time. A very short space of time through very short times of space' (Joyce 1993, 31). That *You* and *I* marks the doubling and division, the difference *of* and *within* the self. And while, 'I am' is readable conventionally as the response to the statement 'you are walking', we may risk an alternative reading of it, thereby connecting it to the becoming-space of time and the becoming-time of space that the movement of both Stephen's consciousness or psyche (as this reflexively moves in tandem with his physical motion) and the following sentence perform. For 'I am' articulates being, it affirms an ontological location of the self. However, this is spaced, displaced, not only from that 'you are . . .' and in the condition of the affirmation as response to the self as other, but also in its motion from the self's past into its future recorded as a series of *nows* in the second clause – 'a stride at a time'. Effectively there is given us to read the motion of being, one spaced and temporal moment next to and after one another. 'I am' is exceeded by the immanence of 'I become, one stride at a time'. Should this seem a little fanciful, we would do well to acknowledge along with Stephen Dedalus the interweaving of the short times of space and short spaces of time by which not only is the subject articulated and inscribed, but also the retracing of the event of becoming is inscribed by Joyce in the performative mechanics of the sentence. In effect, Joyce's act of narration writes (in the narrow sense) the writing (in the Derridean sense) of the subject's ineluctable becoming. 'I am' thus overflows from within itself its own self-generating illusion of presence and stability, through the Joycean revelation of 'a certain inscription of the same, which is not the identical'.

VI TRACE AND ARCHE-WRITING

A comprehension of the condition of writing brings into relief questions concerning the generation of meaning, whether semantic, epistemological or ontological. With that arrives the interrogation of the origin of meaning as emerging neither in nor from the unified sign, nor in undifferentiated notions of presence or being, or some metaphysical concept, but in difference. In addressing the origin of meaning in difference, Derrida turns to the *trace*. I shall speak elsewhere of the *trait*. What is sketched here as we come to a conclusion for this chapter serves less as a comprehensive determination therefore, than as a series of indicative, orientating adumbrations. In order to move on to the topic of the trace allow me to offer a recap of persistent matters informing the present chapter.

The evidence concerning the sign by which the Western tradition organized itself is 'as follows':

> The . . . signified is never contemporary, [it] is at best the subtly discrepant inverse or parallel [i.e. spatially or temporally differentiated or deferred] – discrepant by the time of a breath – from the . . . signifier. And the sign must be the unity of [this] heterogeneity, since the signified (sense or thing, noeme or reality)[8] is not in itself a signifier, a *trace*. (*OG*, 18)

The sign is divided into two parts, signifier and signified. The two form a differentiated and therefore heterogeneous unity, the sign. As we have seen however what goes for the structure of the word applies equally to the meaning of being, though of course in a completely different manner. The signifier is always a trace, never the thing, concept, idea, reality or whatever is not the trace or mark. That apparent unity of the sign – saying *I* or *I am* for example – only has its possibility therefore through the play of the trace. This does not mean to say that the trace is simply the signifier, a word like any other. Nor should it be assumed that the trace alludes to or represents any prior presence or some origin secreted below the surface of a textual manifestation, a meaning, an ontology or an identity. Thus, while it may be possible to speak of a literary text for example as being composed and indeed made possible by the gathering of a multitude of traces, this is not to suggest that the traces are simply sources or signifiers pointing to some hidden meaning to be unearthed.

As much as any text, present being or 'living present' then, within these is always the 'nonidentity' of that identity, an element called by Derrida the 'retentional trace' that is neither of the present or of presence strictly speaking, nor of any past that can be presented as such. To clarify what the trace is, Derrida remarks '[t]he trace is not an attribute'. It is not simply a part that constitutes the self. Furthermore, 'Originary-being must be thought on the basis of the trace, and not the reverse' (*SP*, 85). There is thus no notion of being that is not always already informed by the alterity of this trace, which, furthermore, is 'at work at the origin of sense' (*SP*, 85). From the very beginning one might say, there must be difference and disunity in order for one to be able to speak of identity, of meaning, of being, of an ontology. If we admit to this ' "movement" of the trace' as the spacing that makes possible the apparent unity of any sign and as also the *'temporalization of sense'* (*SP*, 86) then such spacing and temporalization is signalled through what Derrida also terms *arche-writing*. The term has a broader sense, to do with the structure of meaning or identity and specifically an inaugural or originary 'writing' (as temporalization of sense and spacing of meaning) or structure. I will come back to the *arche-* elsewhere in this volume, reiterating and supplementing what is found here. For now though, I should say something. The prefix *arche-* or, as is more commonly found in its Latin spelling *archi-*, (from the Greek (αρχι-) signifies any figure that is chief, principal, first in authority or order, as the *Oxford English Dictionary* has it. Thus *architect* for example means *master-builder*. Equally though, it might be translated as 'first maker'. More generally or abstractly, the prefix has come to signal in English as in French the principal or notion of an originary sense or authority.

Derrida's neologism thus might be taken to refer to an originary or authoritative 'writing', as just suggested. After a fashion it does, though not in any simple conceptual manner. For what Derrida seeks to announce through his coinage is that at or more precisely before the idea of the beginning, before any simple genesis or sup-posedly self-contained, non-differentiated and spontaneous creation or origin, there is the 'motion' (temporality, deferral) and structure (spacing, differentiation) of a 'writing'. Therefore, there is the difference by which the broadened sense of writing has been described. The very idea of any start, source or origin, so-called, or any concept, authority-figure, organizing principal or sense is itself structured by the thought of its necessity, and by an *arche-writing*, a structural beginning informed by *différance* before the notion of any spontaneous generation *ab ovo*. It is this which articulates the very possibility of any sense through that spacing and temporalization by which an apparent unity or ontology has the chance of being present and perceived as such. To reiterate, there is no origin, no *arche*, that is not marked, structured, by some trace, which nonetheless is not anterior or exterior to that structure, that architecture – whether by *architecture* we might risk the signalling of the structure of meaning or being. It is not a component, element or attribute, and yet the trace serves in the *inscription* of sense, of meaning and of being. Moreover, if being is written and this strange motion of that which is nothing as such but is only indirectly apperceived as the becoming-space of time and the becoming-time of space, then being as presence is only understandable as a becoming. This becoming cannot be represented directly and yet, as I have insisted, it takes place.

VII KHORA

As has been argued, the history of Western thought has relied upon supposedly stable dualisms, such as presence/absence, speech/ writing, nature/culture, sensible/intelligible and so on. That Derrida's text proposes the reading as well as offering a performative staging of an intervention in such a history suggests that, according to the logical structures of the *trace*, of writing and of *différance* also, it must itself be understood as a project of reiteration – a project and also a projection of the play of the trace, the work of différance, the strange 'movement' of a writing. Always already having taken place, such events nevertheless remain to be read, to come.

Yet, if writing is opened to a definition that escapes framing or determination, while accommodating the *differantial* of its spatial and temporal structuring, can it be said to have any form at all, con-sistent and homogeneous, stable in its design, constitution or con-struction and available for representation? Obviously, the answer is no. How, then, do you describe that which has no form *as such*? Derrida attempts to do just that in a reading of the strange 'figure' of *khora*, in Plato's *Timaeus*. *Khora* opens itself to a telling analysis by Derrida, apropos the relation between philosophy and literature or, to insinuate this binary otherwise, truth and writing. Derrida's patient explication of the text of Plato offers a countersignature to that text. It traces faithfully the very contours by which Plato pro-ceeds, providing ample evidence of Derrida as a good reader, a faith-ful correspondent of the other. In this correspondence, everything hinges on being the good reader, of reading that which remains unread in the text of Plato, as literature arrives at the limits of philo-sophy, in order to expose those limits. Pursuing the threads at which he pulls through the Platonic labyrinth, Derrida aims to illustrate how *khora* can be defined only in ways pertaining neither to the sen-sible – that which has to do with feeling and emotion – nor the intel-ligible – that which is concerned with rationality and intellect. If, therefore, *khora* 'names', it bespeaks the affirmation of an alterity resistant to naming, determination or containment according to any of the conventions or epistemological resources of ontology. Neither negative nor positive, *there is khora*.

How does one speak of *khora* therefore? If at all, one must proceed by analogy. One must move according to the logic of difference, of displacement and deferral, and through apophatic illustration governed by an iterable necessity. If one is to speak of *khora* at all, then 'in order to think *khora*, it is necessary to go back to a beginning that is older than the beginning, namely, the birth of the cosmos' (*K*, 126). *Khora* thus has to do with the *arché-* (that from which one starts, the beginning, the start, the chief, the principal or first in authority), as generally in *architecture, architectonics, arche-écriture or arche-writing*.

We are speaking of a beginning older than the beginning, then. However strange an idea that might be, it needs to be thought through. A beginning older than the beginning: that which, in effect, authorizes and makes possible any genesis, starting point or departure from some location, but which cannot be represented, which is not available to any positivist or negative representation. A beginning older than the beginning: *as if* that assumed inauguration *were* the first time, the inaugural moment. *As if* genesis were that which, being read retrospectively as such, obscures the prior beginning that makes the iterable inscription or articulation of a supposedly pure and undifferentiated origin possible *in the first place* (as it were). Derrida brings back to our view, he *invents*, the necessity of thinking the *arché-* the prior beginning. However, he does not assign this a simple, full, non-differentiated image, such as genesis, or creation. Instead, as the idea of an architectonics implies, a beginning older than the beginning (and note in Derrida's phrase the precision with which he chooses the definite and indefinite articles) must necessarily be thought as structural and therefore differantial.

In the thinking of *khora*, Derrida continues from the commentary on beginnings, 'in that which is formal about it, precisely, the analogy is declared: a concern for architectural, textual (histological) and even organic composition is presented' (*K*, 127). *Histological*, here associated with the textual and architectural as the linked analogical concerns, is the science of organic tissues, dealing with the minute structure of animal and plant tissue. Now, you'd be right in observing that there is nothing obvious relating the architectural, the textual or the histological. Derrida inscribes a chain of relations where there is no relation, a series of figures approximating one another only at the level of complex structure. (One might pursue such figures across Derrida's text, not least in the figure of text, hymen or fold, but also in the matrix, the weave, veil, *Geflecht*, network, knot, the proper name of Penelope or Ariadne, the gesture in knitting of the decrease or diminishing [SOO, 24], the image of the silk worm, the teeth of a crane's bucket scooping up material from the sea, the 'inextricable' interlacing [*OS*, 30], and so on. As one place from which we can follow the clews back, I suggest you unpick the knot, with all its 'guiding threads' of either *Geflecht* or *matrix* in *Of Spirit* [*OS*, 8–12].) What offers the thinking of relation is then only the analogy of radically different types of structure without shared resemblance or similarity beyond that of the formal constitution and institution of an identity. The implication then, apropos *khora*, is that because *khora* may be translated in a number of ways, it cannot finally be defined absolutely. Its meaning is always contingent, and no figure is any more justifiable than any other, except as an analogy for imagining the unimaginable. Unrepresentable as such, unavailable to any adumbration aiming at mimetic fidelity and irreducible to any appropriate representational modality, '*khora* is not . . . anything but a support or a subject . . . which would *give* place by receiving or conceiving, or indeed by letting itself be conceived' (*K*, 95). The language is estranging isn't it? But then this gives place to the difficulty of thinking *khora*. How do we conceive *khora* if it is impossible to receive as identifiable or stable form? Whatever it is or is not, it can only be thought in its resistance to conception, and yet it has already given place to that thinking, even as it is equally (anticipating the chapter on art) the *subjectile* on which reception or conception is staged or takes place. That Derrida offers us either as equally applicable, appropriate, suggests that any distinction between nature/culture, organic/inorganic, 'man-made' (*sic*) or birthed is impossible to make: hence that earlier impossible series: architectural, textual, histological (and so on and so forth). This being the case, *khora* therefore names the deconstruction of, and taking place between, genders, and it must be added, genres and the idea of genus also. Giving place as the support for the ontological project instituted by the question *what is* (for example *what is literature? What is art? What is deconstruction?*), *khora* nonetheless escapes ahead of all determination of any ontology, even as it haunts its possibility, possibly as that which makes possible the thinking of ontology from some place before the *in-the-first-place*.

One of the fundamental problems resides in the question of the taxonomical and epistemological resources and laws of determination. *Khora*, 'which is neither "sensible" nor "intelligible", belongs to a "third genus" ':

> at times the *khora* appears to be neither this nor that, at times both this and that, but this alternation between the logic of exclusion and that of participation . . . stems perhaps only from a provisional appearance and from the constraints of rhetoric, even from some incapacity for naming. (*K*, 89)

You'll have noted the frequency, the temporal pulsation marking the seemingly contradictory appearances of *khora*. Doubly contradictory or paradoxical, you say, and rightly so. For, not only is there the shuttle between *both* and *neither*, but, within this apparent polarity or binary, a doubling – *this nor that, this and that* – within the conceptual terminology of the logic. Yet even this is far from certain. Observe the vacillation in that *perhaps* – and on the very first page of the essay. There is to be read a matrix of sympathetic vibrations that take place as the event of writing and the experience of reading Derrida. Everything resounds harmonically, as the network of traces shake themselves apart. Definition, however provisional or tentative, unravels itself in the very moment that it is being, becoming, adumbrated. Without apparent confidence, the text proceeds to trace the impossible in response to that which the impossible, the undecidable and ineffable give place to: that seemingly hesitant temporary circulation. Derrida's writing stages itself in a performative gesture, *as if* it were a provisional postage stamp, transmitted despite, and yet as witness to, the unavailability of any definitive issue. This is the impulse or semaphore of Derrida's inaugural gambit in this essay. *Descry*, to use an archaism doubly indicative of observation and inscription, the traces, the clues, the *fils conducteurs*, of a web of *traits* and *retraits*: *appears, alternator, perhaps, provisional appearance*. As *subjectile*, khora gives place to the performative that takes place.

Perhaps.

We are suspended from the beginning, in any preliminary approach to a beginning before the beginning and as a response to this, in the experience of the aporetic. *Khora* thus remains to be read, resistant as it is to 'the order of the "paradigm", that intelligible and immutable model' (*K*, 90). While '*khora* receives, so as to give place to them, all the determinations, but she/it does not possess any of them as her/its own' (*K*, 99). As you can see from Derrida's hesitance in translation, a hesitance dictated by the word itself, gender troubles the word. Certain translations of *khora* will give the word as 'nurse', 'wet-nurse'. Others will suggest receptacle, or, imagine the context, womb. If there is the trace of a female spectre here, a 'haunting which allows neither decomposition nor dissolution into the simplicity of a perception' (*OS*, 62), then the intimation is that the female proceeds the male. There can be no beginning announced in logocentric or phallocentric narrative, no definitive starting point, from which some erectile or ejaculatory trajectory might be traced, without a beginning, a beginning *qua matrix*, which is always haunted by the possibility of a female.

So, irrecuperable and wayward, troublesome even. This is *khora*, at least in the face of the demands of philosophy. She/it does, however, make literature possible, and story telling in general. *There* we might say, *there is literature*. Read this two ways at once. Over there, you see, displaced, spaced, spacing itself from any present or presentation, yet *always already* taking place invisibly, secretly. Over there in an other place, the place of the other, the gift of which is to give place. Irreducible to any ontology, literature takes place/there is literature.[9] Though neither nothing nor something, *khora* makes it possible for the (always masculine) philosopher to hide the stories he must tell in the name of truth, borrowing without speaking of the rhetoric, the poetics, the narratives, the languages in which he stages his non-reflective reflections, and pretending not to indulge in representation whilst presenting, and representing, mimicking and re-presenting all the while.

Don't be in a hurry here, don't rush to conclusions. If it's not clear in all that we have said of *khora* so far, here is Derrida on the gender of the philosopher, if not philosophy: 'the figure of the philosopher is, for me, always a masculine figure. This is one of the reasons I undertook the deconstruction of philosophy. All the deconstruction of phallogocentrism . . . has always been linked to a paternal figure . . . A woman philosopher . . . would be a woman who thinks. Not a philosopher' (*D*, 97). Would *khora* be her name? Would *khora* name that thinking which Derrida opposes to philosophy, and which for Derrida is feminine or female?

Are you *khora*, do you think?

Are you *khora*? *Do* you think?

And does the thinking of *khora* haunt you, remaining all the while *impenetrable* to the phallogocentric probings of the philosopher?

Write to me in your name, write to me namelessly, and we'll keep the secret between us, giving place

> to all the stories, ontological or mythic, that can be recounted on the subject of what she receives and even of what she resembles but which in fact takes place in her, *khora* herself, so to speak, [though she] does not become the object of any tale, whether true or fabled. A secret without secret remains forever impenetrable on the subject of it/her. (*K*, 117)

Tell me – how should I think of you?

P.S. Had I the time or space, I would be tempted to trace, perhaps weave or, one hopes, unpick an imagined, impossible relationship between the *khora* of Plato and the *Geist* of Heidegger (somewhere caught up in the knot between *Geflecht* and *Geschlect*), which 'in the first place . . . is neither *pneuma* nor *spiritus*' (*OS*, 32).

NOTES

1. The sentence is an 'invisible' citation, reiterating the first sentence of Derrida's essay 'Différance'.

   Another translation of 'Différance' is available, in Derrida's *Speech and Phenomena: and Other Essays on Husserl's Theory of Signs*. Allison's translation gives the sentence as 'I shall speak, then, of a letter'. Had I the space it might be productive to speculate on the difference between the two translations, and what difference the difference might make, as well as what 'différance' causes to take place in and between the different, differing versions. The essay that Allison translates is taken not from *Marges de la philosophie* but from one of the previously printed versions, in Tel Quel collectif, *Theorie d'ensemble* (1968). This version of Derrida's essay has several 'introductory' paragraphs that precede the 'opening' sentence that speak of the etymology and differing meanings at work in the verb *différer*.

2. I shall come back to this interview shortly, quoting Derrida on différance as a non-concept.

3. This description of Saussurean linguistics is necessarily brief and sketchy, given the space available to me here. Derrida gives a lengthy account of the premises of Saussure's work in 'Différance'. For a full account, see Saussure (1995). For a short though comprehensive survey of Saussurean

structural linguistics and their significance to structuralism, see Eagleton (1983, 91–126). For a commentary on and application of structuralism as practised by Roland Barthes, see K. M. Newton (2001, 33–46).

4. Not a neologism but a rarely used word, and more often spelt in English protension, the term suggests a reaching forward or an extension of time or duration. The use of the 't' spelling indicates that Derrida has taken the word from a specifically philosophical context, that of the phenomenology of Edmund Husserl. Husserl had used the word in opposition to *retention* to suggest the idea that consciousness of a present event extends into the future. It would appear that Derrida appropriates or retains the term in order to exceed phenomenological discourse and its delimitation by the ontology of presence. Moving on from the critique of Saussure in 'Différance' Derrida turns to notions of consciousness in phenomenology, in order to expand the thinking of différance beyond a merely linguistic context to one that apprehends the condition of Being. In this, and as an analogical parallel to the critique of Saussurean linguistics as these are grounded in what Derrida terms a 'phonocentrism' (the privilege of speech over writing; see the fuller discussion of this concept in this chapter), there is another critique, that of the privilege given to the notion of consciousness, its *a priori* centredness, as being somehow outside and before the networks of difference addressed in the essay presently considered. In Husserlian thought consciousness, which is always a consciousness to itself as present and as a being-in-the-present (to which consciousness is the self-reflexive apprehension in its 'presence'), has as a constitutional aspect of its being-conscious *qua* present consciousness horizons of retention and protention. That is to say human consciousness can remember the past and anticipate the future based on that memory and on the conscious experience of the present event. Derrida decentres the privilege given consciousness through demonstrating how retention and protention are aspects of the play of différance, of which therefore consciousness is also a construct, product or effect.

5. See discussion of writing as supplement in the present chapter, below.

6. The very idea of representation suggests the notion of a sign that can stand in for and somehow bring back to presence, to a present, that which is absent, deferred.

7. Although the third definition follows on immediately from the second, without any elision, I have taken the liberty of separating the two for the purposes of schematic presentation.

8. *Noeme* is a transliteration of the ancient Greek, meaning thought, concept, idea or perception. In phenomenology, the *noema* is an object of perception or thought. Its opposite is *noesis*, which is the process or act of thinking or perceiving. Derrida's retention of the Greek not only implicates the Greek philosophical tradition, and particularly Platonic thought in which logocentrism is assumed, but also suggests a signification of other philosophical, linguistic, rhetorical and psychoanalytic discursive registers.

9. The / indicates an impossibility of translation, most specifically, though not limited to a play between the German, *es gibt*, and the French *il y a*.

Idiomatically, *es gibt* is or can be translated as *there is*, rather than the more literal *it gives* (the *it* referring to the other that gives without possibility of reciprocity for the one who receives the gift of the other). That there is an idiomatic translation from German to French signifies that an 'other' resonance resides simultaneously as other within the apparently straightforward or more commonsensical translation. This other of translation, translation's other, is displaced from the more immediate meaning. In its arrival or possibility however, it disrupts notions of presence and absence, primary and secondary, and so on, across the entire gamut of the Derridean logic of *différance* because one cannot justifiably prioritize one meaning or translation over another. Moreover, that there are two identities or meanings performatively enacts a spacing, a differentiation, a deferral both spatial and temporal in the generation and reception of meaning that operates at a pre-semantic level, the oscillation of which cannot be calmed down. That *it gives* but also *there is* literature, for example, indicates how literature is both given, a gift of the other, and spaced, spacing itself as an other. Over there, we might say, there is literature; it is not here, not with me, not me; I recognize its alterity as well as its singularity but this recognition of the singular condition of the literary in no way captures it but only serves to indicate that it is given, as it were.

CHAPTER 3

ART

(Writing in [excess of]) Representation

The most efficient way of putting deconstruction to work [is] by going through art and architecture.

Jacques Derrida

. . . that rather terrible thing which is there in every photograph: the return of the dead.

Roland Barthes

I am not able to see myself. I am blind to myself.

Jacques Derrida

I REFLECTING ON A PORTRAIT OR, DRAWING FORTH

What do I mean when I speak of a portrait? A *por-trait*? *Pro+trahere*: to draw forth, extend, reveal, prolong, to make or to trace. And what is the *trait* that the painting or the photograph, the pencil sketch or other drawing, draws forth, makes visible in its representation of the self? What does the portrait draw out of me? In seeing a portrait of myself, what might I draw out of myself, as the otherwise invisible sign within the image of the same, which is different or other?

In *Derrida*, Jacques Derrida is shown in an art gallery, the Cathedral Gallery, Paris. He is examining a portrait of himself. In response to a question concerning his response to the portrait, Derrida confesses that the image makes him anxious, he has a 'difficult rapport' with his image (D^2, 71). The relationship between self and image, between being and identity, is not without importance in Derrida's text. For now however it is Derrida's immediate and singular response that interests me. He observes, '[i]t's very strange . . . It's uncanny. It's bizarre. But I don't have the desire to destroy it as I so often have with other photos or images' (D^2, 71).

Seeing an image of oneself is strange for a number of reasons, not least because one is taken outside oneself. This is true whether we speak of a painting or a photograph. You see a presence, captured, fixed in place, at a given moment. Time appears frozen. A fiction of permanent presence, of presence to yourself, is given you to understand. You are there and not there, looking at a self, which though yourself is not you, not you looking back at yourself. That other you looks at nothing, it only gives the appearance of looking out, never seeing you at all, as though you were invisible, not there. It is at once fixed in time and out of time completely. It captures you in the blink of an eye. Forever. Seeing yourself in this manner, reduced to a representation of yourself, produced in the instantaneous presentation of the self reduced to an image sent out into the world and over which you have no control (except perhaps to destroy it) – it is *as if* you were dead. We are presented through our representations of ourselves and others with this uncanny recognition. But what is perhaps the most uncanny aspect of this apprehension is not merely that the image is that of the dead person, as Roland Barthes has hypothesized. It is *as if* in standing outside yourself you, the 'living' you, are a ghost. It is a matter of being acted on, agitated and solicited. Confronted by the simulacrum of a presence, the power of its representation imitating life and offering you a memory of yourself as a trace of your being in that representation, you may feel as you would *as if* you could experience your death. You may experience the sensation of experiencing the impossible. It is *as if* you were living on beyond 'your' death, to find yourself having become the spectral visitant, the *revenant*, who returns to the place of living and who can no longer take part in that scene.

The question of representation, specifically here portraiture, introduces a network of traces. It announces a scene of writing, of inscription and interpretation as illustration. Some of the traces in this mesh we have already touched on, while others will be discussed elsewhere in the present volume. For now though, particular traces will be addressed in the present chapter, as we give attention to the relation between writing and the image. The question will have been articulated through attention to that system which produces the image as an apparent totality or immediacy to be received, while the structure of its inscription remains as an invisible ground. In pursuing this, the matter will have been seen to be a concern with the ways in which 'painting [or other visual forms of presentation such as drawing or photography] and writing can only be interpreted as images, reproductions, representations, or repetitions of something alive, of living speech in the one case, and of animal figures in the other' (*D*, 188). The question is one of a hymenal fold: involving itself *on the one hand* with a portrait of a discourse and, *on the other*, with a discourse on the portrait. In perceiving this reciprocal fold of traces, it will be noted that a strange revivification or reanimation takes place through the presentation of a temporal and textual structure of a ' "thing" . . . that presents itself', occluding the temporal and textual by which presentation takes place (*D*, 199). Derrida thus unfolds and unveils the operations of a complex network. To observe at work the network, this is often, no, always, the way with Derrida. In speaking ostensibly of one subject, one thing, he opens to our view the multiple threads of a vast mesh, which, though already there, had remained invisible to us until Derrida arrived to act as a guide. Striking in this question of representation is the role of *mimesis*. As we shall observe, *mimesis*, 'as a system of *illustration*' (*D*, 183), disavows its system as a system, as a network, a writing, a text.

II FRAMING THE SUBJECT

In response to questions of art, aesthetics and representation, I propose here to treat specifically of a few 'subjects' to which Derrida has been drawn, from which he draws certain threads, and around which, in certain framing and unframing gestures, he sketches interpretations in the attempt to open the reading of 'art'. These 'subjects' are: *mimesis, subjectile, parergon, trait* and *representation*. Books such as *Dissemination, The Truth in Painting, Memoirs of the Blind, Right of Inspection* and *The Secret Art of Antonin Artaud* effect an irreversible translation of our perceptions concerning the grounds of representation. Throughout these texts and other essays, Derrida's writing is haunted by the traces of modern discourses on the aesthetic, which appear insistently through the ghostly signatures of Hegel, Kant and Heidegger. Derrida's essays on aesthetics address frequently aspects of art and visual representation best described as marginal to what have been understood, traditionally and canonically, as the so-called principal concerns of writing on art. At the same time however, while Derrida's orientation towards such issues may appear *ex-centric*, his writing unfolds patiently and attentively how the apparently (and occasionally literally) marginal or liminal is of crucial, if overlooked, importance to any attempt to read representation, the work of art, or the discourse of aesthetics.

At the same time, in pursuing the question of the marginal, there is a constant concern in Derrida's writing on art and aesthetics to question the very grounds of aesthetic investigation as this originates in ontological questions such as 'what is art?' Thus, as can be seen tirelessly at work in *The Truth in Painting*, Derrida refuses to move beyond the marginal in his opening chapter, returning to it, tracing and retracing it. A double gesture is underway, which follows the lines of the frame even as it constructs and takes apart the act of framing. He thus engages in a strategy which resists the assumption behind the history of philosophical investigation into art and the beautiful, which takes as first principles such questions without necessarily reading a place before the first question from which assumptions come into play that are not opened to questioning. Derrida multiplies the sides of a frame, and in so moving closer and closer to the question of what the frame entitles and the ways in which the title frames the work of art, he explores how the analyses of Kant, Hegel and Heidegger come to rest in particular unthought or unquestioned assumptions concerning art, the beautiful and aesthetics.

In the case of each of the singular motifs, *parergon*, *trait* and *subjectile*, Derrida's interest is, as you might already have surmised, with the demarcation and/or erasure of borders, boundaries and limits. This is not to say the discourse on *mimesis* does not interest and implicate itself in the question and the figure of the frame. It does. It is merely to alert the reader to the fact that the boundary, and all liminal metaphors and tropes, serve a supporting, framing function. Such attentiveness and responsiveness to the liminal resonates with the endless reformulations of the ontological interrogation concerning the nature of the work of art. He attends to those marks, in short, which determine representation or the work of art as such, while at the same time becoming invisible in the process of making the work appear. As I have already implied, another way to speak of these figures is to suggest that each is a form of writing in the broader sense sketched in the previous chapter, an inscription that, while being largely unread, makes possible the signification of the work of art as art. Moreover, in yet another manner one might say that such figures speak, albeit indirectly, of a certain desire, if not for stories exactly, then at least for an acknowledgement of narrative or, to put this another way, acts of spacing which take place within the apparent totality and immediacy of representation and the visual. I am echoing consciously a phrase, 'your desire for stories', spoken by one of the interlocutors in *Right of Inspection* (*RI*, 1), in which, through the motif of narrative presentation, Derrida effects the dismantling of the photograph as absolute presentation or representation implicitly bound up with the somewhat ghostly retention of *presence* and the *present*. There is an urge confessed here, to translate, construct or unearth, out of the apparent immediacy of the image, that which haunts it, that which can be deciphered or unravelled, 'somewhat in the way one speaks of constructions in psychoanalysis or police (re)constructions' (*RI*, 1). Though addressed in one context to the matter of the structure of image and representation, such reconstructions also touch upon matters of title, signature, discourse, museum, archive and so on.

III SUBJECTILE

Beginning then with the subjectile, we must ask what exactly is a 'subjectile'? Narrowly defined, it is the material or material support on which a painting or engraving is made, so the *Oxford English Dictionary* informs us. A little abstractly, the subjectile is that which is adapted to receive a 'subject' or picture. I say 'abstractly' because while reception can infer the material on which the painting is made having been prepared, there is also the sense that the subject, you or I, can become the subjectile. In this reading, transmission takes place. There is the sign of a sending or *posting*. This is indicated already in my opening reflections on Derrida's reception of his portrait, of what he is prepared to receive or reject, and how that reception determines him as its addressee. Materially and technically, the subjectile is, writes Mary Ann Caws, 'the underlying support of canvas, paper, text' (*SAAA*, xi), or that which makes the image, the text, the representation possible. It is that which makes the text, whether one speaks of words or pictures, appear and yet which, despite its materiality, is immaterial in or to most conventional discourses on art. We might suggest that the subjectile is therefore a ghost of sorts. Hovering in the background of any text, neither there nor not there, it belongs properly speaking neither completely inside nor outside any text, the text of the painting or photograph. It resides as the double border between word or image and world, between representation and the real, between the idea of an original and translation, between representation and interpretation, and of course between the living and the dead, presence and absence. The subjectile haunts that to which it gives a place of appearance. Derrida's interest in the subjectile is focused on its aspect as what 'underlies both language and art like a support . . . and which is not to be translated' (Caws *SAAA*, xii).

In its liminal and only marginally visible location the subjectile cannot be assumed. It '*is something* [which] is not yet a given . . . it does not constitute an object of any knowing' (*SAAA*, 63). Neither something nor nothing, an apparent neologism in the text of Artaud not yet having been received into dictionaries in the 1930s, *subjectile* arrives. Or rather, it returns from older sources in both French and Italian (*SAAA*, 64). Derrida thus constructs the meaning from the archive of traces that the word re-presents, even as he unearths the buried ruins of its sources. The subjectile is both 'a substance, [and] a subject'. It 'belongs to the code of painting and designates what is in some way below (*subjectum*)', occupying – perhaps being – a liminal place or, more accurately, a taking place. It names a process without proper place. It announces a becoming of the *between*, which both is and is not: '*between* the beneath and the above, it is at once a support and a surface . . . everything distinct from form, as well as from meaning and representation, not representable' (*SAAA*, 64; emphasis added). Neither representation nor representable as such, it nonetheless brings about representation. The term marks and remarks a certain crossing and recrossing of borders. It institutes the very borders that it crosses, while having 'no consistency apart from that of the *between*' (*SAAA*, 71; emphasis added). There is therefore no subjectile as such, even as the subjectile writes the possibility for the work of art to happen, as it were. A secret that permits the possibility of meaning and representation, the 'subjectile appears untranslatable, that is axiomatic' or, in every example, singular and so unavailable to determination in any general manner (*SAAA*, 65). Such apparent paradoxes speak of the subjectile's power to mark a text, to inform and make possible its taking place, while, in being marked by both a lack and excess, as well as being both excess and lack, the subjectile is irreducible to any stable location or meaning, other than to its own surface and support: 'the word "subjectile" is itself a subjectile' (*SAAA*, 65).

Hence, ghost, neither 'a subject . . . nor . . . the object either' (*SAAA*, 71). Lack *and* excess, being traced by such marks even as it leaves traces of itself only through the signs of its own lack and excess, the subjectile *is not, in sensu stricto*. Yet, though not an 'it', it is not a negative term: any address to the subjectile cannot be given in terms of a definition that is merely negative or positive, and therefore partaking of some ontological determination. One can no more say 'it is' than one can say 'it is not'. Having no being, the verb of being will not hold when one attempts to 'apply' it to the notion, hardly a motif (*SAAA*, 72), of the subjectile. Making possible the generation of meaning, of representation, of the image through its support, yet being unsupportable through any such act itself, other than through reference to itself, a subjectile belongs to the order of that which leaves its mark in having retreated from the scene of what it causes to appear.

Having called into question the very possibility of the semantic and ontological stability of the term, Derrida admits that the figure is undecidable: 'it doubtless no longer even belongs to being' (*SAAA*, 73), and this is so precisely because 'the subjectile remains *between* . . . whether it constitutes its underlying element . . . or interposes itself' (*SAAA*, 75; emphasis in original). That there are remains, that the term remains as some untranslatable, undecidable, even unknowable remains: this remains all that we can say of 'it'. What remains are the remains, the traces of that which remains in some future never to arrive to be translated or rendered in any final form. Here is the alterity, the haunting condition of the subjectile by which, in turn, one's perception is haunted in seeking to come to terms with 'it'. *Subjectile* names a spectral motion akin to the work of writing, which supports meaning, which places meaning as its surface movements, its temporal and textual structure, and yet which is never that meaning, never what is indirectly represented. In the subjectile and through the play of this impossible figure everything is played out in the work of difference as that which makes possible any representation, image, meaning or being at all. And this difference, this performative inscription is what makes possible the oscillation 'between representation and its other' (*SAAA*, 96).

Were I to move this discussion in a different direction, I would bring it back to what is received in the response to the portrait, illustrated through the example of Derrida in *Derrida*. I would be tempted to consider this in the following way. In the film, we see Derrida, 'the original' and apparently living Derrida, responding to the uncanniness of the image in its manifestation as a painting, a portrait. However, what one 'sees' in the film is not there of course. There is no Derrida there. There is no 'original'. This is yet another 'portrait', a representation of the intellectual as both audience and subject of a particular experience, to which experience of being filmed looking at an image of oneself he is expected and invited to respond. There is no 'true' Derrida. There is only the painted image and the filmed image. Two competing traces exist only through the phantom-subjectile medium of projection for the times of representation, in that apparitional possibility that is endlessly iterable (at least in principle). The 'subjectile', in this case, film, produces the illusion of living, allowing through its spectral medium the uncanny experience for its audience of Derrida living on beyond death. This is a device on which the film plays repeatedly in different ways, as for example in the moments when a camera records one Derrida watching the recording of another Derrida (and on occasion yet another), or when the camera records a 'blind' Derrida who, though looking at his image in the mirror of the hair salon, is blind to being watched and does not see himself seeing himself. The film thus interprets representation even as it performs its representations and so represents interpretation. Folding into one another, a writing or inscription and an image, an image of the image, of what the image occasions on the occasion of the image. These reciprocate one another, a series of echoes of the other being staged in the erasure of Narcissus. And this is only effected through the subjectile being at work.

But we should not rush to understand the subjectile merely as the motion, the rhythm of inscription, which traces the opening and revelation of that becoming which is also a between. It should also be remembered that the subjectile is that on which the subjectile comes to be remarked, though never as itself of course. This is what is seen in *Derrida*, it is what *Derrida* both represents and interprets, as *Derrida* intervenes in Derrida reflecting on Derrida, and the process of becoming the *trait* in *Derrida*. Derrida is written on by the act of filming, becoming the subjectile onto which the image of Derrida is projected, constructed. The subjectile is then, as Derrida says economically, both words and page (*SAAA*, 114). Words, traces, brush strokes, pencil lines, light, projection: all are phantom projections and supports, movements and elements in a structure allowing for representation, and all the while not being that. At the same time, such marks, performing the representation, the image, the visual that they neither are nor are reducible to, require themselves a support, such as the page, the canvas, the photographic paper, the screen. Any image, any representation is only ever possible through such support, and through the violence of appearance and penetration, the weaving motion that is figured through the motif of writing.

Whatever it is we think we mean when we talk of 'art', such discourse 'always implies representation, reappropriation, reintegration, transposition, or figurative translation of the same' (*SAAA*, 116). Yet the excess of that which makes art and its implications possible is, in its force, its violence, not of art. Art is thus haunted by a writing, by a performative event that is not those elements defining art. The subjectile betrays. It translates and traduces the very art it upholds and makes possible. More than this, it may be affirmed that the *subjectile* just is traduction. Subjectile may be said to name the motion or becoming of traduction: transport, transfer, conveyance, derivation. In not being of that 'art', but in belonging a constant motion between the representation and its other, the subjectile announces that 'Being is not, it is not present, it remains to be born' (*SAAA*, 128). Presence and the present are haunted by *différance* on which such notions rely for the illusion, the illustration or representation of their meaning. This is witnessed in *Derrida*, in that scene with which I began this chapter. Support and instrument, a subjectile generates and enacts a matrix, taking 'upon itself' the 'uterophallic form of the father-mother' (*SAAA*, 132), even as 'it' escapes and exceeds this already impossible determination. Thus, the subjectile figures the other (*SAAA*, 137) that we name spectre, ghost, phantom, phantasm. If 'it' is or can be said to be anything, 'it' remains as a trace without ground, a 'figure of the unfigurable' (*SAAA*, 134). Being 'never literally what it is' (*SAAA*, 139), the subjectile bears the trace, even as it bears witness to the traces of the constant un-sensing of meaning, of being, of stable representation, and therefore gives the lie to the promise of presence, and of full meaning that representational art would appear to guarantee.

IV TRAIT

The *trait* is an interesting and complex figure. I have already observed its work in *portrait*. Furthermore, it may be inferred that the term is related to *trace* and to other similar forms, such as *tract*, which shares a common root, *trahere*, meaning to draw or drag, to pull. Earliest uses in English forms acknowledge temporality, which is clearly heard in phrases such as 'tract of time', but the term *tract* also indicates spatial cognition, as in a *tract of land*, the figural image by which Thomas Hardy traces, drawing out the image of, the landscape of Egdon Heath in *The Return of the Native*: 'the vast tract of unenclosed wild known as Egdon Heath embrowned itself moment by moment' (1999, 9). Hardy's sentence is fascinating for the ways it insinuates the relation between pictorial representation and writing, form and content, space and time. Were this the only sentence in the chapter to do so, its remarkable and singular exemplification of the work of différance and writing would alone warrant our attention, as would its 'institution' of the scene and the implications for reading the trait therein. It exemplifies both the movement of différance as that which it indelibly marks and articulates the architectonics of representation and scene and the invisible motions that produce these images.

What is all the more interesting though is that it condenses motifs and tropes that are to be observed throughout the chapter. As the chapter illustrates and traces repeatedly, there is no subject, no consciousness in the work of différance and the multiple traits by which it weaves structure and image. The consciousness of the narrator arrives belatedly to reinscribe what takes place, to receive and so take down the dictation of the other in its response, to what is always already on the move. The sentence, and, by extension therefore the chapter, arrive, in effect, as tracts on the trait. In a gesture of adumbrating frames within frames, they perform what they describe, producing in the process a treatise on the illusory art of representation and the hidden graphic movements that make the absent visible. And, it has to be said, this chapter offers a tract on différance, and on literature itself as supplement and subjectile as the collective trait treating or presenting, staging, both a representation as absent, and a discourse on the différance of, *in*, representation qua illusion, illustration, image, of presence. The sentence stages itself as both representation and the support for the representation of repeated human actions time after time in their iterable recurrence. (Is it not this haunting revenance and iterability that the *return* of the title, *The Return of the Native*, announces as the inaugural coming to being, and what is always to come? Is it not the case that the economy and *trait* of the return dispels once more any discernible starting point or origin?)

The sentence plays economically on the spacing of time and the time of spacing, implicating the tract or trait in his tracing of the land and the time of representation. Coming near the very start of the chapter, and therefore the novel, the sentence opens spacing and temporality through a tracing that follows the contours as much as it re-presents them in their absence, and so may be said to partake of a performative, rather than merely a constative function. Additionally, the sentence, in its folds and motions, the spacing of its structure and the times of its reading and writing, anticipate the chapter as a whole. They inscribe and portray the place and its taking place, as the inaugural condition for the coming into being of both life, initially inhuman or nonhuman existence, and the 'being' of the chapter itself. Or to put this differently, as time moves in the scene so writing enacts a concomitant, analogous becoming. The chapter is interesting further in that it admits of no human form in its representation. However, that 'representation' or portrait of the land is bound up in a convoluted manner in that chapter with temporality. The writing of representation and its complex of interwoven traces is a matter of tracing and treating of spacing and time, specifically different passages, durations, the continuance and measures of time. Understanding this brings us back to tract. The point here is to acknowledge how representation in being constituted through traces, whether written or painted, or drawn, is, as any other writing, the production and effect of the motions of *différance*.

If it is the movement of the *trait* or trace that undoes the apparent immediacy and stability of representation, what else can be said of the trait, apropos of art? As Peter Brunette and David Wills point out, 'much of Derrida's writing on the visual arts has concentrated on the *trait* . . . a word that is itself synonymous . . . with the term "writing"'. They continue,

It is through the idea of the trait, referring to whatever is drawn, as well as more specifically in French to the brush stroke, that the graphic [as opposed to the phonic] emerges . . . there can be no purely pictorial line, any more than a purely verbal line – because the trait is always already a *retrait*, necessarily subject to repetition and subdivision. (1994, 4)

In an essay on metaphor, Derrida examines the metaphor as *retrait*,[1] which may be translated as both retreat and also re-tracing. The metaphor, a figure for something else, is only ever such a mark. It retraces or reiterates, whilst not being a direct representation of the thing, subject or idea it figures. The metaphor's arrival signals the deferral of and differentiation of presence and the present and thereby announces the temporal and textual network as being always already in place in the act of signification. At the same time, the appearance of the trait also signals that presence has retreated. It has left only this *trait* as the sign of its *retrait*, a *retrait* that is doubled, and redoubles, re-dividing itself in the *trait* as representation *and* interpretation. This is why there is neither a purely pictorial nor a verbal line. Nor is the *trait* secondary. It does not come after that which it traces. As we see with the example of Hardy, the trace precedes what it represents, its supplementarity arriving before the 'original'. In what amounts to the *a priori* registration of withdrawal and non-appearance, it may be read that the inscription of the *trait*, as Derrida attempts to 'articulate it in the trace or in difference, *succeeds only in being effaced (n'arrive qu'à s'effacer)*' (*RM*, 125; emphasis added). As might be apparent from the words of Brunette and Wills, the *trait* treats of both feature and mark, drawn line or brush stroke. Importantly, the trait makes appear, to use this already overworked formula, both that which is silent – the graphic – and which also spaces, displacing presence from within the totalizing illusion of representation, even as such spacing, such seemingly invisible differing and deferring (this being a question of spacing and temporality, in that the eye takes time to read what it believes to be the immediacy of reception of any representation), makes such an illusion possible.

That the *trait* is a mark, that is to say transmissible and available to reading (at least in principle), means that it is always already remarkable, even though within the work of art it is usually taken as unremarkable, unless recuperable within the architectonics of form and content, and therefore subservient to representation and ontology. The appearance of a *trait* is therefore always a *re-trait*, as we have said. Never appearing for a first time simply, any *trait* always implies repetition, of withdrawal or retreat, and return or re-markability. Its graphic condition thus attests to the *trait*'s identity as a writing, whether the *trait* is a pencil line or brush stroke, or indeed the play of light in a photograph or film. As we had seen with the subjectile, the *trait* is never itself, although it is not nothing. In its iterability, it is always already supplementary. Both replacement and addition, the *trait* is a figure of, even as it figures, 'an indiscreet and overflowing insistence . . . an over-abundant remanence, . . . an intrusive repetition, always marking with a supplementary trait, with one more turn, with a re-turn and with a *withdrawal* (*retrait*) the trait that it will have left in the text itself' (*RM*, 104). An interruption and an excess beyond identity, the *trait* is that graphic reminder *and* remainder, which, irreducible to – other than – either form or content, representation or meaning, marks a passage *between* the visible and invisibility, and thus has to do with the gaze, with vision. It is, I would aver, the agitation in *trait* which acts on, provoking anxiety in the viewer of his own portrait, the *trait* that in its passage of traduction recalls uncannily to the mind's eye or to memory something of the subject, but as other than the subject who receives the mark in the confrontation with his image, as that image in turn intervenes in the blindness of self to cause one to interpret, to translate and so betray oneself.

Vision is, perhaps obviously, central to all of Derrida's writings on art, even though it is not the only subject. Vision, for Derrida, is implicated in reading. It is furthermore 'about looking and the right to it'. This in turn 'becomes solely a matter of lines of demarcation, marks or boundaries, limits, frames, and borders that leave traces of having *overstepped* the mark' (*RI*, xv; emphasis added). Notice how again overflow, overabundance, excess are emphasized in relation to the trait and the border, the frame, and that in representation which cannot be contained in a closed system – in short, *writing*. I am tempted to hear in this remark what amounts to a virtual thesis on how to read the visual arts, how to see the difference by which art is made possible, without falling prey to a kind of readerly blindness or becoming blind to the necessary act of reading which has to begin again and again. Such blindness is called by Derrida the desire for restitution, to which, in their analysis of a painting by Vincent Van Gogh (*Old Shoes with Laces*) Derrida reads Martin Heidegger and Meyer Schapiro succumbing (*TP*, 255–382). The essay is presented as a dialogue, or to be more precise a 'polylogue' comprising '*n* + 1 – female – voices' (*TP*, 356). Its interlocutors shuttling back and forth, weaving in and out of each other, moving between the essays by Schapiro and Heidegger. The painting depicts two shoes.

Concerning the shoes, they cannot be reassembled as a pair, they cannot be assigned this meaning, *pair*. They are 'detached, abandoned, unlaced . . . ' (*TP*, 374). Inasmuch as the very idea of *pairing* is undone a 'spectrum of possibilities of the possibilities of specters presents itself' (*TP*, 374). The dysymmetry of this may be glimpsed in the English translation, in the motion between *spectrum* and *spectres*, and of course in the overflow, the drift that is irreversible from one end of the sentence to the other, from the classical measurability of a spectrum to the possibility of the impossible that is named the spectral. But this becomes more pronounced, as meaning is rendered dysfunctional through Derrida's use of *le spectre* for both possibilities. Thus, the commentary retraces and performs semantically the dysymmetry and concomitant opening or unfolding already in the painting's double and differential image of the shoes. Each shoe is of course an interpretation and therefore marked by, even as it remarks, the *trait* of itself. But it is also the *trait* of the other. Each shoe figures its other *in* the painting, in an unfolding reciprocity that neither closes the gap between the two as iterable reminders of the other nor completes the circle in the presentation of an image that amounts to the notion of *pair*. In reading the opening of the closed system of *pair* within itself, Derrida acknowledges how each shoe is haunted by other shoes, not least those from which those represented are 'amputated', and therefore impossible to give restitution to, in returning to them the ghostly supplement that each shoe thus figures and by which it is traced.

It is impossible here to paraphrase more of Derrida's lengthy, complex commentary. However, we can say that both Schapiro and Heidegger's commentaries produce meanings having nothing to do with the image as such, but with a misrepresentation as to the possible contexts for the image. In this sense, both Schapiro and Heidegger desire a story that hides itself as story, as narrative subjectile, but which imposes itself as a border, a frame if you will by which the painting may be explained and contained. As Derrida points out, one cannot even assume that the painting is of a *pair* of shoes, just because there happen to be two shoes, let alone remark that the shoes belong to a peasant, as Heidegger does (*TP*, 258–60). Misrecognition and with that misreading figure a kind of proleptic will to blindness, whereby 'the desire for attribution is a desire for appropriation' (*TP*, 260). The perception of attribution *as* appropriation identifies the desire for stories and the projection of meaning as being the will to *meaning-for-me*. One produces and stabilizes the meaning of a text by marshalling and economizing on all the traits in order to situate a semantic totality in which difference is subordinated to the production of an identity that, after a fashion, is *my* identity, identity-for-me. The meaning I read returns a reflection, a restitution that is at bottom an encoded narcissism. Seeing clear and true in the reading of the work of art involves a suspension of attribution, an interruption of one's desire. It is thus to engage in the task of seeing what one does not see by habit.

The interest in what one sees but which is understood as remaining mute in any conventional analytical construction of the visual concerns the graphic. How the graphic *trait* relates to sight and blindness, visibility and invisibility, appears very early on in the discussion between two voices in *Memoirs of the Blind* (*MB*, 2–3). One is afforded insight in the places concerning the self, identity, being, where one is most blind. The *trait* effects a hinge, but also a break in the binaries just mentioned, as well as forcing a passage that erases at least in part the presumed or assumed separability and autonomy of the component terms in each binarism. Once the breach or hinge is traced, the meaning on either side of the break can no longer be maintained. This text considers the structural dislocation or disjunction, the disorder or difference that must perforce take place in any act of self-portraiture and the assumption of auto-presence. There is a structural displacement between the making of the self-portrait and the necessary blindness that accompanies the production of the work. Put simply, if one looks at the line or stroke, the *trait* one is making in the act or performance of self-portraiture, one has to do so from memory, from a place that is blind. Conversely, if one looks at one's reflection in order to commit the image to paper or canvas, one cannot observe the making of the line or stroke, which must proceed blindly.

So, to reiterate the point, the *trait* is the demarcation, the spectral manifestation of *différance*. In ghostly fashion, the line read and the line to be drawn hovers as the phantasmic, (a)material trace of memory. It appears and retreats. It is the *trait* and *retrait* by which one sees without eyes. In perceiving this, we come to apprehend indirectly that there is a relationship between the representation of the 'present' self and the self's temporal alterity. Put differently, the perception or insight opens to our view an all-too-often obscured relation between *mimesis* and *mneme*, representation or image and memory, image and interpretation. Understanding this relation, one begins to grasp the temporal dimension of identity, meaning, ontology and the spacing inherent to such concepts. Once the temporal is apprehended, presence is placed in a relation to itself by which there can be no full or simple, undifferentiated presence. Presence is displaced from within itself by the *trait* that is the signal of a past that has never been present, an alterity irrecuperable and irreducible to the selfsame. Nothing is seen as such then, but a certain revelation takes place in *and* as the temporal disjunction of the *trait* and its iterability, whereby there occurs 'an unveiling that renders visible' (*MB*, 122). In this, and there, *there*, there is always already some supplementary phantom. The *trait* retreats. It is always already a *retrait*. Haunted by the *retrait*, it is 'not then paralysed in a tautology that folds the same onto the same. On the contrary, it becomes prey to *allegory* [or analogy] . . . given over to the speech and gaze of the other' (*MB*, 2–3). Comprehending the *trait* and its relation to seeing as thinking or reading (one says 'I see' when one means 'I understand'), rather than to what blinds one to comprehension in being seen. (Arguably, in their non-receptive restitution of the text of Van Gogh, Schapiro and Heidegger see before seeing and therefore do not 'see', do not interrupt what Joyce calls in *Ulysses* the 'ineluctable modality of the visible' as the modality that maintains the illusion of presence and logocentrism [*MB*, 31].) As Derrida remarks 'in losing his sight man does not lose his eyes. On the contrary. Only then does man begin to *think* the eyes . . . he sees *between* and catches a glimpse of the difference' (*MB*, 128; second emphasis mine).

To fold back upon ourselves, and to unfold again this point from another perspective already implied in the response of Derrida to his portrait. This difference just announced, once caught in the blink of an eye as it were, we might name on this occasion the *trait*. Moving beyond the immediate frame of reference for this chapter, I would conclude this section by pointing to the fact that it is also, significantly, the difference by which we are known, and which survives us, as the proper name. For the proper name, the name you read here, *Derrida*, or the name on the cover of this book and which I sign elsewhere is what comes back to me as a *trait* which be-trays, surviving, living on beyond me. This is what the *trait* gives us to see and to think. And like that portrait with which we began, the proper name returns to us as this uncanny spectral trace. It returns and retreats as the future anterior ghost of ourselves. Our signature, our proper name, as *trait* guarantees and countersigns us as an other, which, as David Farrell Krell emphasizes, mourns us (2000, 10–11). Supposedly the sign of a living being, the equivalent of living speech, this strange *trait*, the signature or the proper name is haunted. It is ghosted by its own iterability and transmissibility as *trait*. Amputated from us, the proper name improperly can only function seemingly paradoxically as the mechanically iterable signature of our singularity. For the signature to prove its 'originality' or uniqueness it must be repeatable. And to borrow from Krell once more, such technicity 'means my death' (2000, 11).

V PASSE-PARTOUT

The *trait* leaves a mark, one which returns and retreats. Being of the order of some *revenant*, the trace is always already this ghostly reminder and remainder of the incommensurable relation without relation between sign and object, material mark and immaterial resonance. Whether one is speaking of *trait* or *subjectile*, one is therefore concerned in addressing the work of art, those 'lines of demarcation, marks or boundaries, limits, frames, and borders that leave traces of having overstepped the mark'.[2] The boundary or limit is always that which, in being crossed, attests to the transience, as well as the translation, of the spectre. Such an act of overstepping 'doubtless dismantles the most reassuring conceptual oppositions'. Binarisms and oppositions such as presence and representation, visibility and invisibility, text and context, representation and reality, presence and absence, alive and dead – all are disjointed. Thus, we are brought to a border, which is not fixed but rather which unfixes any stability in its articulation, every time it takes place. This border is named the *parergon* in *The Truth in Painting*. In the delightfully – and perhaps deceptively – titled first section, 'Passe-Partout', Derrida situates what the 'insistent atopics of the *parergon*' as this appears in an enfolded and intimate relation with the 'great philosophical question[s]' such as 'What is art?', 'the beautiful?', 'representation?', 'the origin of the work of art?' (*TP*, 9). Again, one witnesses Derrida issuing the fundamental ontological questions in order to step back before their arrival so as to initiate the dismantling of the grounds on which the ontological interrogation is itself built. If the ontologies of 'art', the 'beautiful', or 'literature' are at stake, so also are the epistemological and therefore institutional habits by which ontologization gets underway repeatedly and is maintained blindly, without the necessary reflection and insight into the very grounds of the question of ontology itself. Before speaking of the *parergon* however it is important to acknowledge the *passe-partout* as *trait* and *subjectile*.

The *OED* tells us that the *passe-partout* is both a master-key, a shibboleth allowing access anywhere to any encrypted secret, and a frame composed of two sheets of transparent material mounted back to back. Moreover, it is the adhesive tape holding the two sheets together. The figure of the *passe-partout* is thus an excessive *trait* in its own right. It has no single or proper identity of its own, but operates as the machinery by which is opened the possibility for decryption and framing the reading to come. At the same time, this *trait* is not simply double in its semantic resonances, it is also a double border. 'It' divides itself. Of course, all borders are double in that, neither simply an outside nor inside edge, they touch on both inside and outside, thereby doubling – and dividing – by the mark that takes place, and providing a support in the manner of the sub-jectile for that which is framed, and thereby deciphered as work of art, if the frame is explicitly 'around' the painting, drawing or pho-tograph. Derrida ups the ante however in choosing the figure of the *passe-partout*, because it figures as an exemplary instance of the double border, and because, used specifically in photography, it is transparent. It is therefore a semi-visible and semi-invisible support, a *trait* neither completely there or not there, not simply a border but doubled in and of itself.

The *passe-partout* is thus a particular example of the *parergon*, the frame, margin or framing device or effect. It is situated in the book as a margin before the margin, the outside border to the inside border but also an inside border to that which is outside, namely the book title, for example. It therefore names an 'atopic' as Derrida puts it because it is

> neither work (*ergon*) nor outside the work (*hors d'oeuvre*), neither inside nor outside . . . it disconcerts any opposition but does not remain indeterminate and it *gives rise* to the work. It is no longer merely around the work . . . it puts in place . . . the instances of the frame, the title, the signature, the legend, etc. (*TP*, 9)

Parergon thus establishes the grounds for determining text and context, inside and out, the work of art as such, without being accounted for, and so receding into the background or invisibility in having this determining function for the ontology of that of which it is not considered properly speaking to belong. Derrida's *passe-partout* does not merely describe or speak about his project, it behaves in a performative manner, as a performative interjection that frames, constituting itself as *parergon*. It becomes the mark or *trait* on and *as* the text. Neither inside nor outside the book (as with any introduction or preface), it is that, which, in supporting the text, also doubles itself by performing the function about which it speaks. Once this is recognized, we cannot go back to seeing the border or frame as merely a delimitation. Derrida's articulation marks an irreversible doubling, appropriate to the figure of the border as an act of inscription, whereby the constative utterance is transformed, translated from within itself, to become what Derrida unveils as always already being – a performative gesture without which no work, no text is possible.

As singular manifestation and performative 'taking-place' of the *parergon*, the *passe-partout* gives us a glimpse of what is to follow in *The Truth in Painting* as successive frames open and close around one another. Being the first chapter 'proper', 'Parergon' is, as David Farrell Krell describes it, 'a text within a text', its logic being dictated by this internal fold that constitutes it. It is 'folded back into and upon itself, or reproduced within itself, after the manner of a Russian Baba or Chinese box, but into abyssal infinity – the phenomenon that Derrida himself designates as *mise-en-abyme*, a mirroring without end' (Krell 2000, 26). The *parergon*, which includes but exceeds the idea of the frame, and of framing in general, thus partakes of the condition of both *trait* and *subjectile*, in all their possible, excessive significations, as well as in their ruination of stable signification, ontology, representation. Yet all are merely singular examples of what the parergon signifies in Greek, 'by-product, marginal side effect, mere avocation, addendum, or supplement' (Krell 2000, 26). Seeing through the *passe-partout* (the key which is also a lens, and also a passport) then, 'seeing' becomes translated, vision transformed, as support and mark, as frame. All the 'ghosted figures' (Krell 2000, 26) become visible in all their destabilizing yet necessary functions in the secret, yet quasi-visible technicity which makes possible and causes to appear the work of art, and without which no work of art is possible. Coming to see what we have been blinded to, we see how conceptual divisions such as internal and external no longer function. Coming to terms with the work of writing within the work of art, as *parergon, subjectile, trait*, we come to see how illusory is the implication that 'art – the word, the concept, the thing – has a unity and, what is more, an originary meaning' (*TP*, 20). We also come to recognize how '*there is* frame, but the frame *does not exist*' (*TP*, 81). Once more, a phantom effect then, the trace of a ghost disorganizing all ontologies, leaves its signature, the otherwise unreadable graffiti of the apparition.

VI MIMESIS

Mimesis will direct us, serving as a guide to literature, being, circularity, and from there to the matter of excess in writing as the excess beyond representation. It will do so first in terms of that which cannot be represented but which nonetheless demands reading. Second, it will direct our attention to that within representation and the present, as well as the presence that representation suggests as commensurate with the present, the traces of history. These arrive not as reminders of presence having passed, but as remainders of the historical, occluded in the aesthetic work of representation. It is not certain that one can even pretend to encompass so vast a topic as *mimesis* or represent it in a sketch such as this, not least because the history of its reception in Western philosophy is a history marked by avoidance. As Derrida comments, 'one cannot avoid missing mimesis as soon as one identifies it, and wants to decide on its truth value' (I:D, 25). The assumed and historically repeated relation between mimesis and truth put in place over and over again, as for example 'in Plato, Heidegger and Girard . . . in very different, but finally analogous ways' (I:D, 25), testifies to how such avoidance takes place when one decides on this simulacrum of a relationship.

The 'concept' of *mimesis* is as old as that of art. One figures the other like two shoes that are not necessarily a pair. But if one figures the other, there is no saying, no deciding on which comes first. Each becomes the other of the other, a figure of, for, the other. Yet before rushing to assume *mimesis*, we would do well to remind ourselves that one cannot properly define *mimesis* because, as Philippe Lacoue-Labarthe cautions us on the subject, there is nothing proper to *mimesis*, it has no property of its own (1989, 116). It cannot by definition be defined but can only be exemplified through singular manifestations of art, which are read as being *mimetic*, and which are read therefore as being faithful or true to *mimesis*, even as in circular or framing fashion *mimesis* as concept is what is taken to measure the representation of what is true in art. *Mimesis* does not exist therefore. It is a phantom-discourse, a spectral support or subjectile on which the 'truth in painting' is wagered.

Derrida writes 'The Double Session' as two halves, as a double response to two passages, one by Plato, from the *Philebus*, the other from the work of Stéphane Mallarmé, from a text titled *Mimique*. Of the two halves, Derrida comments at the outset of the 'half' printed in second place, that they exist 'only through the fiction of a crease' (*D*, 227). By virtue of the hinge, then, the crack or bracket, the fold or *brisure*, is the text doubled. The two 'sessions' or scenes are not whole in themselves, Derrida confesses, nor together do they form a finished or symmetrical structure or presentation. In 'The Double Session' Derrida not only draws our attention to Plato's marriage of art with *mimesis*, as though the two 'halves' did in fact form a whole, but also how, in a wedding which is more a welding, there takes place the instantiation of a tradition in Western philosophy of perceiving *mimesis* predominantly in terms of the idea of truth. From *mimesis* and through his reading of the *Philebus*, Derrida coins the neologism *mimetologism*. He does so in order to illustrate the *homohegemonic logic* of the mimetic, as that which is already at work in the tension between the extracts from Plato and Mallarmé. On the one hand, what is staged is the extent to which the mimetologic has dominated literature throughout the history of Western culture. On the other hand, Derrida's purpose is to demonstrate literature's potential for calling into question this mimetologic demand and, we might suggest, its law.

Beginning by disturbing the assumptions that underpin the ontological interrogation 'what is literature?' as a question destined by the desire for truth, Derrida illustrates, through a deployment of figures of speech signifying the constructedness of a work of art, how literature stages a resistance to the demand for truth and the mimetologic imperative. He effects this not through dialectical opposition – for otherwise there would be re-established two implicit halves to a whole, with the binarism, truth/literature cemented in place – but through what we have already identified as a more affirmative resistance to the demand for truth. This affirmative resistance is carried out specifically through performative gestures of mimicry and imitation and through the insertion of 'the poetic text into the very "process of truth" which has always been philosophy's exclusive concern' (Kamuf 1991, 169).

In doing so, Derrida dismantles the frameworks that hold in place concepts of truth and fiction, illusion and reality, original and copy, and so on. At the same time however – and as on so many other occasions – Derrida does not simply unhinge the frame, thereby effecting a structural undoing. He also erases the boundaries that keep in place concepts of presence and absence, present and past. In this manner, through the agency of Mallarmé's prose poem, Derrida traces the deconstruction of philosophy by that which it has always sought to condemn or exclude (Kamuf 1991, 169).

Having announced, apparently disingenuously, that this 'double session' is 'concerned with the question *what is literature?*' (*D*, 177) – a question that Derrida insists takes place 'between literature and truth, between literature and that by which the question *what is?* wants answering' (*D*, 177) – he then proposes that the 'mimetic system . . . as a system of illustration' (*D*, 183) is, itself, illustrated in this mode by Mallarmé's *Mimique*, that short piece inserted by Derrida into Plato. If you pause for a moment to reflect on the internal parenthesis that I have inserted into the, admittedly, lengthy and somewhat circuitous sentence with which this paragraph begins, you might notice something. This interjection, which qualifies the question *what is literature?*, already cited from Derrida's text, folds into itself another quotation. The second citation is divided between two clauses. Derrida's syntax is arranged in such a way that the initial ontological query is located not as an originary inquiry, but as itself already located *between*. The question therefore is a mark, the sign of an anterior postulation. The logic implicit here is that though the ontological question is conventionally understood as a founding question, and therefore an opening of the discourse on the way to truth, in reality, it arises belatedly. For it can only be asked if truth and literature are situated as opponents *as if* they were already in place in the first place, where the latter is either marginalized, condemned or excluded by the former. I say *as if* they occupied this *a priori position*, as though this were somehow established, a given, and not a convenient rhetorical illustration of a binarism for Plato. Truth on the one hand, and literature (and its more or less spectral cognates, fiction, lying, perjury) on the other, into the midst of which, belatedly, there arises the question *what is literature?*.

Derrida therefore unfolds, in his inaugural gambit, the folds of a structure conventionally assumed, in order to dismantle the conventional, the habitual, the institutional; in this gesture he exposes all that haunts all such forms, forms which, as we shall see, mark not only Plato's text but

> if one reconstitutes the system, the whole of a history . . . And this history, if it has any meaning, is governed in its entirety by the value of truth and by a certain relation, inscribed in the hymen in question, *between* literature and truth. (*D*, 183)

Hymen might strike you as an odd word, and this would need reflection were there space.[3] However, for now, we should continue with the parenthesis above, for what I have just described is not all that takes place. Returning to my cordoned citation, it will be observed that, having marked the *between* as the place on which the ontological question hangs, Derrida then unravels a further clause: *between literature and that by which the question* what is? *wants answering*. Truth is replaced here, the previous neat formula taken to pieces. The logic of what lies behind or before truth is thus unveiled in that *that by which* and what comes after it. Truth is therefore not assumed by Derrida, it is not accepted as a *philosopheme*, a self-evident, simple metalinguistic or universal, metaphysical concept. Instead, one is invited to step back before 'truth' to investigate the structure of this concept, what it includes, what it excludes. Although only at the beginning, Derrida proceeds through a necessary caution and rigour, and above all else perhaps a suspension, an interruption almost before one gets underway, of habits and assumptions of thought. A framework is being revealed here, as that same framework is being opened outwards beyond itself, into the figure impossible to represent directly, the *mise-en-abyme*.

We appear to have travelled a long distance from art, and from aesthetics. Much of what Derrida has to say though of the relation between literature and truth can also be thought through apropos any possible relation between art and truth, especially as this may be reflected through the category, the concept of *mimesis*, which ' "precedes" truth in a certain sense . . . destabilizing it in advance' (I:D, 27). If I may risk a detour here, I would like to ask in the light of this statement, how does *mimesis* destabilize the truth which supposedly it proves, or by which 'concept' the philosopher supports his presentation of truth? Let me frame this for you. First, if *mimesis* is nothing as such but must always be exemplified and, second, if every example is singular and therefore differs from every other, it therefore follows that *mimesis* does not exist. It is not reducible to an 'it-ness', some stable, universal ipseity, which holds true each and every time, or from time to time. In order to equate *mimesis* with truth, the assumption has to proceed that *mimesis* is a stable *a priori* category or concept, having its own internally coherent truthfulness, to which it is always and equally faithful. So the concept of *mimesis* precedes truth in the philosopher's construction of his or her aesthetic reflection on a work of literature or art, in order for that work to embody through its interpreted, allegedly illustrative mimetologism, the truth in painting, the truth in literature. Yet, the radical singularity and emptiness of the mimetic has to be comprehended as arriving before the truth only to destabilize the very idea or concept of Truth universally perceived as constant, as having its own internal coherence and conceptual, ontological or structural undifferentiated cohesion. Returning though to the discussion of this subject in 'The Double Session', there is at work a chain of words. These are easily missed, if one thinks of them as *merely* rhetoric, *simply* figures of speech, and so passes over them, or sees through them. Reading on the way to somewhere else, as though the sentence were a route map, you do not see necessarily what is being staged, how the presentation is being framed. Let me illustrate what I mean by picking up on some of Derrida's intermittent stitches that hold the text together:

> fold . . . outline . . . mark out . . . a few rough strokes, a certain number of motifs. These strokes might be seen to form a sort of frame, the enclosure or borders of a history that would be that of a certain play between literature and truth. The history of this relationship would be organized by . . . a certain interpretation of *mimesis*. (*D*, 183)

The excerpt just cited comes before the extract already quoted and considered. In folding back on the passage, I want to draw your attention to the figural language by which Derrida both stages and frames his analysis of a particular history as interpretation, rather than being a history of *mimesis* represented as without support. Playing between the motifs of adumbration and the *parergon*, Derrida draws us an illustration of what is to come. He anticipates his own interpretative illustration that is to be unfolded through the chapter. At the same time, he constitutes the frame into which the very same illustration, of which the frame is a part, not merely the marginal enclosure or border, is to be presented. The caution Derrida exhibits here doubles the framing gesture even as it opens or unfolds to a certain perspicacious gaze – as though from an angle of parallax – the 'secret' that *mimesis* understood as copy or illustration and therefore key to, representation of, truth, is always already inhabited, haunted, by interpretation, narrative, displacement and deferral. *Mimesis* cannot be represented as such, it must be explained and so, in recognizing this, one sees how *mimesis* itself is not direct representation however much its mode of envisioning appears as a faithful copy of some displaced original no longer present. Instead, *mimesis* is anticipated in its interpretative role as a mimicry of the real, itself an interpretation, a translation and not the truth of some reality, some thing. *Mimesis* is a writing that exceeds in being sketched, drawn, framed, narrated, that for which it is taken as being a true and faithful copy.

Derrida's complication of his own phrasing is itself illustrative in its semantic, as well as grammatical iterability. Reiterating itself, folding and unfolding itself through the cautionary reflux and variation of motifs, tropes and figures, it structures its form, framing and unframing itself, opening up the interpretative process in the gesture of anticipatory illustration. In so doing, there is maintained a certain distance from the semantic or signified content, the truth of its argument. However, simultaneously, there is apart from this distanciation that amounts to a framing, a performative dimension to the commentary also, for that performative amounts to the 'interpretative' aspect of framing that defines the illustration and provides its borders as being an illustration of something, it being a discourse *of* and *on* its subject. This 'truth' is therefore always already displaced, deferred, within the very folds of its unveiling. Never present or a presence but perceived indirectly through the work of writing and *différance*, truth as such is never available in any pure, simple form. *Mimesis* and, more importantly, *mimetologism*, or, at least, a certain history of *mimetologic discourse*, has always aimed to deny this differentiation through the *logos* of its truth, the truth *in representation*. Put simply: illustration is always already an interpretation. It is a mode of mediation that hides more or less skilfully the structures and framing devices of its translative powers.

Having thus complicated the picture, we can proceed. Derrida announces and sets out four *traits*, thereby 'framing' what he takes to be the crucial elements of the *Philebus*. The first *trait* is the observation that Plato proceeds by dialogue. The book 'stands as a substitute for dialogue, as it calls itself' (*D*, 185). Writing is made to stand in as a mode of discourse for the silent soul. As representation of this, the model of dialogue seeks to bring what it imitates back to itself, giving back life and voice, which are absent, deferred, displaced by the detour of writing. Dialogue thus operates as a *mimetological* substitute for presence. As a result of this, the second *trait* appears: '*the truth of the book is decidable*' (*D*, 185). Although the dialogue is an invention, a fiction belonging to the work of art, what it has to convey is truth. The book therefore serves truth, inasmuch as the author sets out in writing truthfully the truth of that which he seeks to represent, according to the 'tribunal of dialectics and ontology' (*D*, 185). Writing is therefore judged according to its mimetic fidelity, according to 'whether it is in conformity . . . to the true' (*D*, 185). Truth, the true, it must be seen in the Platonic dialogue, is an absolute value. And it is over the question of value, the value of the book, that Derrida then identifies and traces the third *trait*.

Writing 'is neither good nor bad, neither true nor false' in the Platonic context, its value is not intrinsic. The Platonic notion of the book, 'which copies, reproduces, imitates living discourse, is worth only as much as the discourse is worth' (*D*, 185). In that writing is a dead and exterior form of voice, and therefore life and presence, it can never be worth more than the living discourse in its truthfulness, it can only be less in value. Writing is therefore always secondary, a debased if necessary modality, 'interpreted as an imitation, a duplicate of the living voice or present *logos*' (*D*, 185). Derrida is quick to point out that writing in general is not literary writing. In the *Republic*, 'poets are only judged and condemned for being imitators, mimes' (*D*, 186). Although historically what we think of as literature is a relatively recent historical invention having to do with a certain epoch in Western culture associated with particular legal rights and the concept of the individual subject, yet, as Derrida comments, from Plato on 'the whole history of the interpretation of the arts of letters has moved and been transformed within the diverse logical possibilities opened up by the concept of *mimesis*' (*D*, 187).

And finally, 'a fourth trait, to finish out the frame of this text' (*D*, 187), playing still between interpretation and illustration, between the illustrative interpretation of the Platonic text, and the interpretative illustration that the Platonic text affords the interpretation of illustration, representation, and of course *mimesis* as representational modalities subordinated to the true. The book, already conceived as copy, is moreover taken to be a particular form of copy, an '*image* in general . . . the imaginary' (*D*, 187). In other words, writing illustrates, it serves to occlude its translative, copying powers, when put to work to produce the faithful image, identified as a 'phantasm' (*D*, 187), as the truth, as phantasm of the true. However, if the book and the soul are compared to one another, then both imitate the other equally. Each is therefore read as a phantasmatic image, a likeness of the other (*D*, 188). This has profound ramifications. If the soul resembles a book and vice versa, then the order of original/copy collapses. The book then, 'reproduces the *logos*' (i.e. the true, Truth, which implicitly remains unavailable to representation)

> and the whole is organized by this relation of repetition, resemblance . . . doubling, duplication, this sort of specular process and play of reflections where things . . . speech, and writing come to repeat and mirror each other. (*D*, 188)

Far from stabilizing meaning, identity or truth, writing opens onto that hall of mirrors, as a *mise-en-abyme*. Painting and writing 'can only be images of each other [in Plato and after him, as Derrida has it] to the extent that they are both interpreted as images, reproductions, representations, or repetitions of something alive' (*D*, 188). And as soon as one seeks to speak of the relation between literature or art and truth, one immediately opens up the possibility that truth or something alive, the living word or the living animal for the writer on the one hand or the painter on the other, is always already haunted by the possibility of doubling and division, spacing, duplication and 'the enigmatic possibility of repetition within the [implicitly *mimetic* or *mimetologic*] framework of the *portrait*' (*D*, 188). Once again, Derrida draws on the metaphorical resources of mimetic art and its supports not merely to structure and present his argument, but also to perform the image of the counter-Platonic argument. *Mimesis* comes into play as the driving force, the ghost in the machine producing even as it undermines the classical model of *mimesis* as truth.

Paintings or images illustrative of a truth that is taken as *mimetic* and therefore faithful and truthful remain always copies, the sum of their traits, produced in distinction from whatever is held to be the original, as we have argued. They expose the inherently ineluctable iterability of the copy, and the signs of the copy within what is supposedly any 'original' or 'unique' meaning, destabilizing in advance the truth. It therefore follows from this that the mimetic work, the text as copy is, as we have seen, both a double and a displacement. The image precedes the original after a certain fashion, being both copy, duplication and memory of a past present and the image of an anterior ideal to come, always already a supplementary double, 'the same as and different from what it duplicates' (*D*, 191). It always enters into this relation, and structure, in coming into being. Never the thing as such, in order to be read as mimetic it must be always already the composite or constellation of *traits*, which in the sheaf or mesh of their network signal the retreat of the original, the real, the true, in coming to appear as they do in a more or less mimetic form. *Mimesis* in the singular forms of its manifestations is therefore operative only through an identification of the other, however close the resemblance or representation, and so takes place through the force of what it 'ruins, destabilizes, (de)constructs' (I:D, 30). It is not that there is no *mimesis*. Rather, it is the very mimetic condition of *mimesis* that the radicality of what I would call the *mimetic-performative* disavows, ahead of and in resistance to all efforts to theorize finally *mimesis* as a codifiable and repeatable *mimetologism*. All the *traits* gathered and woven in the simultaneity of a formal 'de/construction' that is the possibility of a pictorial work of art such as a portrait therefore are a writing, not an undifferentiated representation. Any mimetic illustration is haunted by the motions of writing, the text that it stages and by which it takes place, by which the stage or scene is staged, giving to meaning or identity the very possibility of their projection, even in their undoing and ruination.

VII LOOSE THREADS

But – coming back to painting, creating an image as though we had completed a circle, and completing this doubtless distorted portrait of Derrida as an art critic.

The idiom in painting: this is a fragment of a phrase on which Derrida plays at the beginning of *The Truth in Painting*. First and foremost, idiom has to do specifically with the singularity and untranslatability of an expression, with specific characters or properties by which language is mistakenly identified as one's own. It is also one form which that singularity takes. It is thus akin to, analogous with, the subjectile. We might therefore propose the following statement: painting, drawing – both are writing, and writing remains: to be read. It remains to be read, however, only according to the idiom, each time and every time demanding that we attend to the idiomatic, the singular.

This appears to be a rather bald summary. Another summary of sorts might be risked, though this is not of course to have the last word. No such thing is possible, there being many more strands to tease out, many other equally justifiable locations from which to begin. In summary however I would suggest, somewhat provisionally, that Derrida's writing on art is also concerned with a discourse on vision, and with coming to see the impossibility of any full restitution of the other within the visual or what are called the visual arts. Or if one cannot speak of restitution exactly, then one may perhaps suggest that what takes place indirectly when one sees writing (as being [let us multiply all the frames here, as secret affirmation of the impossibility that they will hold]) in (excess of) representation is a revelation of the other's coming to countersign. There might be given to be read the invention of the other, despite and in the face of any *mimetic* attempt to represent the other as the same, to gather up the other into the same, and thereby still the disturbances of difference by which the other is apprehended. If Derrida's writing on philosophy and literature, from Socrates to Freud, or from Plato to Mallarmé has frequently, if not constantly, opposed the graphic trace to the phonic, then his writings on art situate the graphic as the place of motion, of rhythm, oscillation and textile weave within the static, fixable presence assumed in particular forms of representation.

Derrida pulls at the loose thread that unravels the certainties of mimetic adequacy. In doing so, he unveils the ways in which the mimetic functions through an often brutal suppression of the heterogeneous, of the mark, the ruin, the trace, in favour of the image without remainder, or what Derrida has described as the 'effect of full silence' and 'mutism' of the work of art (SA, 12). The work of art cannot be presented without trace, the graphic remainder in excess of representation and irreducible to any mere matter of form or content: 'the thereness, the being there [of presence in the work of art], only exists on the basis of this work of traces that dislocates itself' (SA, 16). Such dislocation occasions the anxiety, the uncanniness that haunts the narcissistic self-recognition in the face to face with the portrait, with which I began. In its iterability, seriality, discontinuous movement, and spatial and temporal work, the graphic produces the fiction of presence in the image of an identity complete to itself. The graphic movement, *motif*, *motivation*, makes the illusion, the ghostly simulacrum of presence possible even as it dislocates the truth in presence by making this very representation possible.

So, to take the summary further: if Derrida's writing on art addresses vision in different ways, it is also an exploration of what vision does not see, what is both a secret and yet in full view everywhere. Such texts speak of what is materially there and yet which is, in a particular way, invisible. Derrida's texts on art and aesthetics remind us that we are blind to the dislocating work of vision until our attention is drawn to it, until we redraw our focus, learning to see differently. Thus haunted and structured by the mark, by the spatial play of the visible/invisible within and yet other than representation, art appears only by virtue of the ghost in the machine, by the 'functioning of a *techne*' (*RI*, xxxvi). *Subjectile, trait, parergon*, all make possible the assignment of the condition of art to art, even though they are in excess of and incommensurate with that condition, that identity. *Mimesis* is all the more disturbing because its fidelity to life only causes to appear that mechanical iterability as the countersignature to our own inevitable death sentences. Reading for this functioning of the *tekhne*, where the work of making is also, already, a making appear (thereby placing in plain view everywhere the secret that *tekhne* and *poiesis* are not as dissimilar as some might believe), 'revelation is seen revealed, exposure exposed, presentation presented, and so on' (*RI*, xxxvi). Yet, acknowledging this writing of the other, and this other writing within art, of which every *trait* invites us to remember, if we now *see* the truth in painting (drawing, photography, the so-called 'visual arts'), then we are also called to bear witness to the fact that 'we can no longer discern the limit' (*RI*, xxxvi).

VIII REPRESENTATION

Despite this impossibility, limits in the guise of representations are found. Imagine my surprise when I came across JD on MySpace. Jacques Derrida is in your extended network, says the page. Apparently, Jacques has 603 friends, including Heidegger, Camus

and, perhaps surprisingly, Slavoj Žižek. It struck me that this representation has to do with a certain narcissistic identification rather
than with Derrida. If you pause to reflect on the idea of a website or
photograph, a performance on stage or screen, or one's public role
or 'face' as opposed to one's allegedly private perception of oneself,
a great deal more than art and aesthetics or other merely formal concerns are involved. That's not to say that art is merely formal, only a
matter of aesthetics. It is though to admit that representation
escapes any merely aesthetic attempts to frame it, to represent it
through a consideration of its structural or formal representational
means or properties.

Take the MySpace webpage. It gives to Derrida a certain representation *as if* it were an actuality. Its *actuvirtuality* occludes though. It's
just enough of a representation of representation for some people to
imagine themselves reflected in, inflected by, and produced as the
subject of that particular virtual posting. As Derrida reflects, in an
imaginative scenario, 'we' find in an archive a sentence opening an
'introductory address', which reads ' "one might say that we represent
something (*nous sommes en représentation*)" ' (SOR, 295). In this line,
the idiom *en représentation* communicates or, in the legal context,
'transfers' the sense of being the representative of some office or position, representing or standing for its regulations, structures. Derrida
speaks of this, noting that 'in the political domain, we can speak of
parliamentary, diplomatic, or union representation', which he distinguishes from representation in the 'aesthetic domain . . . in the sense
of mimetic substitution' (SOR, 298). So, politics and aesthetics (SOR,
299), from the poles of which *representation* crosses and recrosses,
undergoing silently certain translations in its transport, and translating the discourses, subjects or 'domains' in which, on behalf of which,
representation takes place. In addition, as Derrida goes on to explain
to the audience of philosophers in Strasbourg to whom he is speaking, he and they are, jointly, a representational body. They are in a
given place representing philosophy.

In turn, implicitly therefore, that office or institution which one
represents determines one as a subject. There is thus a sense in the
phrase of being interpellated, of an interpellated subjectivity. This
need not be a material 'post' or public role as a conference delegate.
It can amount, as with the MySpace page, to something more spectral, a community-without-unity, a tele-technological or *mediatic
actuvirtuality*. Rather than MySpace however, you might consider

www.humanities.uci.edu/remembering_jd/. This particular webpage was produced at the University of California, Irvine, as a memorial, and an act of testimony to the legacy of Derrida, initially in response to a particularly deplorable excuse for an obituary, an *atrocity-in-representation*, published in the *New York Times*, on 10 October 2004, two days after Derrida's death. A collection of more than 5,000 names, the page affirms how each and all those names are 'in representation', and transmit themselves as the traces of that which Derrida may be said to represent (each representation being of necessity different from every other). A gathering of signatures announces an imagined, yet painfully real, found representation in death. Derrida has been misrepresented. We represent Derrida, multiple Derridas beyond any single representation. We bear witness to the summons, the citation that excites in the proper name, and is irreducible either to representation or the ontology of representation. This is, these are our representations of Derrida, in the name of Derrida, in our names, Jacques Derrida – apophatic presentation through the trace of the proper name.

Returning to that phrase Derrida imagines finding. At the most naïve level, one could translate the French phrase, *nous sommes en représentation*, as 'we are in representation'. One is never not 'in representation' even if all that one believes one represents is oneself. How often, on the phone, through instant messaging, or whatever medium you care to think of have you said, self-evidently and apparently needlessly, *it's me*? Or, equally, conversely in the face of some hesitation, silence or poor connection have you said, *is that you*? A call goes out for a transmission of the self, a transmission involving the representation of oneself, *as if* one is carried away from oneself, or *as if* one seeks in saying *it's me* to gather in, reel back, what one sends of oneself. The complications become more distinct if you pause over the possible echoes that are on the line. When Derrida opens the archive, when the sentence cited arrives, sent from somewhere as an enigmatic transmission, a number of signals bounce around, problematizing translation, and leaving a remainder, even were one to remain, or seek to remain within French. For example: *en* – in, at, to, of. *Représentation* – representation, performance, picturing (a mental image, a phantasy or phantasm), portrayal, depicting.

Turning to the essay from which the phrase above comes, 'Sending: On Representation', asking if translation is 'of the same order' as representation Derrida opens the problem of the remainder, what remains as trace of the other, between Latin and German, between *representation* and 'the *Stellen* of *Vorstellung* or *Darstellung*' (SOR, 297), and, in what does not pass between the two, what remains to be read. While *representation* (in French or English) names reproductive and repetitive processes (mimesis announces and employs both) *Darstellung* does not. It speaks of *presentation* rather more than representation, of a staging, a taking place, and thus implies event, as, for example to use Derrida's choice, *exhibition*. Moreover, *Darstellung* raises inescapably a concern with and a discursive context of epistemology. Although profoundly a question of languages then, this is also an interrogation directed on the one hand to the representation across languages of differing epistemological models, while, on the other hand, being a question of the epistemological problem concerning representation. Derrida's investigation in 'Sending: On Representation' involves itself in the languages and history of philosophy, addressing, as you might imagine, what passes between so-called 'national' traditions of philosophy. This should not be thought only in terms of institutions, cultures, philosophers as collective representations of the history of thought in their particular traditions. It is also crucially a question of how translation takes place if at all or in part, from one culture, one language, more than one language within a given philosophical language, so to speak, to another.

Having posed this immense problem, pointing to a knot in need of unravelling but also implicating himself in pulling at the very threads he descries, Derrida then steps outside the institution of philosophy, narrowly defined, in order to recall a differentiation made by Freud. There are, Derrida reminds us, dictionaries that distinguish, as did Freud, between 'representations of words [*Wortvorstellungen*] and representations of things [*Sach-* or *Dingvorstellungen*]' (SOR, 298). The former must include 'representation' of course. One could speak therefore of the representation of 'representation', and then 'represent' 'representation' in other words. (One could also represent 'representation' by some 'thing', a painting or sculpture, if you can conceive this or receive this possibility.) One could even write 'representation's representation' (adding the quotation marks in different places will cause one to pause over that which is being represented, which representation is represented in the representation that is in part determined by diacritical marks). However, this is not being entirely fanciful. With or without quotation marks – marks within the marks proliferating and subtracting, closing and opening simultaneously all the framing devices that would give support to the representation of representation – one could always read either 'the representation of representation' or 'representation's representation' in at least two ways. *On the one hand*, there is that representation which is 'representation's'. There is the representation that representation, the idea put to work and so effacing itself in its practical and singular manifestation, causes to come into being. The processes by which representation gives place to representation cause representation to take place. *On the other hand*, there is that representation by which I represent 'representation'. Of course it is through the agency, the law of representation by which, as representation's representative, represents, or re-presents, that which is never available to representation in any direct manner, namely *representation*.

So, you see, you have an image of sorts in mind, that representation cannot, by representation, be represented as such. Perhaps the work of analogy or allegory, symbolism would figure one form, one image in the place of the unimaginable. Art and literature, these would be representation's representatives. What I imagine you, the reader, imagining then – I imagine you sitting there, leaning back, legs crossed, with ample but subdued light in which to reflect on what you're reading – is a 'situation in which a context is never able to be saturated for the determination and *identification* of a sense' (SOR, 299). All the various modes and modulations of representation on which I have touched, and in touching which I have drawn in a few brief strokes a representation or two so as to draw your attention to this subject, are 'not only the grammatical modulations of a single and identical meaning' (SOR, 299), but instead modulations of different meanings, 'variables and divergences from the identity of an invariant meaning' (SOR, 299).

I see the thought dawning. One cannot represent or pretend to represent the work of Derrida thematically, not least for the very important reason that Derrida does not himself work thematically. In response to his work, if we are to be attentive in a responsible fashion, we cannot proceed *as if* Derrida can be represented thematically or *as if* such a thing called deconstruction existed. However tempting this might be, Marion Hobson cautions, 'it is inaccurate to speak as if he [Derrida] had worked in or on a domain' (Hobson 2001, 133). Derrida's thinking (there is no such thing as Derrida's philosophy) cannot be framed. It does not fit 'into preset or traditional [representational] channels' (Hobson 2001, 133).

Representation implies conceptual unity therefore, whether in toto through a mimetic verisimilitude or synecdochally, as in the use of the term *deconstruction* or, indeed, the appearance of the proper name *Derrida, as if* its trait were a kind of nominal siglum or shuttle on a textile loom, weaving in and out to draw together all the threads. It is always a question of negotiating between presentation and representation, and the relation and tension between the two. For what remains to be thought in this tele-mediatic-techno-actuvirtual epoch in which we find ourselves, by which we are represented to one another, to ourselves, one always has to bear in mind that presentation always returns as double, copy, simulacrum in representation (cf. Hobson 2001, 149). Today *we are* in *representation*. Whether or not we consciously *represent something* beyond ourselves, as representatives, 'we are', 'I am' – being in all its conjugated divagations is *in representation*. And the re-presentation that stages identity does so through the virtual, uncanny rootlessness of an *envoi*, a sending incessantly recirculating, folding and refolding upon its own traces.

We are then. But who, or what, is signified by this seemingly self-evident affirmation *we are*? We are, in circulation, the articulation of relays, 'from relays to relays of relays, in a destiny which is never sure of gathering itself, identifying itself, or making itself determinate' (*P*, cit. Hobson 2001, 150). This is where *we are*. *This is where one is.* As Derrida remarks in his reading of *Darstellung* in Heidegger, 'it is the . . . human subject, which is the field in this relation, the domain and the measure of objects as representations, its own representations' (SOR, 307). But then, 'the problematic in which we are caught up' is always already at work in language, between languages, wherever there is found the desire for the representation of presence, wherever there is staged or presented in other words 'the presupposition or the desire for an invariable identity of sense already present behind all the usages and regulating all the variations' (SOR, 303). In any utterance of the self, of one's presence, even, especially in the presence of another, no less than when I write to you, there is, Derrida reminds us, the staging, the taking place of a sending, an *envoi*. The self always sends itself beyond itself in order to communicate with another, and so open up the possibility of a reciprocal sending that marks one with another as a 'being-together'. Yet, 'wherever' I believe I find myself, wherever one is, wherever we are, 'the *envoi* of being divides itself' (SOR, 322).

Let me leave the last word to Derrida, without representing him here, *as if* he were consigned to the representation of all the 'place-holders' of hypertextual mark-up:

> In representation, the present, the presentation of what is presented comes back, returns as a double effigy, an image, a copy, an idea as a picture of the thing henceforth at hand, in the absence of the thing, available, disposed and put forward for, by, and in the subject. *For*, *by*, and *in*, the system of these prepositions (puttings-forth) marks the place of representation or of the *Vorstellung* . . . Doubtless the present which returns thus had already the form of what is for and before the subject but was not at its disposition in this preposition itself. . . . [However,] *Phantasia* names a mode of . . . appearing which is not representative . . . This Greek thought of *phantasia* . . . we should follow here in all its displacements, up to the allegedly modern problematic of 'fiction' and 'phantasm'. (SOR, 308–9, 316)

NOTES

1. On the *trait* and its relation to the *retrait*, see also the discussion of *retrait* throughout *Memoirs of the Blind*.
2. This quotation and the one following are taken from the back cover 'blurb' of *The Truth in Painting*.
3. *Hymen* signifies a certain undecidability as Derrida appropriates the figure. While the term is an archaic or poetic synonym for marriage and therefore symbolic union it is also, obviously, that female bodily membrane that separates, for instance, virginity from its loss or the 'absence' of virginity, or, until it is broken inside from outside, and therefore perhaps self and other, in a strictly corporeal sense. (Derrida also employs the figure of the tympan, the membrane of the ear, in similar ways.) As a membrane that plays on the opposition between inside and outside, the figure of the hymen also traverses and so renders unstable any absolute distinction between the two.

CHAPTER 4

LITERATURE AND BEING

What the writer invents is . . . the absolutely 'other' . . . The author of
a literary work writes that work in response to an implacable obligation imposed on him or her.

J. Hillis Miller

Literature does not belong. Literature does not come home. It is
strangely homeless, strangely free.

Nicholas Royle

Literature does not present themes as such, but rather takes the reader
through a process of summarizing . . . If I am responding creatively to
a work being performed before me, if I am doing justice to its singularity, alterity, and inventiveness, I am still active in performing it . . .
I am caught up in, and partly constituted as a subject by, the event of
performance.

Derek Attridge

I TO LITERATIZE¹ OR, THE EQUIVOCAL SEVENTH

Invention singularity historicity circularity spectrality citation being
et cetera: literature, an 'irreducible plurality of signatures' (*as if*. . .)
My first sentence is odd, restless. It doesn't remain in one language:
seven nouns, more or less, and the rest 'in translation'. Or should that
be: 'and the rest' in translation? 'And the rest' is already a translation
of *etc.* It implies something remaining, something to come. And what
is to come is not a predictable or programmed future, but that which
can always arrive at any moment. In general, remarks a disembodied
voice arriving from nowhere over a scene of the Parisian landscape,

I try to distinguish between what one calls the future and 'l'avenir.' . . . There's a future that is predictable, programmed, scheduled, foreseeable. But, there is a future, l'avenir (to come), which refers to someone who comes whose arrival is totally unexpected. For me, that is the real future. That which is totally unpredictable. The Other who comes without my being able to anticipate their arrival. So if there is a real future beyond this other known future, it's l'avenir in that it's the coming of the Other when I am completely unable to foresee their arrival. (*D*, 53)

Here is the unpredictable other that – or who – remains to come, a ghost (*l'arrivant*) arriving at any moment. The present moment or one's supposedly secure presence to oneself can always be transformed by such an arrival. Where one is, who one is, these conditions of being are always open to such eruption, to the translation of the other. And what goes for being goes also for reading. I cannot predict the reading to come of what I am writing at this moment. As much as an idea or identity appears to be encapsulated or *framed*, that which is other or to come within the structure promises to exceed or traverse the boundary. This can always take place, even though that which promises to do this is not immediately or, indeed, ever visible. Just like that 'voice-over' from *Derrida*. Whoever speaks at that moment is always out of time, always arriving whenever we watch the film. Its articulation comes to pass *as if* it were the passage of that metro car, passing over the Seine. It comes and goes, the trace of another, haunting the field of vision and irreducible to that, excessively so, and in its retreat, in the *retrait* (the retreat that is also a retracing) that the recording of the voice already is, it leaves the trace of its trace, nowhere as such but as the recording and the memory. The technology that makes possible the scenario is not that different from what literature stages and makes possible. Before film or any other tele-technological medium, there is literature, as the haunting of being. That is why we read. It might be said, that is where there is literature.

Back to the 'sentence' from which we have not yet departed: instead of *et cetera* one could also write: and so on and so forth, as in the title: 'Et Cetera . . . (and so on, und so weiter, and so forth, et ainsi de suite, und so überall, etc.)' (EC, 282–305). As you can see here, not only is there Latin, but English, German, French and so on. There are parentheses, implying the attenuated indication of everything else that cannot be spoken of but which, in speaking of a particular subject, such as 'literature' (not supposing what we mean by this yet), needs to be acknowledged. And there is that ellipsis, ending nothing but implying a path off, into the future, into all that remains to come, into the abyss or infinity, and so on, and so forth, *as if* it were possible to imagine, or even begin to signal the impossible that might be read – or invented – in the etc., the so on and so forth, and . . . and . . . and . . . (*as if* one could imagine the possibility of the impossible – imagine). This returns us to my sentence. We return to it as a beginning without punctuation in its principal part until the arrival of a colon, from which hiatus are issued further signs. The colon authorizes a continuance *and* a break. But moving back, once more, *as if* we were turning in a continuous circle, taking a step or two forward only to find that the step was not, but instead that we were back where we thought we had started, thus: seven nouns, more or less.

You would be forgiven for thinking that I cannot count. There are either seven nouns or not. Well, language does not come down to calculation. One cannot count on language. While there are six nouns to begin, it is the equivocal seventh that in a different reading presents problems, especially as it comes before that *et cetera*. While *being* is a noun, it can also be read as a modification of that noun, *as if* it expressed the subjunctive mood or was a gerund promising to lead to a definition of the previous terms, as in an imagined sentence such as 'invention, singularity, historicity, circularity, spectrality and citation[2] being repetitive and significant elements to be found or otherwise to serve in the difficult if not impossible definition of the concept or idea of "literature"'. That this imagined sentence appears as a possibility here and yet does not make itself visible initially or now, without qualification, indicates a difficulty I have with such a sentence. Principally, that difficulty has to do with the fact that, whether or not you can see the reasoning behind the choice of nouns in the definition of literature, you could equally add many others. For, if these are constituent 'qualities' in the ontology of literature, or may be agreed upon as signifiers of that which constitutes literature for a large number of people, it is undeniably the case that the list of such terms can be extended, perhaps indefinitely, hence that *et cetera*. It has to be admitted that, whatever we think we mean whenever we speak of *literature* or *the literary*, such figures figure within themselves or on their surface the endlessness of the *etc.*, rather than being delimitable by any single term or any constellation of motifs, however seemingly exhaustive or comprehensive.

Literature is therefore a quasi-concept only. It is always improper. Within its genres, it exceeds and dismantles those institutions of literature. The strange condition of the literary is that it is to be observed as becoming transformed, as it transforms itself in each of its singular expressions. Literature exceeds its own proper identity, its properties, in the motions of its narrative, however much we may wish to assign structurally repetitive similarities. And it is transformed with every reading, every reader. Literature is a strange noun, a self-emptying ghost of a concept that can only name everything or nothing. It is irreducible to any stable or permanent universal, which would not have to revert to inclusive and exclusive choices involving historicization, periodization, cultural definitions, juridical or theological discourses and institutions, and so on . . . For example, there is 'literature as historical institution with its conventions, rules, etc.' (SICL, 37). Literature 'is dependent in its modern form on the rise of constitutional democracies in the West from the seventeenth century on, and on the radical democratic freedom to say anything, that is, to put everything in question' (Miller 2005, 31). The radical unconditionality of literature is to be free in principle to express everything and anything. One would have to begin therefore by acknowledging that literature cannot, by definition, be defined, except by this unconditional condition of the

> power to say everything, to break free of the rules [that have been established historically and institutionally in the process of defining literature], to displace them, and thereby to institute, to *invent* and even to suspect the traditional difference between nature and institution, nature and conventional law, nature and history. (SICL, 31)

Every example must perforce be singular, differing from, and deferring the authority of, every other manifestation. Certainly there are iterable qualities. The same and yet not the same, their transformative repeatability attests though to the singularity of literature, however paradoxical such a statement might sound. What is literature, then? Let us begin by returning to the first of our nouns: *invention.*

II INVENTION, SINGULARITY, HISTORICITY

Implicit in thinking the question of literature in relation to the 'invention' of reading, of reading history differently, and reading the difference of and in the signs of a text's historicity, a series of questions announce themselves. What do writing and representation have to do with the concept of invention? What is the relation between invention, memory and the witness of literature to the past? How does literature in the nineteenth century (on which I shall focus for my examples) *invent* the traces of the cultures from which it seeks to mark a distance, but which idiocultures it nonetheless inherits, receives and mediates in its narrative and poetic inventions of English history and identity? And, if a certain questioning of history begins with a question of rethinking history differently according to problems of different models of temporality and cultural memory, what in the questions of invention, singularity and history concerns the nature of being, and the ontology of subjectivity?

To reduce unreasonably all the questions here to a single interrogation: in reading literature, '[w]here it comes to the subject and where the subject, the essence of the subject comes to itself and sees itself come [the] question becomes then, and will remain . . . how can (and may we) see *ourselves* coming to *ourselves* . . . ?' (Atf, xiii). In this demand of the subject, put to the test of a seemingly endless motion of self-reflection, the historicity of being is implicated in a teleological circling, and recirculation. Past and future interweave themselves in the figure of the subject who, touched by past and future, is unveiled as gathering or nodal point of a circular temporality. For, there would be 'no future, no future as such, no novelty [or *invention*] at all, without some sort of historical link, memory, retention or tradition, thus without some sort of synthesis' (Atf, xiii). And this 'synthesis', always changing, always appearing, disappearing and reappearing, is figured in the 'circularity' of being (see below). Subsequently, I will address this motion of becoming visible and invisible, advancing and retreating, through the discourse of the spectral, as this may be illustrated *apropos* the fundamentally spectral condition of literature by the work of citation.

There are a number of semantic resonances in *invention*, not all of which may spring to mind readily. *Invention* speaks of a creative process. It announces the production of something supposedly new, original, that, in short, which has never been seen or imagined before. *Invention* is thus closely tied to notions of *innovation* or *discovery*. It implies a work of fabrication, of the imagination, a fabulation, fantasy or possibly a narrative phantasm. There is then that sense of fabrication associated with invention involving the composition of a work of art. Most commonly, invention in this sense is linked to literature, but can also be used of music. At the same time, perhaps somewhat more implicit, hidden or invisible in the term, there is a more technical sense. *Invention* bespeaks design, a contraption or device. Recalling the Latin – *in-venire* – we hear that something enters, it comes into being. There is always something 'to come' in invention. But what remains in invention to come is not simply the new. In coming back, the 'advent of time-to-come' that haunts *invention* in another language returns 'to fold back toward the past . . . it envelops in itself a repetition, it unfolds only the dynamics of what was already found there' (PIO, 59) – or *literature* let us say: the unfolding of which takes place in the invention of citation, a production of the new on the basis of the repetition of another's language. If invention '*begins* by being susceptible to repetition, exploitation, reinscription' (PIO, 28), then under the law of this hypothesis citation is apprehended, and is thus re-marked as the motif and movement of a certain *trait*, a spectre that comes to leave a signature, a countersignature of the other. Invention (*invenire*) is therefore always already haunted by that which, though unpredictable, is to come (*l'avenir*), by a coming of the other. As the graphic affiliation between the French and Latin affirms, the to-come as an in-coming haunts invention even as invention marks the temporality of the unprogrammable advent (*ad+venire*). Literature is, if anything, ad*vent*itious. It is the possibility of this adventitious spectrality. This is in principle literature's secret, a secret always exposed on every page.

But I am getting ahead of myself. Invention names an opening in itself, awaiting the arrival of some other that circles back on itself as another. Invention finds therefore, *as if* for the first time. But this *as if*, a trope that always insinuates the possibility of the impossible, is also the trope, the motif, for the origination, the invention of fiction as always already originary. *As if* names the fiction of genesis – *as if* there could be a for-the-first-time-never-before-having-been-coming-into-being-spontaneously-from-no-prior-source-whatsoever. *Invention* makes possible this impossible thought, and so finds its fictions as *and* in the circulation of repetition with a difference and the circularity by which the fold unfolds and refolds, and which is therefore radically anachronic. And invention

> unveils what was already *found* there or produces what, as *tekhne*, was not already found there but is still not created in the strong sense of the word, [defined just before this citation as 'creation of existence *ex nihilo*] is only put together, starting with a stock of existing and available elements, in a given configuration. (PIO, 43)

A *given* configuration such as a novel, a poem or the idea of genre.

A suspicion arises that *invention* might not be creative. It produces nothing out of nothing. Instead, *invention* is the sign of a response. It is a reaction to, or a finding out of that which was already there. It is a discovery that is also an *uncovering*. Something, to paraphrase Freud, comes to light, which had been forgotten or buried. Invention, in opening to the other, is uncanny. From out of that configuration by which invention takes place comes the possibility that it 'gives rise to an event, tells a fictional story and produces a machine by introducing a disparity or gap into the customary use of discourse' (PIO, 43). Making a broad historical claim, this I take to be the aphoristic summation and motivation of much narrative in the nineteenth century. Narratives of the past, what we call too easily 'historical' narratives, in the nineteenth century function as so many double readings. Take the inaugural sentence of *The Pickwick Papers* as exemplary of this doubling gesture.

> The first ray of light which illumines the gloom, and converts into a dazzling brilliancy that obscurity in which the earlier history of the public career of the immortal Pickwick would appear to be involved, is derived from the perusal of the following entry in the Transactions of the Pickwick Club, which the editor of these papers feels the highest pleasure in laying before his readers, as a proof of the careful attention, indefatigable assiduity, and nice discrimination, with which his search among the multifarious documents confided to him has been conducted. (Dickens 2003, 15)

This 'first sentence' is double and invents the gap in the customary use of discourse in a number of ways. That first ray of light is both literal and metaphorical, it brings light onto its subject, even as it will come to illuminate Mr Pickwick's rise from bed. It also illuminates the fact that the sentence is not a direct representation but the 'translation' or invention of already existing documents, on the part of an 'editor'. The novel begins therefore with repetition and doubling. Moreover, the novelty of Dickens's first novel is that the sentence is in mock-heroic style, and so 'invents' Victorian literature with the novelty of a historicized transformation occasioned by pastiche, an invention that finds its authority and departure, in borrowing on the resources of a different set of historical and cultural co-ordinates. The novel in the nineteenth century thus becomes instituted through a doubling that is also a displacement of the earlier institutional forms, norms and laws of a particular genre and mode of address belonging to the previous century. An other voice returns from the past, doubled and reiterated in the invention of the editor, to comment on a recent present, and so disorder both the conventions of representation of the present and also the subject matter of the genre's historical conventions. Giving rise to a 'fictional story', invention thus introduces a gap in the customary use of discourse. It 'forms a beginning and speaks of that beginning, and in this double, indivisible movement, it inaugurates. This double movement harbors that uniqueness and novelty without which there would be no invention' (PIO, 43). Here in Dickens's first novel, an event takes place. All that is to come in literature in the nineteenth century is invented, through a repetition and a finding of the past as this pertains to the modernity of national identity.

Providing for the middle classes a mediation of their modernity and national identity, narratives such as *The Moonstone*, *Wuthering Heights*, *Cranford* or *Middlemarch* also present encoded archives of decisive cultural and historical ruptures and inventions, thereby effecting those disparities, opening those gaps of which I was just speaking. Such disruption or eruption marks the representation of identity and memory as in conditions, simultaneously, of becoming and crisis. Invention is therefore highlighted as the possibility of a surprise or novelty of an event, a 'coming about (*survenue*) of the new . . . due to an operation of the human subject' (PIO, 43). Here is where what we call literature arrives. Here, invention finds the past and so intervenes, taking place. Intervening between two subjects – the one who reads and that about which one reads – and also between two distinct temporalities – the time of reading and the time of which one reads – invention opens, through its phantasmagoric staging, the presentation of some other that is all the more haunting because it is, in so many ways, familiar. Impossibly distant, it is also unnervingly close.

To take briefly a few examples with regard to crisis, disruption and identity: there are to be read the traces of national identity given particular historicist narration through the science of optics and tropes of visuality from Hooke to the 1830s in *The Pickwick Papers*, a novel which plays on the 'found' cultures and modalities of Romanticism, in its parodic invention of earlier generic modes. Through this, the novel simultaneously posits the impossibility of knowing the past except as a series of sites from which ruins may be recuperated, and which are then to be read precariously *only* as the anamnesiac traces of cultural memory having meaning in the present of the novel, solely in relation to one another. In *Pickwick* the singular event becomes the iterable ghost of itself, imagined comically as the historical repetitions of cultural and scientific misreading, or more seriously, the ethical demands of bearing witness to one's past as this is crystallized in the circular temporality of the Christmas celebration. Christmas is effectively singular and iterable. Every Christmas invents itself, it reiterates the times and instances of every other Christmas. It thus functions according to the iterable and doubling condition of invention but also with that mode of citation involving singularity and iterability that is dating (on which subject see below). To move to different examples, in very distinct ways both *The Moonstone* and *The Ring and the Book* focus on historicity's competing claims, and the impossibility of arriving at a single perspective when confronted with the past as multiple, competing, often fragmentary textual traces. The 'true' narrative of the past is opened from within the evidence attesting to that past as unreliable, if not undecidable. Representation of the past is shown to be liable to a contest in presentations through competing narratives. Despite this, the ethical demand of history is that one attests to that which one can no longer see. Faced with the aporetic experience in narrative contest, the reader must 'invent' a past in order to move beyond the undecidable impasse. Both novel and poem present a mid-Victorian crisis of consciousness in relation to the past, demonstrating how cultural memory is a labyrinth as well as an archive. Everything that *is* appears to be known. Yet, not everything can be connected. There is in the nineteenth century the apprehension of a virtual web, on which identity relies in its attempts to economize endlessly on an abyss in becoming aware of itself.

Alternatively, if we are to talk of invention apropos eruption and crisis, there is, in *Cranford*, the exorbitant and singular, seemingly irrecuperable narrative of cat vomit. Mrs Forrester's pussy swallows and is made to vomit a lace collar (Gaskell 1998, 125–6). The melodramatic events do not take place in the novel. They are recounted as a narrative, and the inference is that the narrative is itself regurgitated on several occasions, brought up repeatedly in 'polite company' as a form of social binding. Vomit, never mentioned directly, becomes an inventive and excessive trope, which as *trait* is inventive because it disorganizes and so ruins notions and competing claims of relevance, propriety and a hierarchy of interests in the recounting of cultural history. At the same time, it is an inventively, unforeseen and radically democratic trope. Other than history, as trope its invisible motivation in the text invokes and brings up or calls forth multiple historical traces without order or privilege. Its eruption in social circles lays bare the institutional and narrative structures of class position. Now, there is no cultural history of vomit as such, much less one either of feline spew in particular or the discourse of retching, bringing up or regurgitation in its appearances in English literature as far as I am aware. Yet, Gaskell's small, interpolated narrative would constitute an undeniably significant moment in such a history.

The narrative of pussy's mishap arises in Chapter Eight of *Cranford*. Told by Mrs Forrester to Lady Glenmire, the story intervenes in an interweaving of social, cultural and historical discourses and institutions in an especially complex and fascinating way. The important thing to distinguish here is that one is speaking of a trope, not of vomit as such and its relation to the abject, as does Julia Kristeva. Speaking of vomit apropos the abject is still to maintain vomit in a dialectic of taste and disgust, self and other. Kristeva's model is limited by maintaining an economic inscription according to hierarchies of taste and aesthetics. The trope of vomit as absent sign of the eruption of history is unassimilable to this order. 'Thus', as Derrida avers, 'it is no longer a question here of one of those negative values [such as are privileged by Kristeva], one of those ugly or harmful things that art can represent and therefore idealize'. As the very structural absence of the trace, in its phantasmic tropological force admits, 'the absolute excluded . . . does not allow itself even to be granted the status of an object of negative pleasure or of ugliness redeemed by representation'. It is

unrepresentable. And at the same time it is unnameable in its singularity. If one could name it or represent it, it would begin to enter into the auto-affective circle of mastery or reappropriation. An economy would be possible. (E, 290)

The vicariousness of vomit in Gaskell is then a rhetorical spectre, which 'cannot even announce itself as a *sensible* object without immediately being caught up in a teleological hierarchy' (E, 290). It is a figure for what is not figured and what cannot be figured in the conventions and institutions of historical narrative, of history as narrative and of 'literature' as a historically specific system or institution. The tale operates on these other traces by the rule of analogy or iterability, the forcing of which does not admit to identification or the subordination of homogenization. This rule functions through a structure suggestive of equality of interest without resemblance or relationship between two or more different subjects, objects or matters. The principles of singularity and exemplarity without hierarchy, order or preference thus motivate and govern the rule.

Sifting the sediments of culture can involve one in being open to certain unexpected and, to some, excessive instances of disconcerting overflow. In Gaskell's trope of pussy's vomit the big picture of historical rationalization gives way before a rhetorical and emotional force admitting that, with regard to the past, not only can one never know it absolutely, but neither can there be assumed a 'proper perspective', if only because there is no 'it', no one past to which one can give adequate account. That which we try to contain by the facile notion of history cannot be accounted for. There is no final account, no economy of ordering. Cultural memory, like waves of antiperistalsis, will come back upon us, arriving unexpectedly. In the resurgence of memory's traces, what comes up is that which is unassimilable to any system, order or economy of representation – and we can only bear witness to it, seeking a response commensurate with the event and our subjective experience of that.

It may appear of course a prurient, not to say perverse interest on my part to persist on the subject of vomit-as-trope, especially as this is not a word Gaskell employs. That she does not use the word though suggests the singularity and radicality of the other in relation to 'history' in this particular example. At the same time however Gaskell's concern is with the aesthetics of history and the historicity of aesthetics and aesthetic relations, grounded through the communal class-relation experience of *taste*. So much of *Cranford* negotiates ironically the questions of historically specific gender and class experience through the codes of cultural aesthetics articulated and mystified as matters of taste, that the mnemotechnic trace of absent vomit remains irrecuperable to any discourse on taste. And yet, it comes up in the midst of a refined and tasteful gathering, of the ladies of Cranford. So irrecuperable to any mode of directly sensible or intelligible apprehension is the idea of vomit in *Cranford*, as that which in polite conversation or society is considered in excess or beyond all question of taste and propriety, that it remains unnameable. It appears *in absentia* as an excessive trace without and resistant to determination.

To stress the point once more, in a novella concerned with propriety and etiquette, the cultural shifts and intimate interplay of details in class-relations, this singular *narrative* interruption is striking. It is all the more noticeable I would argue given the frequent allusion to various historical and political backgrounds including the Napoleonic Wars, English colonial activity in India, Victorian xenophobia, repeated national financial collapses between the 1820s and the 1850s, the Irish famine and so on. Gaskell acknowledges through the *ne plus ultra* of excess that the aesthetic is historical and moreover that one's subjectivity is held in place historically by the discursive parameters that mediate that historicity in all its various practices and discursive forms.

The absent figure is not simply a mute metaphor. It is an analogy of analogy (E, 278), which in Gaskell serves to affirm all the silenced discourses and languages of history, and therefore of all the occluded historical and material traces, which the material situation of aesthetics excludes from narrative and literature. Yet, and because of this trope of cat vomit, we perceive the 'exemplary secret' of literature, which, in its inventions, has the chance 'of saying everything without touching upon the secret', by which gesture 'all hypotheses are permitted, groundless and *ad infinitum*, about the meaning of the text' (PIO, 43). Never mentioned, Gaskell's vomit remains only as text or trace, and thus the sign of an obliqueness. Undoing the 'hierarchizing authority of logocentric analogy', it is not vomit but 'the possibility of the vicariousness of vomit . . . unrepresentable, unnameable, unintelligible, insensible, unassimilable', which resists the 'power of *identification*' (E, 293). 'No more than a word', and a word that is never admitted, 'it cannot be seen' and so points back endlessly 'to the other or to something else' and so 'holds us to the other' (PIO, 44). The vomit thus announces through its absence, its structural absence, the place of literature's secret.

In such examples of narrative anomaly and radical alterity, and others by which one is compelled to read again, and which one cannot reduce 'to some aesthetic quality, to some source of formal pleasure' (PIO, 42), one finds the registration, however indirectly perceived, of that which arrives or is immanent, however unpredictable. One is forced to take note of the anomaly as that which is oncoming, about to happen, shortly to take place, or come about. Invention is therefore marked by that which comes not only from the past but also from the future, becoming visible. It is therefore given form, but one which, it has to be admitted, is already there in however invisible a manner. To such *invenience* (to coin a word[3]), an uncovering and bringing to light is touched by the possibility of the novelty of an event, which makes possible the 'singular invention of a performative' writing that bends the rules 'in order to allow the other to come or to announce its coming in the opening of a dehiscence' (PIO, 59–60).

In considering literature and the literary in relation to identity and cultural memory as so many experiences of invention, one must reflect, necessarily, on the extent to which invention responds to singularity. One should be wary of fetishizing singularity though, for if we do we risk making absolute or otherwise universal that which can only be known through iterability, through a relation between the epoch of an event and the trait by which it comes to be available *as singular*. The paradox of reading the singularity of a text is that while a text may be perceived as other than every other text, yet its transmissibility, its reception, relies on the fact that its signs, the forms it assumes, these are iterable beyond any original or finite context. It is this iterability that opens up the present situation to that which is to come, and which therefore ensures in principle at least that a sign is always readable. Thus in reading a text, in its constitution of a world through the constellation of signs, a singularity arrives as the actualization of its traces into an iterable and transmissible form. Reading this form, I am opened to a singular encounter with an other. Invention then is always 'invention of the other'. The other however does not 'exist as an entity but is lived through as an event' that leaves traces, marks and signs (Attridge 2004, 43). One aspect of this encounter and invention is acknowledged in the experience 'of the past [as] an encounter with alterity'

(Attridge 2004, 46). If it takes place at all then, invention does so in that response that finds the coming of the other, and therefore marks its responsiveness in relation to the experience of the singular, which is read retrospectively and always belatedly. Referring back to Gaskell, Dickens and the other Victorian writers to whom I have turned, to be modern in the nineteenth century and to articulate through narrative traces and texts of the past as a confession of being's historicity is then to experience, in distinct and singular ways, this shared singular, yet iterable condition of belatedness, and with it the experience of a haunting anachrony, in which perception comes to be understood *as memory*.

From Dickens to Hardy, let us say as a schematic trajectory for Victorian literary identity, becoming conscious of one's modernity and the modernity of one's being is to inhabit a relation, and so produce for oneself an identity, of disjointed untimeliness. Being, being haunted by '[t]his logic of the *supplement of invention*' (PIO, 59), affirms and so performs a being distinct from but informed by the coming of the other. It is, simultaneously, to describe the sense of *where one is* ontologically and historically, to inscribe oneself in a location dependent not on being closed off from the other but on the precarious sufferance and affirmation of difference and iterability. And in this, for as much as one articulates a reflection of the historical and cultural place that one inhabits or is at home in, and with which one is most familiar therefore, there is also a becoming-conscious of being's unhomeliness. If I admit to being inscribed by that which is not me, I must always be host to a somewhat spooky parasite, a *para-citation*, whereby my identity is written, and constantly reinscribed, by my invention of the other as that which informs 'me' in my historical situatedness, and so in response to the other's coming. This coming can always take place. It is the adventitious 'to come' of and in *l'avenir* and not the predictable or programmable future.

Being Victorian then (risking a generalization), in the literature of roughly 1830–80 is an endlessly iterable and citational series of bearing witness to, and experience of the other. Specifically it is a question of inventing forms for the experience of one's being haunted by the other and one's being as a material and historical condition of experiencing modernity in countless singular ways as the experience of anachrony, as this informs the disjointedness, the fracture of being. In its relation to the traces of the past, literature in the nineteenth century arrives at this inevitable recognition: every perception *will* differ, and so proscribe the notion of an authorita-tive, commanding perspective. What being shares, if anything, is the iterable sense of an unhomely, uncanny singularity that is haunted historically and called by the traces of the other. Moreover, there is no perception that is not informed by a 'multitude of remembered elements' as Henri Bergson has it (1991, 150). Hence, we read at work the pervasiveness and popularity of nonlinear analogical models of culture and society, such as the web, the network, the mesh, the weave. While Darwinism and geological or archaeological paradigms provide two forms of hierarchical and stratified models of being and historicity, through their metaphors and narratives of diachronic overlap, interaction, transformation and embeddedness, tropes of the matrix and mesh, the network and web offer alterna-tive, radically rhizomic figures of culture, society and identity struc-tured by difference, without locatable genesis, or eschatological or teleological completion and so the promise of a finite ontology appropriate as an analogy for one's being and one's modernity. Figures such as web and weave are everywhere to be found, from coaches to trains, from telegraphy to telepathy, from social interac-tion and divisions of class to the postal system – and of course in the most monstrous form, that *khora*-like phenomenon, literature.

For the Victorians, one's relation to the past involves an endless negotiation with, and invention of the past, so as to weave together threads that might offer the possibility of provisional connections between the countless singularities of being's experience, or what Matthew Arnold describes as being 'in the sea of life enisled' (1979, 130, l.1). This is what, in the examples to which I have had occasion to refer, literature invents through its realist modes in the nineteenth century: it invents a radical opening of history in relation to memory and being. The self or the present in the nineteenth century always affirms, as it is shaped by, the iterability of a 'minimal remainder'. What constitutes the modernity and therefore the self-consciousness of historicity, of being historical in Victorian literature, is the sense that the trace of history, of the other as minimal remainder must of necessity be reiterated, 'in order that the identity of the *selfsame* be repeatable and identifiable *in, through*, and even *in view of* its alter-ation. For the structure . . . implies both identity *and* difference' (*LI*, 53). We will see this worked out shortly in an example from *Far from the Madding Crowd*. However, for now, it has to be acknowledged that in order for the singular historical and material experience of the nineteenth century to be recorded as a double acknowledgement of identity and difference, there is the demand that a literary work bo both familiar and estranging.

To put this another way, the Victorian sense of responsibility to the other demands that 'for the work [such as the novel] to be singular . . . [it] must repeat itself singularly, to alter itself in order to preserve or conserve itself as singular . . . iterability makes of the thing or text a ghost, something that begins by returning' (Kronick 1999, 67). Whether one were to take, again, *The Pickwick Papers*, with its singular relation to the mock epic, the eighteenth-century picaresque traditions, or its invention of *Don Quixote* in a nineteenth-century model grounded in class relations, or to examine the ways in which Robert Browning, having found the old yellow book, the text on which he bases *The Ring and the Book*, works through the material in that text in a dozen different narrative voices, one would encounter those texts as singular inventions. In this condition, they respond to the haunting trace of the iterable remainder, so as to situate the spook-ridden modernity of Victorian identity in untimely relation to countless pasts. As Elizabeth Gaskell suggests through the narrative of absent but remembered vomit, the traces of the past are unorderable, hierarchization being only a violent economy to stay – or pretend to stay – the ineluctable phantom revenance. In distinction to such violent ordering and economy, as the examples of Dickens, Browning, Gaskell and Hardy affirm, the Victorian writer recognizes 'the power of the writers of the past, or of the ghosts to come who spoke to each other through' them, 'in turn provoking [them] to speak, to make or let them live', thereby orientating themselves 'in this heritage while understanding each other very quickly, with scarcely a word' (*WM*, 128). One can only hope for communion with both the others of one's own time and the others of the past, every other living and dead, through being open to an exorbitant, inventive regurgitation, while barely speaking of the past, if at all, except in apophatic silences, 'aporias of writing' (*WM*, 128), or codes of intuition at which one can only guess, and thus be forced to invent. If this is regurgitation, then, it is also inescapably the experience of mourning, given highly ritualized encryption.

If what I have suggested so far about the literature of the nineteenth century sounds as though it is equally applicable to other historical moments, what I believe marks the so-called Victorians is the pervasive sense, if not celebration and affirmation, of mourning. Literature marks the passage of one's coming into being, one's own historical modernity by reiterating the traces of the past and so bearing witness to those signs whilst moving away from them. In this manner, when each 'unique death is taken up into all the codes and rituals of mourning, when the singular event comes to be marked by the designated spaces and times of mourning' (Brault and Naas 2001, 17), all the singular modalities by which the Victorians *literatize* the self (to use Thackeray's neologism) are available to us, they come back and so reveal themselves to us as events and experiences of mourning. And what they share therefore as the encoded admission of their historicity is, possibly, that all their 'mournings are but iterations of the one death that can never be identified' (Brault and Naas 2001, 17). The trope of vomit and the inference of vomit's vicariousness confesses silently to all that cannot be swallowed in the work of mourning (E, 291). In this manner, Victorian writers such as Gaskell bear witness to being cut off from the historical, or seeking to cut themselves off from the haunting experience of historicity by which their being is determined, and is located as a *being-there* but always cut off from the past for which one mourns without the possibility of a proper representation, which would amount to a restitution.

In this fashion, time after singular time, literature makes possible a 'historicity without history – historicity without direct references to actual occurrences but only direct exposure of its field' (Fynsk 1996, 223). The signs of this historicity without history are those minute and multitudinous scratches in all directions, revealed by George Eliot in *Middlemarch* through the perspective of what is otherwise invisible on the surface of a table which comes to be revealed by chance in the light of a candle (Eliot 2003, 264). Here we have refraction, reflection and mediation. We are positioned by perspective on perspective governed not by a subject but through the chance agency of illumination and location, from out of which the hidden traces emerge, causing one to reflect. That which is experienced as singular is necessarily other. Furthermore, the figure of a perspective – taking a position, and therefore risking an invention of perception – affirms its singular positionality, but that there are always other 'multitudinous' traces and therefore 'directions'. In Eliot's image, an image of a subject of history having revealed to her the network of traces awaiting deciphering, and in the implicit gaze of the narrator's perception addressed to a *you* to come, the 'conventions and resources of historical truth-telling . . . give space for the possibility of a meta- or supplementary witnessing' (Clark 2005, 156). Like the vomit, the scratches may be deemed to be irrelevant, but literature's inventiveness admits to its 'right to say anything in any way' (Clark 2005, 156) so as to articulate and invent history and the material conditions of being otherwise.

Were I pushed to isolate, unreasonably, a single feature by which literature of the nineteenth century might be defined it would be this very idea of *invention* therefore, in its ability to open the sites of memory and the past, and so give space to vomit, mourning and the invention of the other in such a manner that one's identity is doubled, haunted by its other. In this manner the Victorian subject is displaced from itself in its experience, and in this comes to apprehend its modernity through the singular sense of being as witness to its own expulsion, its existential homelessness. The Victorian text addressing history through a reflection on the singular historicity of being taps time, entering into the temporal core of what has taken place, and which imprints itself indelibly as a signature. I am myself, says the text, but where I am, what I am, is countersigned by an other. I thus invent myself in singular fashion, through 'finding', *inventing* the traces of the past through the experience of alterity.

None of this is to say that one can simply appropriate *invention* as the latest critical tool or keyword however. What is *invented* comes about as and when it does, in each example and on each occasion. Arrival or reception cannot be programmed. In speaking of so many singular inventions, one should therefore resist or avoid the programme or attempt to capitalize on the trope of invention *as if* it were programmable, as far as this is possible. In the case of every motif causing one's reading to pursue the unexpected path, there is a demand for response as constant attentiveness to the simultaneous demarcation and erasure of boundaries and limits. One is attentive to those marks of memory and the past that determine representation, identity or ontology while becoming invisible in the process of making the work appear in its present. Motifs such as invention should not dictate the readings. What ought to be clear though is that one works through motifs, tropes, figures in given instances, rather than through programmes and methodologies. They serve merely as one form of hook on which to hang the textual thread, and so to suspend from it other elements in the weave. They also offer the illusory comfort of knowable co-ordinates across a series of virtual maps, in which each of the lines are constantly in flux, undergoing endless realignments. Singularities are not merely the differences between works. They announce themselves as that which arrests one's attention through exceeding certain conventions, forms or habits, and so bring about a disruption, a discontinuity irreducible to habits of organization or closed representation. They are the differences by which one comes to receive and apprehend the text as it is. It is where one finds oneself in literature. In such glimpses as we are afforded, invention therefore offers a motif by which to imagine an open system in which we are *in representation*. This open system can be imagined as constantly finding and redefining itself according to the needs, the demands and the desires of the culture in which it is situated. In this we find, we *invent* an image of literature. This is *where one is*, where *I am*. Between fiction and reality.

III BEING-CIRCULAR OR, WHERE ONE IS, IN LITERATURE

Wherever one is, one must take responsibility for that. This is what is announced whenever one says 'I' (J, 228). Between fiction and reality, 'the fictional and the real, the phantasmatic and the actual, and like all the genres' though, this is where we are, where we find ourselves as an other *in representation*. This is where we are *in literature* (*H.C.*, 13). This is where we find ourselves as another. If what I am remarking is provocative or obtuse, this is done to 'provoke the reader into awakening: analyze, scrutinize yourself along this line, the thin edge of this passage between the public and the secret, between waking and dreaming, between fiction and reality' (*H.C.*, 13). That line, the double border where we might find ourselves is traced here, in two comments in three languages at least concerning *being* (emphases added):

> Da   There   Then
> war ich   was *I*   I still
> noch ganz   yet whole   was whole
>
> (Celan 1995, 111/112[4])

and

> Il faut redire en altérant le même / *One* must repeat while altering (it all) the same. (Deguy 2005, 84/85)[5]

Notwithstanding what Paul Celan has called 'the inalienable complexity of expression' (2003, 16) – which phrase is applicable to either of the above quotations – we must take responsibility for what appears to be reiterated in the two locations. Despite their different languages, something circulates between the two citations from, respectively, Paul Celan and Michel Deguy. Something of the spacing and temporality, the différance by which being comes to know its identity, appears here and there, now and then *as if* there were an attempted communication, *as if* something were passing, were coming to pass, were appearing between the *one* and the *other*, without admitting of any precedence or priority on either hand. If anything at all can be said of what *comes to pass* between both reflections on the subject, of the coming to pass of being as it announces its own passage, then it is undeniably a matter of temporality, and also tempo. It appears *to be* a question of tempo; but it appears also, and at the same time, *as* an interrogation marked by the problem of tempo and temporality because both mediations of being mark time – the time of a being's reflection on itself and, within that, the motion, the *retour* and *ostinato* of the not-self, of an other. There is traced not simply an other singular, but instead the other as being-singular-plural. The matter of temporality is nothing as such in the two poems, yet it is everything here. For the self does not reflect on some temporality exterior to itself, but that which cuts one off from oneself, reminding oneself of the not-self. *Being* returns to itself in a circular and iterable motion, but never as itself. Identity is thus not a unified and undifferentiated locus or meaning, but 'a place of *absolute* resistance and remaining'. This affirmation, 'passes through me, it institutes this "someone in me" rather than being actively chosen by me. So it remains for all the others in me . . . to be *negotiated*' (*PM*, 35).

What might come to be seen and read here is that the subject's reflection on itself does not admit of a fall into any vulgar concept of time, thinkable as being external to the subject.[6] Both remarks serve to illustrate the 'originary temporality' (*OS*, 27) of being and with that, the circulation of that temporality, inseparable from being, in a motion 'from time to time, one time into another' (*OS*, 28). In this, being is read as a 'becoming-temporalization'. This is a 'becoming-temporalization' that always already *is*, and which, in this paradoxical though nonetheless inescapable and possibly unbearable condition, puts 'itself' invisibly, repeatedly under erasure as the erroneous assumption of its being the sign of *where one is* – hence the deconstruction of a unity or identity articulated in the chiasmus that articulates the subject every time one remarks *I am*, whenever one says 'I', *as if* to say *I am here* (which is always a response to an other, as you'll know).

In the case of the second citation, from Michel Deguy, this chiasmus, this *X* that crosses through the unity of the self is seen. Time is the time of a necessary repetition as the sign that iterability transfigures any movement into a *now* which is to come and which is irreducible to the *now* of the *one*. In Deguy's apprehension of being, time is both continuous and discontinuous. It is simultaneously the motion of time and two temporal punctuations – *now* and *now* implicit in the acknowledgement of the inescapable iterability that proves singularity. In the case of the first quotation, from Paul Celan, the subject is apprehended, re-membered even. And the subject is mourned also in that apparent nostalgia for an impossible unity that has never taken place, and yet which haunts the language of subjectivity, being and ontology. The subject is recalled nevertheless, called to and remembered in a single location that is already, irrevocably doubled, split. The division announces itself. It performs itself, from within the single word, and does so spatially – *there* (*da*) – and temporally – *then* (*da*). But this takes place also, always belatedly. It thus reveals the *itself* as subjected to, subject of the experience of *Nachträglichkeit*, that moment of coming to consciousness as an *après-coup*. That simultaneity of space and time undoes itself and remarks itself from within itself. In this, and also in the temporality of the gaze that informs Celan, language marks the spacing and temporality of being as the 'reality' of being narrated in two singular performatives as the countersignatures of a fiction of a self-identical being which one attempts to articulate every time one says 'I' and seeks to situate *where one is*.

While Pierre Joris' translation of 'da' as 'then' is certainly reasonable, justifiable even given Celan's repeated use of 'als' earlier in the poem to indicate a prior temporal moment, I have chosen 'there' as indicative not only of the temporal but also the spatial dimension of being's reflection on itself. Thus, there becomes readable as the merest possibility nostalgia for the notion of a previous unity to identity, which the subsequent spacing and reflection of the 'I' emerges from, and disrupts irrevocably. *Then* is a time past. *There* on the other hand is both a sign of that moment lost as such, whilst being also a sign of the place where that moment has taken place.

There are other troublesome resonances at work in the passage apropos the circularity of being. While 'ganz' obviously means whole, entire or complete, it can also mean 'quite' depending on context. 'Noch', meaning 'yet', 'still', 'just' or 'even', would seem to share a partial semantic resonance with the more occluded trace in 'ganz', and the temporal disturbance inflicted by reflective consciousness on the temporal recognition of being is signified, however slightly, in 'noch' and its function in particular words such as *nochmals* (once again), *nochgeschäft* (option to double) or *nochmalig* (renewed) indicative of iterability. Finally, the word order in German of the declined verb of being – *war Ich* – evinces a sense of the temporal and spatial placement of an *I* (hence my emphasis), which arguably gets lost in Joris' translation. Celan's German admits of a subject position discrete or quasi-discrete, and therefore discontinuous from, other than the *I* who recalls its other self to itself. In representation, *I* literatizes. I displaces the itself *in literature, in representation*. I cites itself as another self, the other one. On the one hand, 'I is the only one able to say of himself, autoreferentially, autodeictically, that he is himself . . . ineffable' (J, 237). On the other hand, this 'isolation, the insularity of whoever is "selved" – and one should say "severed," "separated," "cut off," "removed" – is the experience of a "selfbeing," a "selfhood," a "self-awareness" ' (J, 238).

The second of my two quotations is available to different readings, if *one* risks forcing the translation, which, it has to be said, is demanded by the line itself. Such an unavoidable forcing of the subject takes place for us to read. In a sense, this is what *one*, as anonymous cipher of my being, does within the line itself. Moving on from the reflection on being's becoming-conscious to itself, I wish to turn to the circulation of this becoming-being and being's becoming in its/their always dissymmetrical singular iterability as such disfigured figures are articulated and disarticulated in two poems. It should be stressed at this juncture, this *turning point in the circle that we are de-scribing*, that both Deguy and Celan are taken to offer felicitous examples of the circulation of being's consciousness to itself in the poems in question, and the significance – to reiterate and extend one of the citations – of the 'interval or the gap, of the trace [of being] as gap [*écart*], of the becoming-space of time or the becoming-time of space' (*FWT*, 21).

But to return to Deguy's meditation on being's iterability, its revenant motion of becoming other in the return of becoming itself to itself: *Il faut redire en altérant le même.* Key to this forcing is the phrase 'en altérant'. Both the work of the preposition and the various meanings of the verb must be taken into account. Take *en*. One must repeat *when* altering the same. One must repeat *in* altering the same. One must repeat *with* altering the same. This of course leaves out any acknowledgement of where a particular pressure arises, in *one*, in *must*, in *one must*. As for *altérer* – to impair, to affect, to spoil, to mar, to alter, to change, to fade, to distort, to falsify, to adulterate. There is an alarming alterity to *alterer*. The condition of transformation or translation is intricately interwoven in a matrix of possibilities to do with the circulation and circularity of the one, of the ways in which it folds back on itself in coming to a consciousness of itself, but only in that structural condition of distorting and change, of alteration and falsification.

At the same time, as Deguy's phrase admits in the copula of the preposition, *one* not only repeats *in* altering (or falsifying, or distorting and so on) the same, one also speaks again. *One* reiterates itself in itself and from itself, as both itself and not-itself, as the simultaneous trace of self and other within the repetition that one names, thereby giving the lie to unity, ontology and a subjectivity undifferentiated either spatially or temporally. Taking this further, as the line already does, it is to be observed that *one* arrives and comes to speak once more (re-dire) *when* and *where* one alters, where the alterity of *one* arrives *in the re-speaking that is repetition as reiteration. One* thereby announces, as we have already indicated, the *itara*, the other, within the circling enunciation of consciousness to itself as not-itself in naming it-self. And this despite the apparent in-difference that is assumed, silently evinced in that figure (*all*) *the same.*

However naïvely, or however one assumes the posture or performance of a strategic naïveté for the purposes of opening the circularity of being's articulation to itself, as this is dictated and marked by its own necessary difference in its articulation and repetition, it might be asked, even parenthetically – *as if* the very question would not bear the weight of the inquiry it demands – 'comment l'un "traduirait" -il l'autre?' / 'how could the one "translate" the other?' (Deguy 2005, 108/109). Something is missing in the given translation, the appended reflexive subject, that 'it', possibly 'itself', so that allowing this silent graphic mark to return, one would be given to read: *how would one translate it-lone-self the other?* Clearly I am once again forcing the translation, to open the problem of recirculation and retour, to bring into plain sight the frustration of an impossible communication that takes place, and which, in taking place, gives place to being.

All of which is unravelled and wound, folded and unfolded, over and under, in this, the last citation from Michel Deguy, this time the poem *Catachrèses* (2005, 102/103).

Retournant l'endroit et l'envers, tournant à l'endroit l'envers: ce qu'il attend n'est pas là – visiblement: ce qui n'est pas, ni l'endroit ni l'envers.

First Wilson Baldridge's translation, then mine:

Turning outside to inside over and over, turning the inside out: what he is waiting for is not there – visibly; that which is not, neither the outside nor the inside.

Returning, turning again, the right side wrong side, turning (towards) the outside inside: that's what he's waiting for, what is not there – visibly: that which is not, neither right nor wrong, out nor inside.

I have forced open the translation here quite unreasonably, yet again. I have risked this however in order to stress, to enflame and irritate the catachreses of circulation *and* iterability, being here shown to be neither absolutely continuous nor discontinuous, and yet an uneasy and paradoxical interweaving of the continuity and discontinuity. At the same time, what also comes to light here is the sense of circulation as not merely a matter of a relatively straightforward or 'progressive' temporality, however much traces might remain in play, however 'overdetermined' by the ghosts of one's past selves one's present self reveals itself to be. What we see here at play in Deguy's Moebius-matrix is a circulation or *matriculation* of apparent surfaces. In this play is the appearance, the making of or giving birth to that which is not. It is not nothing exactly, even though it is not something. It is not the sign of the absence of some thing anterior to the sign. This is what is not there – visibly: being, circling around and returning, appearing/disappearing in the very gesture of turning outside inside and turning inside outside.

IV BEING IN LITERATURE

I have been moving in circles. A circle anticipates and reflects on a movement 'round'. It implies a round, a rondel or roundel, a rondeau, rondo or rondelet. It is an identifying mark, a frame, a figure of nothing, a form informing a motion composed through structural reiterations. It is incorporated as a refrain. None of these words means the same thing exactly. Sharing a semantic kernel, they figure the bursting open of the kernel's enclosure, epistemologically and teleologically in an embarrassment, an *exorbitance* of disseminative excess. (*Ex-orbis*: getting off track, escaping the circle.) A round is not necessarily circular, it doesn't close or complete the circle, at least not simply. As with the idea of a musical ground, for example the *ostinato* or *rondo*, the round, the idea of a round, announces series and sequence, and also cycle. The circular, to reiterate the refrain (in repeating one appears to restrain oneself, holding oneself back, whilst moving beyond one's being 'enchained' thus), thus opens out from within its own structure, moving beyond its apparent closure or foreclosure. In this, and in the guise of the *rondo*, it involves language in a game of chance. It does so via a succession, chain or cycle of gestures that, while appearing to mimic that seemingly closed, 'first' figure, remain the same and yet move on, in the enactment of 'the becoming-space of time and the becoming-time of space' of being's being. So: the round as the insistence on the impossibility of the stability of any ~~Ground~~ is placed under erasure in that gesture of mapping that takes place. What goes around comes around. As Rimbaud knew, and wrote repeatedly in an affirmation anticipated above, 'I is an other' (1957, xxvii, xxix).[7] I am in representation, I am in literature, but I is an other.

There is both a luminous obscurity and an obscure luminosity to this phrase. For as much as it has been read or not read at all, misread, it announces with perfect economy the abyssal topography of a being, which always where it is, is nevertheless nowhere as such, other than in spatio-temporal *différance* that one can glimpse as having been always already shadowed in those motion-signs of *becoming* and *between*. Thus *one* always becomes other again and again, and this takes place, to reiterate the point, *where one is*. This is *where one is* in circularity, in the question of circularity. *One* is placed, *one* takes place, in the staging and framing that circularity *de-scribes*, in the (ana)logic of which all surface and depth, exteriority and interiority, originary ground and the myth of temporal fixity give way. Or, rather, say *give place* in the limiting-delimiting of the inherence of being's circular recursive revenance. I am never myself, as such, but neither am I the apparently transcendent possibility of past moments of *I* that I might recall when *I* was, yet whole, quite complete. Yet language gives the lie to the logocentric dream of or desire for origin and/as completion. Language – that obviously which gives place to the articulation of I before there is an I to announce itself – is 'precisely what does not let itself be possessed but, for this very reason, provokes all kinds of movements of appropriation . . . language can be desired but not appropriated' (LNO, 101).

As a consequence (and this is the gift and secret of literature apropos being), if every 'being-there is a being-in' (Lacoste 2004, 9), *where one is* is always traced by, even as it enacts, both the poetics and 'logic of immanence' (Lacoste 2004, 10), but this immanence never fulfils itself. Immanence would be merely the appropriation to come. This is what is most idiomatic in language: announcing I as my proper self, in the taking place of that 'proper' self-designation, there is simultaneously a citation of an other I, of each I and every other I, other than the I that I am. *I* cannot be appropriated by my auto-affirmative articulation. This is what Celan discloses: articulating the self *in literature* or *in representation* (which effectively is only to say *articulating the self*) approaches, idiomatically, 'that which, throbbing within language, does not let itself be grasped' (LNO, 101). *I* comes to be disclosed *as an other, as every other and wholly other*, as *I* is simultaneously placed and displaced in the taking place of this immanent othering, this radical ecstasis one names being. This is what a poetics of being/the being of poetics unveils, what it reveals as it suspends the intuitive and steps momentarily 'outside *one's* ordinary mode of seeing' (Gosetti-Ferencei 2004, 238; emphasis added). Poetic modes of staging, presenting (*Darstellung* as opposed to *representatio*) being as the performance of a simultaneous 'disorientation and clarity' (Gosetti-Ferencei 2004, 241) admit the phenomenal contingency of that reflective apperception of being as *where one is*. Such staging is never merely a commentary upon the experience of being, though. It is not a copy, mimetically faithful, and cannot be appropriated as a *representation* of being. It is the very trace of being returning, always in other words, as the attestation of the unbearable circulation of being that the literary makes possible to glimpse.

Literature is then this, if it is anything: 'the irreducible plurality of signatures and an ethico-juridical vigilance, a political one too, to the effects of hegemony of one language over another, between one language and another' (EC, 290). Being that there is literature, literature stages the endless textile weave of the traces of being. Being – that, where one is, in literature. (Submit this statement to an endless series of openings.) Being that there – *there* – is 'literature', this is where 'one is'. This is where being comes to find its singular and historical invention 'in' literature, in 'literature', 'in literature'. 'One' is: *one* defines the provisional intersection, hiatus and interruption, the knotting or mesh of traits, coming into being as a singular instance, available to iterability, and momentarily formed as the material and historical determination staged as an ontological form 'in literature'. This is where one is in circularity, in circulation in the circularity, the circulation that is named variously the literary or the poetic, before and beyond, circling around any merely philosophical logic, and exceeding that logic repeatedly.

This is where one is. Given birth to, being is matriculated. And this is where one 'begins' in circularity. *Matri(x)circulation. X* marks the spot, the hinge, the refrain of the (re)trait. This is where one comes to be. One comes (in) to being, touching the thinking of an event or experience. This is 'what "I" can sight and what "I" can say that I sight in this site of a recitation where I/we is' (LG, 229). Again and again: 'the genre "I"' (LG, 226). And if language is never owned, if I only have one language but that language is never mine, my every utterance announces the 'opening *of self*' that exceeds the 'autonomy or auto-affection' of self-presence in that it '"distends [*itself*]"'. In this, I let myself be opened. I am 'hetero-affected', translated by the other (*hetero*). The *I am* is utterable only on the condition of being opened in this place, where I am and where I say and reflect that I believe I am, because I am 'also opened by the other' (*OT*, 29). Every time I open my mouth, or hear myself speak '"in my mind"', it is *as if* my being were formed in the form of the circle made by my mouth – even '*o*' – I touch myself. I touch myself not in closing the circle that affirms my presence. In an experience of ghostly refrain marked by syncopation, I touch myself as an other (*OT*, 33): *Ex-cited*, I gain sight through the insight of the other, *incited by the other*. I am cited. I – *as if* I were citation of the other. I am thus given, 'in the difference between *making* or *forming*, on the one hand, and *being*, on the other':

The excess of *fashioning* over *essence*, with . . . one coming in lieu of the lack or impossibility of the other; all that, no doubt, is the law of *fiction* . . . [w]here the taking-place of the event [of the utterance of the self] doesn't find its place . . . except in *replacement* . . . [isn't that] the place for the phantasm as well, that is to say, the ghostly revenant (*phantasma*), at the heart of (self-) feeling? [And citing ourselves thus in the fictions of circulation and the circularity of being] The revenant, between life and death, dictates an impossible mourning, an endless mourning – life itself. (*OT*, 35)

V LITERATURE IS CITATION

Citation is a genre. But it is not a genre *comme les autres*. It is not representative of a genre, it cannot be gathered into an order or hierarchy of genres. It bespeaks a certain phantasmatic vicariousness. Thus, in its iterable singularity citation performs a participation that 'never amounts to belonging . . . because of the *trait* of participation itself, because of the effect of a code and of the generic mark. Making genre its mark, a text [in the interruption that we call citation] demarcates itself' (LG, 212). Citation thus remarks a belonging without belonging, by which 'genre' or other 'designation [such as saying *where one is*, affirming *I am*] cannot simply be part of the corpus' (LG, 212). Like a dismembered limb, or discarded prosthesis, *there is* citation. Literature affirms this. Literature is always the singular articulation of such vicarious haunting. Literature, if it amounts to anything at all, is nothing other than citation. Citation touches on the untouchable. It imagines proximity.

Yet, citation or quotation is something, the nature of which we believe we understand and can justify in that it partakes of, as it constitutes, a 'substitutive structure of [phantasmatic] prosthetics or . . . *technical* supplement' (*OT*, 223). It is part of conventional academic practice. It belongs to the very nature of literary studies, if not in some senses literature itself. It assumes an authority by which we bolster our work, by which we make claims for our own arguments. The authority of one's analysis rests not on its own particular uniqueness therefore but on the scaffolding of prior authority on which one builds one's presentation of an interpretation, a hypothesis or truth. If one cites without giving the source in some fashion, this is considered to be plagiarism. One must therefore acknowledge one's sources. This is the purpose of the footnote or endnote, the list of works cited and, by extension, the bibliography. A bibliography may well contain items that are not cited or alluded to, but which have had an invisible yet significant influence on one's thinking, analysis and writing nonetheless. Yet, can one make such distinctions so clearly, so unequivocally? Where does one stop in compiling a bibliography in considering those publications or other sources, in short those texts, which have shaped how one thinks, how one reads and translates the other's text? In asking such questions, I have moved from a purely formal and academic question (in either the narrow or the more 'metaphorical' sense of an academic question) to one that opens up a broader concern with epistemology, memory, and it has to be said the nature or ontology of identity or being. All this being said, let me switch directions somewhat abruptly. An imagined quotation arrives, someone else's words, a certain voice rehearsing or performing the following statement:

Writing without citation is impossible.

Such a bold statement warrants a challenge. After all, is it not the case that only certain 'types' or 'genres' of writing demand or employ citations, quotations, references, acknowledged illustrations, excerpts and extracts? To say that writing without citation is impossible *as if* to imply or insinuate that no writing whatsoever can take place without quotation or reference is, if not patently absurd, then at least open to question from those places where common sense speaks.

Citation appears as traces, apparitions arriving from some other place. It announces however obliquely a relationship between spectrality and literature. They are the ghosts of writing that take place in the name, the authority and institution of scholarship. Academic or critical writing is always haunted in the very act by which authority and identity are claimed. However, citation, far from being the remark of an absolute authority, constitutes and affirms a force of dislocation, a certain incapacity to close the system. While making the work of reading possible, citation renders any ontological coherence impossible through a certain phantom dysfunction or disadjustment. Risking a provisional definition of what takes place internally within systems or institutions, deconstruction 'often consists, regularly or recurrently, *in making appear* . . . a force of dislocation'. Deconstruction consists 'in remarking, in the reading and interpretation of texts, that what has made it possible for philosophers [and anyone who writes] to effect a system is nothing other than a certain dysfunction or "disadjustment," a certain incapacity to close the system . . . this dysfunction not only interrupts the system but itself accounts for the desire for system, which draws its *élan* from this very disadjoinment, or disjunction' (IHTS, 4). That displacement and dis-adjoinment that takes place in the name of deconstruction, and which deconstruction names as taking place, is unthinkable without the force of haunting or 'the logic of spectrality [which is] . . . inseparable from the very motif (let us not say the "idea") of Deconstruction' (*SM*, 178 n.3). This ghostly force of dislocation, dysfunction or disadjustment within the unity of a system finds its appropriate visible figure in the intrusiveness of the citation, which arrives like some ghost in the textual machine, some poltergeist throwing business as usual out of whack and giving momentary disturbing manifestation and form to 'the idea of the idea' (*SM*, 178 n.3). In short, citation materializes ideality. At the same time it performs and gives every time singular manifestation to the immanent revenence that haunts every word. Citation shapes itself in singular fashion and each time with a difference, through its iterable appearance to the contours of an otherwise invisible past, irretrievable event or a disembodied and unrepresentable concept. And inasmuch as this iterable apparition takes form, then it might be ventured that all literature comes down to, and has the chance of a survival, according to the spectral logic of citation. Literature is citation.

VI AS IF

Dysfunction or disadjustment, dislocation when witnessed allows the reader the possibility of paying attention to the literariness or fictionality of writing, that is to say to notice what is already taking place otherwise invisibly in the figural, imaginary, tropological, narrative, symbolic and therefore 'citational' effects of all language. What I am calling the literary or fictional in language here amounts to 'the essential possibility of an "as if"' (*N*, 354), which has to be taken into account. *As if* – as if for example one were to utter what Derrida has called 'exemplary phrases such as . . . "it's as if I were dead"' (SOO, 25), and subsequently attend to what such an utterance might mean and how it operates. Clearly, there is at work the thinking of the possibility of the impossible here. A phantasmatic ghostly occurrence is imagined. The revenance of the other arrives. In its utterance, *as if* articulates the staging, the presentation (*Darstellung*) rather than representation (*representatio*) of that which is neither true nor false but which may be conceived, brought to mind in what amounts to a kind of fictionality. While the quotation immediately above situates the question of a condition of being, Derrida also speaks of the analogical signalling of *as if* in literary and spectral terms: '[b]ut above all else, the essential possibility of an "as if" ha[s] to be taken into account, an "as if" that affects all language and all experience with possible fictionality, phantasmaticity, spectrality' (*N*, 354). To risk reading sequence as equation, fictionality, specifically the fictionality of the *as if*, is compared with the phantasmic or spectral condition of the same figure. *As if* defines that which citation stages. At the very least, (it is *as if*) it can be read as performing in interruptive fashion, within the illusory presence of an unmediated voice that presents itself in writing, as the 'voice' or, more precisely, the trace of a voice – that is, a recorded tele-communication, a writing – of some other.

However, as is implied, the question of citation is not merely a formal matter. Instead, the figure of citation serves as a singular example, on the one hand, for the obligation one has to the other and, on the other hand, for that which ruins any identity or totality, any auto-affection. The relationship between any single essay, chapter, book and their citations is always double, therefore, having to do with strife and economy. But one can neither control nor limit the motions or traces of the phantasmatic or the spectral. Why though, to repeat the question *as if* I were citing myself, myself *as if* I were an other, 'why stress spectrality here?' (*AF, 84*). Because, in considering the ontology and concept of the archive, this form or institution is perceived as being spectral 'in the first place . . . spectral *a priori*' (*AF*, 84). While I do not wish to rush to a comparison or an analogy, I would like to suggest that literature is one form of spectral archive. Literature gathers in any moment of its production all the resources of the culture that it mediates and from which it emerges. It produces narrative, representation, image, as the literary 'instituting' of such traces. And it does so moreover affirming *where one is* (*nous sommes en répresentation*). As we know, such traces are not things in and of themselves. The institution, structure or form of the literary 'begins' then with the appearance of that which is not, that which is therefore spectral. Citation is only the most obvious manifestation of the trace. It haunts criticism. It haunts literature. It haunts being. More generally therefore, it can be said to haunt all reading and writing. Citation, as we have seen, admits (to) disorder within any system: that of the time of citation, *as if* a future perfect is wrapped up in the past (SOO, 33).

What might take place is merely a certain registration, recognition or admission of the work of haunting within any textual form, as that work comes to disturb the identity or identification of, or distinction between, the forms of imitation or mimicry (the shaping of an apparently original argument in the more or less discernible lineaments of another) and the function of citation itself as a somewhat spectral authority. Citation haunts precisely because it arrives from some other place as an authority, the authority, aphorism or signature of the other, which intrusion of the guest is paradoxically conjured so as to assert the very idea of originality in argument or research. So, we have to remark again that 'writing without citation is impossible'. As so many precarious, disembodied figures, then, citation disorders and phantomizes the text as the haunting revenance of some other. The concern is with the arrival of something haunting within the place of the habitual. The trace of another arrives where I am, and where I believe I am in writing or speaking. Where one is, there is another, and so that uncanny sense, in receiving literature, of a being-two-to-speak. This revenance, this apparition is neither simply real nor not real. Yet, in being neither being nor not being, being neither presence nor absence, and yet not being nothing, one is placed in a strange position. For,

> beyond all perception, [one has] to receive the other while running the risk, a risk that is always troubling, like the stranger (*unheimlich*), of a hospitality offered to the guest as *ghost* . . . There would be no hospitality without the chance of spectrality. But spectrality is not nothing, it exceeds, and thus deconstructs, all ontological oppositions, being and nothingness, life and death. (*AEL*, 111–12)

Less a question of habitation than of haunting (Avm, 18) even though the one always implies the other (*AF*, 86), 'by interrupting the weaving of our language and then by weaving together the interruptions themselves', the spectrality of citation arrives as a summons calling us to respond, to acknowledge it, to act as host.

Nonetheless, in the face of the demand, this strange process of citing and quoting confesses to a desire, despite itself, to proceed by that most conventional or predictable of literary-critical methods. Academic language arrives *as if* this guaranteed what might be called a kind of proleptic autoimmunization through the control of what is taken into the host. In this fiction, which is all too real, citation is therefore introduced through prescribed methods *as if* it belonged to a regime of inoculation against the very ghost by which all text gets underway, and without which spectral figure, no survival would be possible (FK, 51).

VII THE BARN AND THE BONFIRE: THE EXAMPLE OF HARDY

But of course we are not talking simply about academic writing, with its protocols, procedures and institutional habits, as I hope is clear. If anything, academic writing as supplement of literature serves to make manifest that which is always already underway in literature, as the condition of the exemplary secret of literature. This secret is the right to say anything, but it is also the possibility that everything is being said through a mode of encrypted citation. Such citation does not simply take place as a somewhat spooky version of intertextuality. It is also the citation of the material and historical, that which is considered exterior to the interior of literature, to literature's realist, modernist, conventional or experimental 'representations'. Literature represents nothing. Instead it presents the historicity of being *as if* this were available to representation, given support and form through the phantasmatic weave of traces. Allow me a somewhat lengthy digression here around two scenes in literature, each of which stages for the reader a historical event and a phenomenal, spectral experience of the traces of the past, *as if* this could illustrate the argument.

My first example comes from Thomas Hardy's *Far from the Madding Crowd*. Now, from particular critical perspectives Hardy can be accused (and indeed has been) of romanticizing the rural working classes with regard to his representation of their historical and material conditions. However, what I would like to suggest here, apropos questions of literature, being, historicity, circularity, spectrality, invention, citation and so on, is that on the one hand, his understanding of his present, and present conditions, is mediated and formed by the perception of a phenomenological historicity that exceeds and accommodates the persistence of particular traces. Such traces are iterable. They circulate and give shape to any present moment. Thus being must be presented or staged differently, with a difference. It must be staged in a manner that does not avoid the historicity, the materiality of being, but rather engages in an accommodation of that which haunts being in its Englishness. Narrative therefore is performed as the experience of a sense of Englishness. Effectively Hardy *invents* the singularity of historical experience and event for his reader, through opening the present to the exorbitant signs of all the haunting forces of the conditions of being.

On the other hand, though not separate from the question of being's historicity, is a more formal concern. Hardy's disinterest (if I can speak of his 'romanticism' in this way) stems from his rejection of 'realism' as art. During his quarter decade as a novelist, Hardy repeatedly sought to experiment within the formal constraints of realist narrative, so as to transform its parameters and institutions from within. Art, Hardy asserted, should 'disproportion' the real in figuring, or rather, 'distorting, throwing out of proportion . . . [the representation of] realities, to show more clearly the features that matter in those realities' (Hardy 1962, 229). What is seen in reality, what is empirically observable, takes second place for Hardy to that higher, visionary or phantasmatic mode of perception in the mind's eye: 'the seer should watch [one] pattern among general things which his idiosyncracy moves him to observe . . . the result is no photograph, but purely the product of the writer's own mind' (Hardy 1962, 153). What the mind's eye is capable of decoding from the merely real or material is simultaneously a matter of reception *and* deciphering, of receiving the encrypted citation of the other. Moreover, it is not a matter solely of opening oneself to hidden patterns but also to the otherwise invisible echoes of the past, which vision distorts and disproportions the present of the gaze, as we shall see shortly. Hardy's novels speak not so much from a single, identifiable voice as from some form of phantom narrating machine that recites. It cites the traces of the past in rounds, in circular iterable patterns its refrains capable of translating into narrative or poetic form site, topography, trace, history and collective memory.

The interwoven patterning of lives, locations, narrative strands, discursive traces and other material details of Hardy's writing – whether topographical, architectural or archaeological, spatial or temporal – can be said to produce and at the same time generate or form themselves into a matrix of iterable and recursive structures. Moreover, Hardy's interlacing of countless aspects and facets that go to comprise his narratives finds its echoes in both the formal levels of the text and their archival and encrypted preservation of disparate, heterogeneous literary, cultural and historical traces. Every Hardy text, it might be said, offers a singular archaeological or archival formation, albeit one from the reading of which an origin or source cannot be traced. In its presentation it deforms mimetic representation. Seen from another perspective, Hardy's text displays repeatedly a rhizomic ingenuity, through a complex of endless inter-dependencies that are unavailable to any architectonic prioritization or ontological ordering. The patterns of tension and resistance to easy comprehension suggest that the more we seek a single narrative thread, the more we come to realize how each thread is interwoven into, shot through by and generative of countless others. There is thus given us to read in Hardy's fictions a haunting excess irreducible to the very site from which such flows are glimpsed, as reading *deterritorializes* the very *territorialization* which the act of reading strives for and supposedly guarantees.[8]

The question of excess and rupture takes place within vision, specifically that kind of vision given formal coherence through mimetic representation of reality through Hardy's acts of 'disproportioning'. That matter of that other vision within vision already alluded to through reference to Hardy's journal entries above is figured by the eruption of the past within the present moment of recording, as the image of the sheep-shearing barn in *Far from the Madding Crowd* makes apparent. The passage with which we are concerned is long and complex, but worth quoting at length:

One could say about this barn, what could hardly be said of either the church or the castle, its kindred in age and style, that the purpose which had dictated its original erection was the same with that to which it was still applied. Unlike and superior to either of those two typical remnants of mediaevalism, the old barn embodied practices which had suffered no mutilation at the hands of time. *Here at least the spirit of the builders then was at one with the spirit of the beholder now. Standing before this abraded pile the eye regarded its present usage, the mind dwelt upon its past history*, with a satisfied sense of functional continuity throughout, a feeling almost of gratitude, and quite of pride, at the permanence of the idea which had heaped it up. The fact that four centuries had neither proved it to be founded on a mistake, inspired any hatred of its purpose, nor given rise to any reaction that had battered it down, invested this simple grey effort of old minds with a repose if not a grandeur which a too curious reflection was apt to disturb in its ecclesiastical and military compeers. For once mediaevalism and modernism had a common standpoint. The lanceolate windows, the time-eaten arch stones and chamfers, the orientation of the axis, the misty chestnut-work of the rafters, referred to no exploded fortifying art or worn out religious creed. The defence and salvation of the body by daily bread is still a study, a religion, and a desire. (2000, 125–6; emphasis added)

The paragraph prior to this is straightforwardly representational, mimetic. It records in detail the barn, drawing attention to particular aspects of its medieval structure. Utility and beauty are registered in equal measure, and the overall aesthetic impression given is determined by the announcement of a preference for the ageing barn over the design of the majority of 'our modern churches'. So Hardy draws a picture, the order of description following, responding to, the architectonics of structure, observation of the spatial relations admitting of historical knowledge, and serving to contrast the medieval with the modern.

Were the passage to stop there, one might be mistaken in reading this as a continuance of that romanticized medievalist aesthetic captured in the work of Tennyson, William Morris or the Pre-Raphaelites. However, Hardy's second paragraph presents precisely those more ostensibly abstract issues around which this chapter has circled. Not only does there occur a shift from a minimally inflected but largely objective observation, resulting in a mostly realist representation, to one in which the mind's eye of the 'seer' (as Hardy has it) takes over. There is also an overfolding as well as an unfolding of discrete temporal moments and differences in the experience of the subject's translative gaze. The spirit of the past arrives in the present moment of observation, to exceed the framed empirical and realist vision. The image of the barn is itself a form of structural frame, opening itself from within itself, in the writing of which there is enacted its building in previous centuries, tracing the lines of construction and with that the invisible hands of the medieval workmen.

There is then the disorder of present time, the time of the modern through its resonance and revenance. This is most immediately captured in those sentences highlighted. Two spirits conjoin and communicate as an inner vision is unveiled from within the reportage of everyday function. This is of course already anticipated, if not captured, in the intimation of cyclical function, the barn being put to use in the same fashion generation after generation, and century after century regardless of the histories and ideologies for which churches and castles serve as symbolic reminders – and of which they, unlike the barn, are also ideological and temporal anachronistic remainders in the modern moment. Thus the ghosts of labour, of building and shearing, return, given an archive in the presence of the barn, and cited by the actions of the present farm hands.

What is significant also in Hardy's interpretive description is that perspective is doubled. First, it is a question of *what* one sees, and, more to the point, that there is someone at least hypothetically or in the imagination *to see* in the present moment what is otherwise overlooked. Perspective doubles and divides itself, it stages itself as a structure or formation rather than essential because narration envisions someone who could be on hand to see in this particular phantasmic manner. Narration, itself a phantom articulation, posits an imagined perspective on, and opened from the construction of an imagined viewer. The present of this viewer is then structurally displaced through the citation that the perspective enacts, so that the reader 'sees', *as if* he or she had access to that past present. There appears some shadowy figure neither of the scene nor in it exactly, but capable of gazing at the barn (or landscape, or church, or cliff face). From this, what emerges is that it is a question of *how* one sees and, therefore, *what* one comes to see and what comes to be seen in a visionary communion with that which is of the past but irreducible to the material reality of the structure in a given present, and what is cited in that construction. In this act of envisioning, an act which disproportions reality, the aesthetic perception figures not only 'a transformed *encounter* with' the empirical world, but instead and more forcefully 'an epistemic *overcoming*' of that world (Seel 2005, 7). Hardy deploys an 'aesthetic attentiveness' as an articulation of the 'here and now' of being, 'as it becomes accessible only in openness to the play of appearance of a given situation' (Seel 2005, 16–17). Beyond merely a history of the building, it is *as if* one is vouchsafed an image of labour in its generations.

The 'openness' is precisely that which gives the possibility of such revenance as we witness above, in which the historicity of spirit comes to be articulated, the past apprehended in such a singular fashion. Hardy exploits this through the echo of details from the first of the two paragraphs in the second. In their structural return, they present the reader with an apprehension that, because of the somewhat ghostly presence of Hardy's modern 'beholder', perspective on mere architectural detail has been transformed. The *now* of the scene is translated by the persistence of the past. While it is true then that the 'synchronic and diachronic . . . intersect in Hardy's metaphor of landscape' (Bivona 1990, 96), the landscape is not the only place in which this occurs. In Hardy's writing it can take place through the reading of buildings, through the play of documents, in marks left on roads or on walls, or in the practice of rituals such as midsummer dances, mummers' plays or the repetitious seasonal lighting of bonfires as a 'custom of the country' in *The Return of the Native*, a novel set in the 1840s, as Hardy remarks in his Preface to the 1895 edition (1999, 429).

Having described the activity around the bonfires, through the vision of another of those hypothetical lookers-on (who move like so many phantoms throughout Hardy's narratives; 1999, 18), the narration provides another markedly temporal vision of countless previous moments similar to the present one being recorded. The present is haunted by the cyclical revenance of the event, and the ghosts of all those who repeat the moment and experience its taking place. Again the 'present' moment (already displaced, in the past, sometime between 1840 and 1850 and so at a generation's remove at least from the time of Hardy's readers) is disproportioned, and with it literary realism:

It was *as if* these men and boys had suddenly dived into past ages, and fetched there from an hour and deed which had before been familiar with this spot. The ashes of the original British pyre which blazed from that summit lay fresh and undisturbed in the barrow beneath their tread. The flames from funeral piles long ago kindled there had shone down upon the lowlands as these were shining now. Festival fires to Thor and Woden had followed on the same ground and duly had their day. Indeed, it is pretty well known that such blazes as this the heathmen were now enjoying are rather the lineal descendants from jumbled Druidical rites

and Saxon ceremonies than the invention of popular feeling
about Gunpowder Plot. (1999, 20; emphasis added)

That *as if* (which is an echo of the exact same phrase in the previous
paragraph) introduces us into the realm of the fictional, the phantasmic, which opens the present moment to the traces of multiple
historical singularities. Hardy's disruption of the real is felt forcefully here not because any single past is recorded as leaving its traces
in the present, but instead because the passage signals several times
– of Druids and Saxons, Vikings and other pagan cultures. The pasts
do not simply erupt from within the present. The ritualistic nature
of the activity suggests the fiction of time travel on the part of the
heath's inhabitants, the disquieting, uncanny suggestiveness of the
moment found in the suggestion that it was *as if* those involved in
the ritual had travelled back in time to return to the present expressly
for the purpose of bringing those 'past ages' into their own time. As
with the scene of the barn, the 'spirit' of pagan revellers is *seen* in
that visionary manner to be in communication with, as Hardy puts
it, *the spirit of the beholder now*. (Which beholder we might ask? That
ghostly figure who may have seen the bonfires, had he or she been
there? The narrator, so-called? Or the reader? Every *now* is other
than every other *now*.) The scene is disturbing for other reasons also,
I would aver. For not only are there multiple times, thereby informing the moment with the perception of anachrony, but through this,
knowledge is overthrown and one reads a subversion of received historical wisdom, and with that the location of the 'origin' of bonfires
being linked to the Gunpowder Plot of 1605. It is as a result of such
disruptive temporal flows emerging out of any one given location
that Hardy's art can be said, with all justification, to be 'a haunted
art' (Reilly 1993, 65). But what goes for Hardy, goes for all writers,
albeit in distinctly different, singular ways.

VIII SPECTRALITY

All writing then, we have to say, without citation is impossible,
whether directly or indirectly. Writing could not take place without
the trace of some other text already underway and which survives.
Writing would not be possible without the manifestation or the *revenance* that is named, on occasion, iterability, that very effect or force
of citation that opens any system beyond itself. This *just is* literature,

this strange identity without ultimately determinable or programmable form. For, if literature is a gathering or binding of threads within a frame or genre, such as the novel, the historical and cultural traces belonging to otherwise heterogeneous discourses and practices, and which are hetero-affective, then literature, defined within its given frame, is nothing other than a haunted house. Literature plays host to the coming and going of all the ghosts of who we are. It stages where one is at any given cultural or historical moment. However, at the same time, but with the untimeliness of the revenant, it figures itself in *khoric* manner. In every singular event or experience of literature, literature becomes the receptacle of the remainders and translations of those discourses and practices of the past that leave their phantom marks on ourselves, on what we call our present, on identity today or *where one is*, in (that strange thing called) literature.

Writing is thus haunted, and in being so maintains through reproduction and representation the haunting-effect of the touch of the other always in circulation. Citation haunts, even and especially when the diacritical signs by which it is made manifest seem obviously not to be there. It can come from any past or any future. Writing, and specifically *literature*, the *literary*, is, if it is anything, citation's haunt, a haunted house disturbed at its very foundations, through the motion, the phantasmic motif, of quotation, reference, allusion, recollection, acknowledgement, the proper name and, in addition, all the signs of each and every other.

Pausing for a necessary digression and *as if* I were responding to a ghostly question I seem to hear arriving from somewhere, I feel required to answer why the motif, the figure of 'motif', is considered phantasmic. Inscribed in the word, and as that which the word inscribes, is movement or motion, process, taking place, rather than fixed identity or ontology. A motif such as *invention* or *singularity* is 'nothing', but 'so singularly a nothing that it never lets itself be constituted in the stasis of a being' (TUS, 72). The motif, that recurrent and therefore iterable device or pattern within an artistic or literary composition, recurs so as to impress on one or give to one a ghostly impression or perception. As such, citation is of the order of the motif, and thus is wholly typical of literature, inasmuch as 'there is no essence or substance of literature: literature is not. It does not exist. It does not remain at home . . . in the identity of a nature or even of a historical being identical with itself' (DFT, 28). Citation finds its 'home' in literature, in that, like literature, it has no self-identity, it does not remain in place. Taking place *as if* it were a motif, punctuating and in-forming the motivation of literature, citations haunt citations' haunts: *literature*. And literature is not even a haunted house fully realized and always the same, but merely the ghost of countless architectural and archival ruins. It haunts as much as it is haunted. It arrives with its secret even as it presents without representing the secrets of the other, of each other and every other.

If in this simulacral binarism *spectrality/citation* neither term equates, defines, reflects or is reducible in any neat or unproblematic manner to the other, what remains of interest in opening this consideration is the possibility of beginning to read how one comes to take place in the place of the other, in a place to which the other gives place. A destabilizing force is felt. Apropos citation and the institution of academic discourse, spectral disturbance in and as the work of language returns repeatedly, as that which haunts – and is, too, *the haunt of* – all scholarly habit. It marks and remarks all that is habitual, within the most familiar locations inhabited in the name of scholarship. That citation partakes of the spectral condition of 'literary' writing, and that what appears is not simply some prior text being quoted, may be comprehended if one acknowledges that the spectral is not merely what returns from a past, or from some anterior location. It is also that which is to come. It is that which can arrive at any moment as you will now be aware. It haunts me in the most familiar places.

This unpredictable possibility affirms itself in the disfiguring figure already mentioned, *l'avenir*, which announces simultaneously the future-as-programme and that which can always arrive, some unexpected ghostly apparition or visitant, returning from the future. 'Deconstruction' then, to risk this word here and its possible misunderstanding, takes place within the naming and concept of the future, and not as something I do, something taking place as a critical operation or act of reading. I do not 'deconstruct' the future. Instead, deconstruction is always already at work in what *l'avenir* says and what is written – a ghost writing within its visible form – in the signifier and concept of the future. As the phantom voice-over affirms in *Derrida*, one takes the future as that about which one is certain, about which one can say with reasonable certainty that it will arrive. But, to illustrate the invisible erupting unexpectedly from within the visible: the voice-over in any film is always an unexpected *arrivant*. You simply don't see it coming. The 'future' is witnessed in

the film, as successive frames arrive at each moment of that programme. The to-come however, let us remind ourselves, is that which
cannot be predicted. It is that which, arriving from the future at any
time, can take place unexpectedly and for which I can never be prepared. That *a* in *avenir*, written on occasion by Derrida as *a-venir*
(PIO, 28) and tied to that which comes in invention, figures the possibility of a coming (*venir*) which displaces presence, the present, and
which can always come at any moment. The border of the present
and presence can always be crossed, and so one cannot give finite
determination to such concepts or contexts because these are always
open, to reiterate the point. Context is always subject to this: 'the
context is open because "it comes" [*ça vient*], because there is something to come [*il y a de l'avenir*]' (IHTS, 13). Univocal meaning or
identity is disrupted and so there is indicated through the formal
eruption what one cannot help but hear, but which nevertheless is
not visible. Ontology gives way from within before the unexpected
arrival of its own parasite, the other named throughout *Specters of
Marx* in a French homophonic play as hauntology (*ontologie/
hantologie*). A ghost of an other haunts form, even as the ghost of
an unprogrammable event haunts even the most predictable future.

Thus, what one receives is that articulation of the other haunting
the simple figure of the future, disjointing in the process the time of
reading. Reading, one significant activity overlooked in some definitions of the constitution of *literature*, is therefore revealed as a form
of vigilant passivity. What may come to arrive in reading is this sign
of an alterity, the trace of the voice of the other, arriving indirectly.
Its articulation is an 'oblique offering' (POO, 5–36). I cannot tell in
my reading what is to come, I cannot programme my reading. This
is why there is no programme or method to 'deconstruction' even
though one may believe one can programme other modes of critique, whether poetic or political. Strictly speaking, and against all
such programmes, there is no route map for reading. This is what disturbs those who desire either a programme for, or the death of so-
called deconstruction. Despite the desire for programme and
authority however, the place where one is *in literature* is always
already haunted by its other, the unpredictable. If I am open to the
possibility of the impossible, a reception of some other to come
which can never be anticipated with any certainty, I cannot anticipate what I will read until it is already taking place and has come to
pass, the *trait* read belated in and as *retrait*. It is *as if* reading stages

the experience of *déjà vu*, for an experience of the impossible (the fictional world) that can never be mine.

But it is not even necessary to resort to French *l'avenir* in order to demonstrate the truth in reading, the truth in literature. For, having written above the phrase, *now being quoted*, we should pause to consider the interruption, the suspensive modality of this – or that – *now* (but which one?), which is itself, every time, indicative, if not performative of a certain citational iterability irreducible to any present or presence. The phrase spaces, and so displaces. This is more than familiar, but no less disturbing or disruptive for all that. In appearing in this manner, this figure operates on and thereby countersigns the text and the experience of reading the text in a particularly uncanny fashion. Acknowledging this, it has to be admitted that citation opens one to that mode of anachrony discernibly at work. Reading, properly understood, 'programmes' us to the impossibility of the programme. Reading is always involved in a circular structure, a circularity marked by its own impossible time:

> even before [reading] enters the dialectical circle of cognition, even before the active consciousness grasps itself at work there, this reading is still not yet what it already is . . . it is not yet the immanent movement of self-reproduction which it already is. (Hamacher 1998, 3–4)

Wherever one is, there is this opening of oneself to that which is to come, the haunting reminder of that which it already is. In this experience of the impossible time of reading, there is acknowledged therefore the fact that reading remains to come, and that we will never have done with it. We are never on time with reading.

Citation or quotation are the signs of the priority of a reading that is displaced from within itself, made improper by the necessary and inescapable dialogue by which it must take place. Citation disturbs the remarking of the present from within itself therefore. All presence, all presentation of the present is internally disturbed. This is the condition of text and of writing, and therefore, one might argue, the very secret of literature itself. This is all the more so when narrative assumes or feigns the presence of the subject – first person singular – in relation to the temporal instantaneity of utterance who is not the same as the author. It would appear to be this simulacrum of a presence, this supposedly authoritative 'I', guaranteeing and gathering to itself, that which is supposedly immanent in its appearance: all possible authority, all possible intimation of a presence or origin. But of course nothing could be less certain: for the movement of 'I' to take place, it has to be capable of being detached from any source, any authoritative appearance. 'I' thus remarks the uncanny force of citationality and, with that, the citation of a phantom-effect. Even those inscriptions that are not assumed to have a voice in any 'human' sense, and yet which are read conventionally as singular or unique, dates for example, are available for reiteration. Indeed, as you know now from previous discussions of different signs in different, differing contexts, the force of the date's singularity is only guaranteed by the possibility of its being reinscribed outside of the supposed authenticity of its apparently proper occurrence, in effect in the condition of its being iterable, its disinterrence from its 'proper' place or self. Thus, while the date can never return *sensu stricto* it nonetheless can find itself remarked in a spectral fashion. Moreover, this *revenance* of the date is also a *revenance*, a phantasmatic oscillation, which always already haunts the structure and the possibility of dating: 'a date is a spectre. But this revenance of impossible return is marked *in* the date' (SPC, 18).[9] The date cites its impossible other as the ghost of itself within, and yet always other to, its own signature. There is remarked therefore the apparition of the trace of what could never return as such, encoded in both the iterability of the date and the memory of the non-return of another date which is the same but not the same.

Of course, the question does not come down only to a matter of dates or, to invoke another well-known instance, the articulation of saying 'I'. Neither example guarantees the proper identity or meaning that they appear to promise. Neither the date nor the 'I' maintains any singularity except by the chance of its being spirited away, reiterated or cited. What is not fully acknowledged however is that the iterability which guarantees the recognition of singularity is itself the experience of haunting which is all the more uncanny in that it admits to the unassignability of any absolutely discernible or traceable originary location, as just remarked. Citation is admitted as having no source from which it comes or to which it could be assigned. In both cases, the date and the 'I' are marked by a certain citational *revenance at or as the origin*, and as the affirmation of the impossibility of origin, from the very start. In this, acts of dating or articulations of the 'I' betray a citational relationship to writing in general, despite the fact that the reader habitually or conventionally reads them as inscriptions belonging to a different order of signification such as that accorded signatures or proper names, which also supposedly operate according to laws quite different from other inscribed apparitions and yet are shown to behave as typical modes of inscription. The phantasmatic or spectral condition is not only what comes to haunt citation and all acts of quotation in certain specific situations, particular expressions and their rhetorical deployment, or simply in certain 'forms' of writing. All writing may be said to be spectral, though spectrality is equally just another name or one possible substitution for the endlessly citational structures that are called or otherwise invoked in the name of literature. Nothing comes to rest or finds authority in any one term more than any other. The spectral disrupts pure singularity and thus manifests its performative effect in the mark, the trace, and those places where one 'begins' with iterability, and with what returns. And this, appearing to complete the circle but opening ourselves to move on, is to say nothing other than *literature*.

The idea of a mark that is not iterable, which cannot be cited or re-cited, is unthinkable. The citationality of every and any sign is commented on at length in *Margins of Philosophy*, anticipating the discourse of spectrality to come, an anticipation which is also an echo of a particular discussion from *Dissemination*. As you will be aware from Chapter 2, every sign, spoken or written,

> can be *cited*, put between quotation marks; thereby it can break with every given context, and engender infinitely new contexts in an absolutely nonsaturable fashion. This does not suppose that the mark is valid outside its context, but on the contrary that there are only contexts without any center of absolute anchoring. This citationality, duplication or duplicity, this iterability of the mark is not an accident or an anomaly, but is that . . . without which a mark could no longer even have a so-called 'normal' functioning. What would a mark be that one could not cite? And whose origin could not be lost on the way? [. . .] would a performative statement be possible if a citational doubling did not eventually split, dissociate from itself the pure singularity of the event? . . . Could a performative statement succeed if its formulation did not repeat a 'coded' or iterable statement, in other words if the expressions I use . . . were not identifiable as conforming to an iterable model, and therefore if they were not identifiable in a way as 'citation'? (*MP*, 320–1, 326)

There is nothing, no sign, no utterance, vocable or writing, no graphic mark whatsoever, which is neither a citation nor haunted by its own citationality, at least in principle. The structure of the sign is always haunted by its own spectral condition. Signification relies on being spirited away from itself, from any proper or unique, singular or 'original' articulation or inscription. In this, the possibility of signification, its very operation, becomes the citational embodiment of an ineluctable disembodiment. Every sign, in order to function as a sign, therefore must have given up the ghost. Hence, let us insist on this once more, *literature, if it is anything, is the endless iterable reinscription of the otherwise indecipherable. That is to say, citation, and citation is always already the phantomization of the sign*, as I have indicated through the mediation on the matrix of being's circulation.

One implication here is that to cite is also to call, and to recall. Citation is marked by anamnesis and response. It is to set in motion that which, invisibly, is always already underway, and which does not wait for any perception, any consciousness to set it in motion. What I call reading, and what I might call *my* reading, is only ever this act of response. The call of citation and the displaced writing that remarks the act of citation (which is citation also) comes from some other place, as has just been suggested. It doubles and divides itself, as can be witnessed. Citation both is and is not citation. It disrupts the authority of identity and of origin, being always already in motion. Destabilizing itself both internally and from the location or locution of the other, citation thereby engages or tropes itself as other than itself in the transport from and as a condition of the command, the injunction, the order: *remember me* says the ghost of Hamlet's father. *Do not forget*, the words of Arthur Clennam's father in Dickens's *Little Dorrit*, returning as the merest trace, *D.N.F.*, embroidered and secreted inside a pocket watch. A citation thus returns as the terrible but touching injunction, the gift or giving of the other, in which the command enjoins one to inescapable response and responsibility.

Arriving at this comprehension places us in a closer relation to the condition of citation. We find ourselves involved in a process that has no beginning. At the same time however what is also observable is that all we can do is begin repeatedly, if only so as to get to the point of beginning *and* departure. The principle of citation is therefore readable as citing, indirectly, not simply some anterior, originary source. Instead, citation in principle and in effect acts as any number of spectral threads or traces – what is referred to as *un des fils conducteurs* (*SPIP*, 121): one of innumerable conductors and clews/clues in which is also to be heard the trace of a relation, an *invention*, between father and son (PIO, 28), the signs of a genealogical, if not genetic, imprint hinting at frayed inheritance and heritage, which in turn is at once generative and generational, and yet also discontinuous and coming apart at the edges, so many threads acting *as if* they were bookmarks. The father's message, the trace of his phantom, returns to haunt the son, as we know all too well from *Hamlet*.

This thread attests to a vast and complex network. It announces and enacts the impersonal making and marking of an archive and an archiving of memory, all the more uncanny for being irreducible to any human origin, presence, identity or location. To insist on the point, *this is literature*. Literature is the impossible archive, the network or labyrinth, irreducible to any origin but always, in its circulation, its virtual library, *where one is*. And of course, *as if* to recall myself, *as if* I were citing myself as an other, the archive, in its very structure, is spectral through and through: 'in the first place . . . the structure of the archive is *spectral*. It is spectral *a priori*: neither present nor absent "in the flesh," neither visible nor invisible, a trace always referring to another whose eyes can never be met' (*AF*, 84). Returning from the archive that we name *literature*, the ghost of and in citation turns our attention toward its own repressed truth. And the 'truth' is that which appears as or in the guise of an indirect manifestation of some other spectre, the spectre of the other, which in turn, internally, as the other of citation haunts the reading of citation as the voice of authoritative origin.

Establishing or, rather, writing itself out of an already woven network or labyrinth of citations and their variations into which it places itself even as it displaces textual organization, a footnote in *Dissemination* recites as it cites an archival structure of responses within the various editions of the texts of Mallarmé, themselves responding to and re-citing the encounter with a text, the pantomime booklet, *Pierrot Murderer of his Wife* (*D*, 196–7 n.20). All the variants belong to the text of *Mimique*. All are caught up in the complex textile weave concerning anonymous origins, omissions, textual fragments, reflections of variations and the simulacrum of citation. More than this though, the 'lengthy quotation' is also 'of interest in that it marks the historical complexity of the text network in which we are already engaged' (*D*, 197 n.20). The question is both *figural* or *formal*, and *historical* and *material*. Historicity is affirmed, not avoided, in close textual exegesis. Form forms, informs and deforms its identities and meanings as a result of what we might a little glibly refer to as the ghosts of history (a phrase which however also serves to announce history as itself having a history of hauntings).

Beyond this, citation mirrors or mimes citation, as absolute priority is forestalled and displaced. Nothing other than citation is possible, even while the very act of citation is itself called into question in the process of citation, whose dense annotated network transforms itself from speaking of the troping of citation, to enacting the disturbing performative condition of citation itself. And what is more, in some kind of parody of authority, (panto)miming let us say the authority of scholarship, Derrida marshals the citations concerning the Pierrot, that silent figure of mimicry who 'cites' in parody the very idea of the human via a series of material gestures, the materiality of which is so counterintuitive that all phenomenal adequation is called into question. As a condition of that performative pantomimicry of scholarly reading, a gesture haunted by the ghost of the Mallarméan text, it is observed that there is no citation: 'the sentence in quotation marks is indeed a simulacrum of a citation . . . such a "citation" is nowhere to be found' (*D*, 197 n.20). The citation returns certainly, but only ever in some ghostly fashion, mirroring and citing its other selves, without source, without origin. Authority attests only to what is absent.

In coming back and in being projected from some other place the provenance of which is undecidable, the citations, far from gathering themselves into a determinable set or act, separate themselves from themselves and from within themselves. Instead, like two shoes – as is known their relationship as a pair is undecidable (*TP*, 373–4) – the spectral possibility opens (onto itself) a spectrum of possibilities as, we are tempted to suggest, the truth in haunting, irreducible once more to all epistemologies, ideologies and anthropomorphic mimeticisms reliant on the prior or anterior location. And indeed (to return momentarily to that note on Mallarmé) the word 'phantom' does not simply arrive in the note on the variations to *Mimique*, the Mallarméan text, whether by that word *phantom* one suggests some so-called literal apparition or the work of metaphor. (But how would we decide on one or the other? In the face of apparition, would this ever be possible?) Ahead of definition, the phantom exceeds all such possibility, disabling the reading by pushing at the very limit of interpretability. This is a case of a radical, reflective mimicry, recalling, and calling to, those oscillations, those numbers of yeses. The mime does not have a referent, even though elsewhere the Pierrot bears apparently some filial relation to the recurrent ghosts of Hamlet which trouble the text of Mallarmé (*D*, 195). The reference is not to that which is real but to another ghost, and thus one is witness to the play of difference, the doubling vibration between two mirrors belonging to what is termed a differential structure of mimicry. The ghost is the ghost of a ghost, trace of a trace. Haunting takes place both in the place *of* and *as* citation. The event of *revenance* taking place otherwise in citation is glimpsed if only because citation promises to make the invisible visible, though never as a presence, never present. In effect, the citational programme, that which is supposed to take place, is displaced in its very act and in the demand that the act must occur.

IX BEING-HAUNTED, IN OTHER WORDS

Thus, the promise or programme of citation is always already haunted within its very structural possibility before a word is written or rewritten. Citation does not merely illustrate the haunted condition of literature as its possibility. In its spectral condition, citation is literary through and through. And what is most haunting is that the movement of *revenance* never comes to a halt, with or without some consciousness to bear witness. It might be said that the spectral is everywhere all the time, yet without a proper time of its own. The protocols surrounding citation are so precise, and the laws have multiplied themselves in the name of citation, citing countless examples along the way, if only so as to seek to calm or protect against the haunting vibrations and thereby keep at bay the haunts of citation. Yet, such haunts are those very places where citation – and therefore *literature* – takes place and to which it appears habituated. These are the places, the non-places and the taking place in which citation finds itself most at home paradoxically in a homeless wandering, and thereby remaining to come. If it comes at all, the spectre of the literary generates the most uncanny effects within the response one names reading, and in the subject of reading, time and again. This is *where one is*: in literature, and in the reading circle, the circulation of a reading that can always erupt from within oneself, when and where there might arrive the being-two-to-speak. I am, in effect, no more myself in my encounter with and experience of literature. Giving the last word on literature to a revenant citation, let us affirm of literature that

> It delivers us over to the experience of the wholly-other . . . literature . . . remains the absolute place of the secret of this heteronomy, of the secret as experience of the law that comes from the other, of the law whose giver is none other than the coming of the other, in this test of unconditional hospitality which opens us to it before any condition, any rule, any norm, any concept, any genre, any generic and genealogical belonging. (*GGGG*, 48)

NOTES

1. This transitive verb is an invention, c.1836, of novelist Edward Bulwer Lytton.
2. To cite is not to quote. To quote is to mark, to distinguish by numbers. To cite however is to excite, to cause to move or put in motion, to call, to arouse or to summon. Ex-citation names an awakening, a calling forth. Hamlet's father's ghost excites Hamlet. It calls him, it summons him in order to awaken his consciousness. While quotation marks a text, citation produces a response. It awakens the reader. As the trace of the other, and thus the movement of all language, citation summons one to respond. It puts in motion, it acts on the present tense of a text, making visible that ghostly motion that is on the move in language.
3. I am *inventing* this neologism from an already existent adjective, *invenient*, finding it in the other word, rather than creating something new.
4. The first page number refers to the poem in German, the second to the facing English translation. Of the three 'versions' of the citation, the second is my translation, the third that of Pierre Joris.
5. The first page number refers to the poem in French, the second to the facing English translation. All further references will be given parenthetically in this way.
6. On the vulgar concept of time, see Derrida's explication of the notion of 'spirit' in Heidegger contra Hegel (*OS*, 23–30).
7. In Varèse's translation, 'Je est un autre' is given as 'I is someone else'.
8. I am drawing here in passing on the work of Deleuze and Guattari, particularly *Anti-Oedipus* and *A Thousand Plateaus*.
9. The paragraph continues:

> And each time, at the same date, what one commemorates will be the date of that which could never come back. This date will have signed and sealed the unique, the unrepeateable, but to do so, it must have given itself to be read in a form sufficiently coded, readable, and deci-

pherable for the indecipherable to *appear* in the analogy of the anniversary ring (February 13, 1962, is *analogous* to February 13, 1936), even if it appears *as* indecipherable. (SPC, 18–19)

Note the way in which iterability and the indecipherable are inscribed as the ghostly arrival, its possibility, in the analogy, the figure without relation, resemblance or correspondence in the *ring*, circle *and* oscillation.

WORKS CITED

Arnold, Matthew. *The Complete Poems*. Second edn. Ed. Kenneth Allott and Miriam Allott. London: Longman, 1979.

Attridge, Derek. *The Singularity of Literature*. London: Routledge, 2004.

Austin, J. L. *How to Do Things with Words*. Second edn. Ed. J. G. Urmson and Marina Sbisà. Cambridge, MA: Harvard University Press, 1999.

Banville, John. *Eclipse*. London: Picador, 2000.

Bennington, Geoffrey. 'Deconstruction is Not What You Think'. *Art & Design* 4 (3–4: 1988): 6–7.

Bennington, Geoffrey. 'Derridabase'. Geoffrey Bennington and Jacques Derrida. *Jacques Derrida*. Trans. Geoffrey Bennington. Chicago: University of Chicago Press, 1993. 3–317.

Bergson, Henri. *Matter and Memory*. Trans. Nancy Margaret Paul and W. Scott Palmer. New York: Zone Books, 1991.

Bivona, Daniel. *Desire and Contradiction: Imperial Visions and Domestic Debates in Victorian Literature*. Manchester: Manchester University Press, 1990.

Brault, Pascale-Anne, and Michael Naas. 'To Reckon with the Dead: Jacques Derrida's Politics of Mourning'. Jacques Derrida. *The Work of Mourning*. Ed. Pascale-Anne Brault and Michael Naas. Chicago: University of Chicago Press, 2001. 1–30.

Brunette, Peter, and David Wills, eds. *Deconstruction and the Visual Arts: Art, Media, Architecture*. Cambridge: Cambridge University Press, 1994.

Brunette, Peter, and David Wills. 'Introduction'. In Brunette and Wills, eds, 1–9.

Caputo, John D., with Jacques Derrida. *Deconstruction in a Nutshell: A Conversation with Jacques Derrida*. New York: Fordham University Press, 1997.

Celan, Paul. 'ALS WENN DAS WEISSE ANFIEL' / 'WHEN WHITENESS ASSAILED US'. *Breathturn*. Trans. Pierre Joris. Los Angeles: Sun & Moon Press, 1995. 111/112.

Celan, Paul. 'Reply to a Questionnaire from the Flinker Bookstore, Paris, 1958'. *Collected Prose*. Trans. and int. Rosemarie Waldrop. New York: Routledge, 2003. 15–16.

Clark, Timothy. *The Poetics of Singularity: The Counter-Culturalist Turn in Heidegger, Derrida, Blanchot and the later Gadamer*. Edinburgh: Edinburgh University Press, 2005.

Cohen, Tom. 'Introduction: Derrida and the Future of . . .' Tom Cohen, ed. *Jacques Derrida and the Humanities: A Critical Reader*. Cambridge: Cambridge University Press, 2001. 1–23.

Deguy, Michel. 'Recumbents'. *Recumbents: Poems*. Trans. Wilson Baldridge. Middletown: Wesleyan University Press, 2005.

Dickens, Charles. *The Pickwick Papers*. Ed. Mark Wormald. London: Penguin, 2003.

Eagleton, Terry. *Literary Theory: An Introduction*. Oxford: Basil Blackwell, 1983.

Eliot, George. *Daniel Deronda*. Ed. Barbara Hardy. Harmondsworth: Penguin, 1970.

Eliot, George. *Middlemarch*. Ed. Rosemary Ashton. London: Penguin, 2003.

Fynsk, Christopher. *Language and Relation: . . . that there is language*. Stanford: Stanford University Press, 1996.

Fynsk, Christopher. *The Claim of Language: A Case for the Humanities*. Minneapolis: University of Minnesota Press, 2004.

Gaskell, Elizabeth. *Cranford/Cousin Phillis*. Ed. Peter Keating. London: Penguin, 1998.

Gaston, Sean. *Derrida and Disinterest*. London: Continuum, 2005.

Gaston, Sean. *The Impossible Mourning of Jacques Derrida*. London: Continuum, 2006.

Gosetti-Ferencei, Jennifer Anna. *Heidegger, Hölderlin, and the Subject of Poetic Language: Toward a New Poetics of Dasein*. New York: Fordham University Press, 2004.

Hamacher, Werner. *Pleroma: Reading in Hegel*. Trans. Nicholas Walker and Simon Jarvis. Stanford: Stanford University Press, 1998.

Hardy, Florence. *The Life of Thomas Hardy 1840–1928*. New York: St Martin's Press, 1962.

Hardy, Thomas. *The Return of the Native*. Ed. Tony Slade. Int. Penny Boumelha. London: Penguin, 1999.

Hardy, Thomas. *Far from the Madding Crowd*. Ed. and int. Rosemarie Morgan and Shannon Russell. London: Penguin, 2000.

Hobson, Marion. 'Derrida and Representation: Mimesis, Presentation, and Representation'. Tom Cohen, ed. *Jacques Derrida and the Humanities: A Critical Reader*. Cambridge: Cambridge University Press, 2001. 132–51.

Howells, Christina. *Derrida: Deconstruction from Phenomenology to Ethics*. Cambridge: Polity Press, 1999.

Joyce, James. *Ulysses*. Ed. Hans Walter Gabler, with Wolfhard Steppe and Claus Melchior. Afterword Michael Groden. London: The Bodley Head, 1993.

Kamuf, Peggy. 'Introduction: Reading Between the Blinds'. *A Derrida Reader: Between the Blinds*. New York: Columbia University Press, 1991. xiii–xlii.

Kamuf, Peggy. Editor's introduction. Chapter Three. Kamuf, ed. *A Derrida Reader*. 59–60

Kamuf, Peggy. Editor's introduction. Chapter Seven. Kamuf, ed. *A Derrida Reader*. 169–70.

Krell, David Farrell. *The Purest of Bastards: Works of Mourning, Art, and Affirmation in the Thought of Jacques Derrida*. University Park: Pennsylvania State University Press, 2000.

Kronick, Joseph G. *Derrida and the Future of Literature*. New York: State University of New York Press, 1999.

Lacoste, Jean-Yves. *Experience and the Absolute: Disputed Questions on the Humanity of Man*. Trans. Mark Raftery-Skehan. New York: Fordham University Press, 2004.

Lacoue-Labarthe, Philippe. *Typography, Mimesis, philosophy, Politics*. Trans. and ed. Christopher Fynsk *et al*. Cambridge, MA: Harvard University Press, 1989.

Miller, J. Hillis. *Speech Acts in Literature*. Stanford: Stanford University Press, 2001.

Miller, J. Hillis. 'Sovereignty Death Literature Unconditionality Democracy University'. Peter Pericles Trifonas and Michael A. Peters, eds. *Deconstructing Derrida: Tasks for the New Humanities*. Basingstoke: Palgrave Macmillan, 2005. 25–37.

Newton, K. M. 'Roland Barthes and Structuralist Criticism'. Julian Wolfreys, ed. *Introducing Literary Theories: A Guide and Glossary*. Edinburgh: Edinburgh University Press, 2001. 33–46.

Reilly, Jim. *Shadowtime: History and Representation in Hardy, Conrad and George Eliot*. London: Routledge, 1993.

Rimbaud, Arthur. *Illuminations and Other Prose Poems*. Trans. Louise Varèse. New York: New Directions, 1957.

Royle, Nicholas. *After Derrida*. Manchester: Manchester University Press, 1995.

Royle, Nicholas. *Jacques Derrida*. London: Routledge, 2003.

de Saussure, Ferdinand. *Course in General Linguistics*. Trans. Wade Baskin. Int. Jonathan Culler. London: Fontana, 1974. New trans. R. Harris. London: Gerald Duckworth & Co., 1995.

Seel, Martin. *Aesthetics of Appearing*. Trans. John Farrell. Stanford: Stanford University Press, 2005.

Spivak, Gayatri Chakravorty. 'Translator's Preface'. Jacques Derrida. *Of Grammatology*. Corrected edn, trans. Gayatri Chakravorty Spivak. Baltimore: The Johns Hopkins University Press, 1998. ix–lxxxvii.

INDEX

Alterity (see Other, Otherness) 34, 59, 66, 67, 69, 71, 78, 85, 93, 94, 127, 132, 137, 156
Althusser, Louis 6
Anaximander 51, 52
Aporia 10–11, 28, 29, 34, 130, 74, 123
Archive 26, 27, 83, 84, 109–10, 122, 123, 145, 149, 151, 155, 161
Archive Fever 4
Aristotle 51
Arnold, Matthe 129
As if (als ob) 2, 3, 9, 12, 18, 22, 39, 41, 42, 45, 46, 53, 72, 74, 80, 100, 109, 110, 112, 113, 114, 115, 116, 117, 120, 132, 134, 137, 141, 143, 144, 145, 146, 147, 151, 153, 154, 155, 161
Austin, J. L. 14–17
Aucouturier, Marguerite 6
Autoimmunization 37, 147

Banville, John 66
Barthes, Roland 77, 79, 80
Being 12, 31, 47–8, 50, 56–8, 60–2, 66–9, 77, 79, 87, 89, 115–65
Belatedness (après-coup, nachträglichkeit) 42–3, 88, 100, 128, 135, 156
Bennington, Geoffrey 24–5
Bergson, Henri 6, 129
Bloom, Harold 7
Browning, Robert 130

Catachréses 138
Caws, Mary Ann 83
Celan, Paul 4, 26, 134, 135, 136, 140
Citation 15–17, 22, 110, 115, 117, 119, 120, 123, 128, 136, 141, 142–4, 147, 148, 151, 153–5, 157, 159–64
Columbia Encyclopedia 21
Communication 16–17, 26, 40, 47, 56, 66, 134, 138, 153
Constative speech act 14, 17, 20, 39, 89, 97
Context 9, 10, 15, 16, 19, 23, 26, 43, 51, 53, 57, 59, 62, 66, 95, 96, 112, 127, 156, 158, 159
Countersignature 2, 5, 18, 19, 60, 71, 94, 107, 108, 120, 132, 135, 157
Cranford 122, 123–6

Daniel Deronda 53
Deconstruction 4, 5, 7, 8, 9–43, 63, 73, 75, 79, 100, 112, 113, 135, 143, 144, 146, 155, 156
De Graef, Ortwin 7
Deguy, Michel 134–8
De Man, Paul 7–8
Derrida, Georgette 5
Dickens, Charles 121–2, 128, 130, 160
Différance 23, 30, 35, 44–77, 78, 87, 88, 89, 93, 103, 134, 139
'Différance' 42, 48, 49, 50, 52, 55, 59, 60

Difference 10, 14, 18, 23, 24, 28, 33, 35, 37, 45–7, 48–50, 52, 55 7, 59–63, 67, 68–70, 72, 85, 90, 91, 92, 93, 94, 107, 118–19, 128–30, 133, 137, 141, 144, 148, 163
Dissemination 35
Dissemination 4, 81, 159, 161
Double-bind 26

Eclipse 66
Economy 27–30, 37, 53, 56, 58, 88, 125, 130, 135, 139, 145
Eliot, George 53–5, 131
Essay on the Origin of Languages, The 64

Far from the Madding Crowd 129, 147–50
Finnegans Wake 25, 27
Foucault, Michel 6
Freud, Sigmund 4, 43, 50, 58, 107, 111, 121
Fynsk, Christopher 37

Gaskell, Elizabeth 124–6, 128, 130, 131
Gap 10, 11, 66, 92, 121, 122, 136
Genet, Jean 4
Ghost 33, 80, 81, 83, 85, 87, 92, 93, 94, 95, 98, 105, 108, 123, 130, 138, 141, 142, 143, 144, 146, 147, 151, 152, 153, 154, 155, 156, 158, 160, 162, 163, 164, 165
Gift 25, 31, 75, 78, 140, 160
Glas 4

Hardy, Thomas 88, 90, 128, 130, 147–53
Hartman, Geoffrey 7
Haunting 16, 17, 18, 31, 32, 33, 42, 45, 58, 59, 63, 73, 75, 76, 81, 83, 84, 85, 87, 88, 92, 94, 95, 101, 103, 105, 106, 107, 108, 116, 120, 122, 128, 129, 130, 131, 132, 135, 142, 143, 144, 146, 148, 149, 152, 154, 155, 156, 157, 158, 159, 160, 161, 162, 163

Hegel, G. W. F. 4, 50, 81, 82, 86
Heidegger, Martin 23, 50–2, 76, 81–2, 92–4, 98, 108, 113
Heraclitus 50, 51
Historicity 57, 58, 115, 117, 119–33, 147–52, 162
Hobson, Marion 112
Hospitality 31, 146, 164
Husserl, Edmund 4, 6, 50, 57, 76, 77
Hymen 23, 73, 81, 101, 114
Hyppolite, Jean 6

Identity 9, 11, 13, 18, 19, 22, 24, 25, 28, 29, 30, 31, 32, 36, 40, 48, 52, 60, 61, 64, 66, 67, 69, 70, 73, 79, 90, 91, 93, 96, 105, 106, 108, 112, 113, 116, 118, 119, 122, 123, 127, 128, 129, 130, 132, 134, 135, 143, 145, 146, 154, 156, 158, 161
Idiom 26, 40, 43, 55, 78, 106, 107, 109, 140
Institution 9, 10, 11, 15, 19, 22, 24, 25, 26, 27, 28, 30, 31, 32, 33, 35, 36, 37, 39, 41, 44, 46, 47, 52, 60, 61, 73, 88, 95, 100, 109, 111, 118, 122, 124, 125, 143, 145, 147, 155
Invention 10, 27, 119–33
Irony 17, 57
Iterability 14–16, 25, 26, 50, 51, 55, 59, 65, 72, 86, 88, 90, 92, 94, 95, 1–3, 106, 108, 118, 123, 125, 127, 128, 129, 130, 134, 135, 136, 137, 138, 141, 142, 144, 148, 149, 153, 154, 157, 158, 159, 160, 165

Joris, Pierre 135, 136
Joyce, James 4, 25, 27

Kamuf, Peggy 23
Kant, Immanuel 12, 81, 82
Khatibi, Abdelkebir 26
Khora 71–6, 129
Krell, David Farrell 94–5, 97
Kristeva, Julia 124

L'avenir 116, 120, 128, 155, 156, 157
Le Soir 8

Levinas, Emmanuel 50
Lévi-Strauss, Claude 56
Literature 12, 25, 26, 31, 32, 34, 35,
    37, 51, 53, 60, 69, 71, 73, 75, 78,
    88, 98, 99–107, 104, 105, 107,
    115–63
Little Dorrit 160
Logocentrism 56–7, 64, 65, 75, 94,
    126, 140

Mallarmé, Stéphane 99–100, 107,
    161–3
Margins of Philosophy 4
Memoirs of the Blind 81, 93,
    114
Metaphor 31–2, 90, 162
Middlemarch 122, 132–3
Miller, J. Hillis 7, 116
Mimesis 98–106
Mimique 99, 100, 161, 162
Mitterand, François 7
Mondialatinisation 41
Moonstone, The 122, 123

New York Times 110
Nietzsche, Friedrich 6, 50, 58

Of Grammatology 4, 56, 57, 64, 66
Of Spirit 73
Ontology 9, 11, 30, 31, 37, 47, 48,
    60, 61, 69, 70, 72, 73, 75, 77, 90,
    93, 96, 97, 104, 110, 117, 129,
    132, 135, 137, 145, 154, 156
Origin, Original, Originary 9, 10,
    16, 25, 42, 51–4, 56, 57, 59, 60,
    61, 62, 64, 68, 69, 70, 84, 89, 95,
    98, 100, 103, 105, 106, 119, 120,
    127, 134, 140, 146, 149, 158,
    159, 160, 161, 162
Other, otherness (see Alterity) 1, 2,
    3, 4, 9, 11, 14, 18, 26–7, 31, 32,
    33, 37, 45, 46, 48, 51, 52, 53, 55,
    56, 59, 60, 61, 66, 67, 71, 75, 80,
    86, 87, 88, 89, 91, 92, 94, 98, 101,
    105, 106, 107, 108, 110, 116,
    120–32, 133, 134, 136–41, 145,
    146, 148, 149, 153, 154–6, 158,
    160, 161, 164

Oxford English Dictionary 22, 70,
    83

Palin, Michael 21
Parasitism 14, 15, 17, 22, 23, 128,
    156
Passe-partout 95–8
Performatives, performativity 12,
    14–17, 20, 27–9, 39–40, 48, 53,
    68, 71, 74, 78, 85, 89, 97, 99, 103,
    106, 127, 135, 157, 159, 162
Pierrot Murderer of His Wife
    161–3
Phallogocentrism 75
Phantom, Phantasm 86, 87, 93, 94,
    98, 99, 105, 110, 114, 120, 122,
    124, 130, 133, 142–8, 151–5,
    158–9, 160–2
Philebus 99, 104
Philosopheme 40, 101
Phonocentrism 56–8, 65, 77
Pickwick Papers, The 121, 123,
    130
Plato 4, 51, 71, 76–7, 98–101, 104,
    107
Play 10, 25, 26, 28, 35–7, 46–7, 49,
    51, 52, 56, 58, 59, 60, 61–2, 66,
    67, 69, 71, 85, 89, 90, 105, 108,
    138, 151, 156, 163
Ponge, Francis 4
Positions 4
Post Card, The 4
Presence 2–3, 25, 32, 50, 56–9,
    61–8, 69, 71, 80, 83, 84, 87, 88,
    90, 93, 94, 95, 98, 100, 103, 104,
    107, 108, 113, 116, 141, 145, 146,
    151, 156, 157–8, 161, 163

Reading 2–3, 8, 9, 10–11, 13, 16,
    17, 19, 23, 24, 26, 27, 28, 30–40,
    71, 81, 90, 91–4, 116, 117, 118,
    119, 122, 123, 127, 132, 136, 143,
    146, 149, 155, 156, 157, 160, 162,
    163
Representation 11, 21, 35, 36, 64,
    71, 73, 75, 79–114, 119, 122, 123,
    125, 131, 132, 133, 136, 139, 140,
    145, 147, 149, 150, 154

Republic 104
Responsibility 33, 38, 39, 41, 130, 133, 134, 160
Return of the Native, The 88, 152–3
'Retrait of Metaphor, The' 32
Revenance, Revenant 32, 80, 88, 95, 130, 137, 140, 142, 145, 146, 151–4, 158, 163, 164
Ring and the Book, The 123, 130
Right of Inspection 81, 83
Ronse, Henri 62
Rousseau, Jean-Jacques 64–5
Royle, Nicholas 15–17, 26, 51, 115

Saussure, Ferdinand de 50, 53–8, 60, 76–7
Schapiro, Meyer 91–2, 94
Secret 31–2, 69, 75, 76, 84, 96, 97, 107, 108, 120, 126, 127, 133, 140, 147, 155, 157, 160, 164
Secret Art of Antonin Artaud, The 81
'Sending: On Representation' 110–11
Shakespeare, William 4, 26, 68, 94
Sheaf 52, 53, 60, 61, 106
Sign, Signification, Signified, Signifier 13, 16, 18, 22, 23, 26, 30, 33, 35–9, 45, 47, 49–51, 52, 54, 55–8, 59, 60, 61, 62, 63–7, 69–70, 79, 82, 83, 85, 91, 95, 97, 99, 100, 103, 106, 113, 117, 119, 121, 124, 127, 131, 135, 136, 138, 139, 148, 155, 157, 158, 159–60
'Signature Event Context' 14
Singularity 5, 11, 12, 24, 25, 26–7, 34, 37, 51, 53, 61, 78, 80, 82, 84, 88, 97, 98, 101, 102, 106, 107, 112, 115, 117, 118, 119, 123, 123–36, 141, 142, 144, 145, 148, 149, 152, 153, 154, 159, 160
Sollers, Philippe 6

Spacing 12, 23, 29, 30, 33, 48, 51, 59, 63, 66, 67, 70, 75, 78, 83, 89–90, 93, 105, 134, 135
Spectre, Spectrality 13, 33, 58–9, 75, 80, 85, 86, 87, 92, 93–5, 99, 100, 109, 115, 117, 119, 120, 125, 143, 144, 145–7, 153–63
Speech and Phenomena 4, 76
Spivak, Gayatri Chakravorty 66, 67
Subjectile 73, 74, 82, 83–7, 88, 90, 92, 95–9, 107
Supplement 56, 60–8

Tekhne 37, 108, 121
Timaeus 71–2
Trace 1, 2–3, 8–11, 21, 22, 23, 30, 31, 35, 36, 37, 45, 46, 48, 52, 59, 61, 62, 63, 64, 66, 68–71, 74, 75, 79, 80–1, 84–94, 95, 98, 104, 107, 110, 11, 113, 116, 119, 123–6, 128–9, 130–2, 136, 137, 138, 140, 141, 143, 145–6, 147–9, 153–4, 156, 158, 159, 161, 163
Truth in Painting, The 81, 82, 95, 97, 106, 114
'Two Words for Joyce' 27

Ulysses 67–8
Uncanny, the 32, 80, 86, 94, 113, 121, 129, 146, 153, 158, 161, 163
Undecidability 12, 17, 18, 19, 27, 28, 29, 30, 31, 38, 40, 42, 44, 54, 62, 74, 85, 114, 123, 162

Van Gogh, Vincent 91, 94

'Worldbook' 21
Writing 2–33, 44–77
Writing and Difference 4, 46, 48
Wuthering Heights 122

Zizek, Slavoj 109